Reexamining Racism, Sexism, and Identity Taxation in the Academy

This book explores the diversity-related labour that marginalized faculty, students, and staff are expected to perform because of their social identities – i.e., "identity taxation" in US higher education institutions. It compiles new research on cultural and identity taxation to highlight how systemic racism and patriarchy perpetuate identity taxation in 21st century US academe.

Amado Padilla coined the term "cultural taxation" nearly 30 years ago to outline the expectations that faculty of colour address diversity affairs on their campuses. In this insightful volume, Laura Hirshfield and Tiffany Joseph expand the concept, adopting the term "identity taxation" to accentuate the labour members of marginalized groups participate in due to their intersectional identities. Beyond bringing these terms into conversation with others highlighting marginalized academics' experience, this volume empirically explores how identity taxation affects students and staff, not just the faculty who were the focus of previous scholarship. It provides insight into the consequences of taxation at a moment when change and dismantling structural racism is most needed in universities and society.

Reexamining Racism, Sexism, and Identity Taxation in the Academy will be a key resource for academics, researchers, and advanced students of race and ethnic studies, education, research methods, sociology, and cultural studies. This book was originally published as a special issue of *Ethnic and Racial Studies*.

Tiffany D. Joseph is Associate Professor of Sociology and International Affairs at Northeastern University, USA. Her research examines race and migration, immigration and health policy, and marginalized faculty's experiences in academia. She is the author of *Race on the Move: Brazilian Migrants and the Global Reconstruction of Race*.

Laura E. Hirshfield is the Dr Georges Bordage Medical Education Faculty Scholar and Associate Professor of Medical Education & Sociology at the University of Illinois College of Medicine, USA. Her research investigates the impact of identity (especially gender, race, and gender identity) on the ways that individuals navigate academic and medical contexts.

Ethnic and Racial Studies

Series editor: **John Solomos**, *University of Warwick, UK*

The journal *Ethnic and Racial Studies* was founded in 1978 by John Stone to provide an international forum for high quality research on race, ethnicity, nationalism and ethnic conflict. At the time the study of race and ethnicity was still a relatively marginal sub-field of sociology, anthropology and political science. In the intervening period the journal has provided a space for the discussion of core theoretical issues, key developments and trends, and for the dissemination of the latest empirical research.

It is now the leading journal in its field and has helped to shape the development of scholarly research agendas. *Ethnic and Racial Studies* attracts submissions from scholars in a diverse range of countries and fields of scholarship, and crosses disciplinary boundaries. It is now available in both printed and electronic form. Since 2015 it has published 15 issues per year, three of which are dedicated to *Ethnic and Racial Studies Review* offering expert guidance to the latest research through the publication of book reviews, symposia and discussion pieces, including reviews of work in languages other than English.

The *Ethnic and Racial Studies* book series contains a wide range of the journal's special issues. These special issues are an important contribution to the work of the journal, where leading social science academics bring together articles on specific themes and issues that are linked to the broad intellectual concerns of *Ethnic and Racial Studies*. The series editors work closely with the guest editors of the special issues to ensure that they meet the highest quality standards possible. Through publishing these special issues as a series of books, we hope to allow a wider audience of both scholars and students from across the social science disciplines to engage with the work of *Ethnic and Racial Studies*.

Asian Migration and New Racism
Beyond Colour and the 'West'
Edited by Sylvia Ang, Elaine Lynn-Ee Ho and Brenda S.A. Yeoh

Permitted Outsiders
Good Citizenship and the Conditional Inclusion of Migrant and Immigrant Minorities
Edited by Andreas Hackl

Fighting Discrimination in a Hostile Political Environment
The Case of "Colour-Blind" France
Edited by Angéline Escafré-Dublet, Virginie Guiraudon and Julien Talpin

Reexamining Racism, Sexism, and Identity Taxation in the Academy
Edited by Tiffany D. Joseph and Laura E. Hirshfield

For more information about this series, please visit:
www.routledge.com/Ethnic-and-Racial-Studies/book-series/ERS

Reexamining Racism, Sexism, and Identity Taxation in the Academy

Edited by
Tiffany D. Joseph and Laura E. Hirshfield

First published 2024
by Routledge
4 Park Square, Milton Park, Abingdon, Oxon OX14 4RN

and by Routledge
605 Third Avenue, New York, NY 10158

Routledge is an imprint of the Taylor & Francis Group, an informa business

© 2024 Taylor & Francis

All rights reserved. No part of this book may be reprinted or reproduced or utilised in any form or by any electronic, mechanical, or other means, now known or hereafter invented, including photocopying and recording, or in any information storage or retrieval system, without permission in writing from the publishers.

Trademark notice: Product or corporate names may be trademarks or registered trademarks, and are used only for identification and explanation without intent to infringe.

British Library Cataloguing in Publication Data
A catalogue record for this book is available from the British Library

ISBN13: 978-1-032-58758-5 (hbk)
ISBN13: 978-1-032-58759-2 pbk)
ISBN13: 978-1-003-45137-2 (ebk)

DOI: 10.4324/9781003451372

Typeset in Myriad Pro
by Newgen Publishing UK

Publisher's Note
The publisher accepts responsibility for any inconsistencies that may have arisen during the conversion of this book from journal articles to book chapters, namely the inclusion of journal terminology.

Disclaimer
Every effort has been made to contact copyright holders for their permission to reprint material in this book. The publishers would be grateful to hear from any copyright holder who is not here acknowledged and will undertake to rectify any errors or omissions in future editions of this book.

Contents

Citation Information	vii
Notes on Contributors	ix

Introduction: Reexamining racism, sexism, and identity taxation
in the academy   1
Tiffany D. Joseph and Laura E. Hirshfield

1   Cultural taxation or "tax credit"? Understanding the nuances of
ethnoracially minoritized student labour in higher education   9
Oswaldo Rosales, Emily P. Schell, Clarissa Gutierrez and Amado Padilla

2   Institutional penalty: mentoring, service, perceived
discrimination, and its impacts on the health and academic
careers of Latino faculty   32
Ruth Enid Zambrana, Diana Carvajal and Jalah Townsend

3   Black women in white academe: a qualitative analysis
of heightened inclusion tax   58
Tsedale M. Melaku and Angie Beeman

4   How women of colour engineering faculty respond
to wage disparities   82
*Ebony O. McGee, Devin T. White, Joyce B. Main, Monica F. Cox
and Lynette Parker*

5   "Diversity is a corporate plan": racialized equity labour among
university employees   104
Laura T. Hamilton, Kelly Nielsen and Veronica Lerma

6 On marginality, socialization, and lessons learned for the future
   of faculty diversity   127
   Caroline S. Turner

   Index   148

Citation Information

The chapters in this book were originally published in the journal *Ethnic and Racial Studies*, volume 46, issue 6 (2023). When citing this material, please use the original page numbering for each article, as follows:

Introduction
Reexamining racism, sexism, and identity taxation in the academy
Tiffany D. Joseph and Laura E. Hirshfield
Ethnic and Racial Studies, volume 46, issue 6 (2023), pp. 1101–1108

Chapter 1
Cultural taxation or "tax credit"? Understanding the nuances of ethnoracially minoritized student labor in higher education
Oswaldo Rosales, Emily P. Schell, Clarissa Gutierrez and Amado Padilla
Ethnic and Racial Studies, volume 46, issue 6 (2023), pp. 1109–1131

Chapter 2
Institutional penalty: mentoring, service, perceived discrimination and its impacts on the health and academic careers of Latino faculty
Ruth Enid Zambrana, Diana Carvajal and Jalah Townsend
Ethnic and Racial Studies, volume 46, issue 6 (2023), pp. 1132–1157

Chapter 3
Black women in white academe: a qualitative analysis of heightened inclusion tax
Tsedale M. Melaku and Angie Beeman
Ethnic and Racial Studies, volume 46, issue 6 (2023), pp. 1158–1181

Chapter 4
How women of colour engineering faculty respond to wage disparities
Ebony O. McGee, Devin T. White, Joyce B. Main, Monica F. Cox and Lynette Parker
Ethnic and Racial Studies, volume 46, issue 6 (2023), pp. 1182–1203

Chapter 5

"Diversity is a corporate plan": racialized equity labor among university employees
Laura T. Hamilton, Kelly Nielsen and Veronica Lerma
Ethnic and Racial Studies, volume 46, issue 6 (2023), pp. 1204–1226

Chapter 6

On marginality, socialization, and lessons learned for the future of faculty diversity
Caroline S. Turner
Ethnic and Racial Studies, volume 46, issue 6 (2023), pp. 1227–1247

For any permission-related enquiries please visit:
www.tandfonline.com/page/help/permissions

Notes on Contributors

Angie Beeman, Baruch College, City University of New York, New York, NY, USA.

Diana Carvajal, The Harriet Tubman Department of Women, Gender, and Sexuality Studies, University of Maryland, College Park, USA.

Monica F. Cox, Department of Engineering Education, The Ohio State University, Columbus, OH, USA.

Clarissa Gutierrez, Graduate School of Education at Stanford University, Center for Educational Research at Stanford, Stanford, USA.

Laura T. Hamilton, School of Social Sciences, Humanities and Arts, University of California-Merced, Merced, USA.

Laura E. Hirshfield, Department of Medical Education, University of Illinois College of Medicine, Chicago, IL, USA.

Tiffany D. Joseph, Department of Sociology and Anthropology, Northeastern University, Boston, MA, USA.

Veronica Lerma, School of Social Sciences, Humanities and Arts, University of California-Merced, Merced, USA.

Joyce B. Main, School of Engineering Education, Purdue University, West Lafayette, IN, USA.

Ebony O. McGee, Peabody College of Education, Vanderbilt University, Nashville, TN, USA.

Tsedale M. Melaku, Baruch College, City University of New York, New York, NY, USA.

Kelly Nielsen, Department of Sociology, University of California-San Diego Extension, La Jolla, USA.

Amado Padilla, Graduate School of Education at Stanford University, Center for Educational Research at Stanford, Stanford, USA.

Lynette Parker, Center for Inclusive Innovation, Digital Promise, Washington, D.C., USA.

Oswaldo Rosales, Graduate School of Education at Stanford University, Center for Educational Research at Stanford, Stanford, USA.

Emily P. Schell, Graduate School of Education at Stanford University, Center for Educational Research at Stanford, Stanford, USA.

Jalah Townsend, The Harriet Tubman Department of Women, Gender, and Sexuality Studies, University of Maryland, College Park, USA.

Caroline S. Turner, Educational Leadership Program, California State University Sacramento College of Education, Sacramento, USA.

Devin T. White, Peabody College of Education, Vanderbilt University, Nashville, TN, USA.

Ruth Enid Zambrana, The Harriet Tubman Department of Women, Gender, and Sexuality Studies, University of Maryland, College Park, USA.

Introduction: Reexamining racism, sexism, and identity taxation in the academy

Tiffany D. Joseph 🆔 and Laura E. Hirshfield 🆔

ABSTRACT

Amid the 2020 COVID pandemic and officer-involved deaths of numerous Black Americans, US colleges and universities stated commitments to improve ethnoracial diversity and address structural racism. This type of diversity-related work, which fell mostly upon faculty of colour, was not new, however. In 1994, Padilla coined the term "cultural taxation" to describe the disproportionate labour faculty of colour are expected to perform. Hirshfield and Joseph expanded on this work by developing the term "identity taxation" to emphasize labour performed by faculty from marginalized groups because of their intersectional *identities*. Scholarship about these concepts has since proliferated. This special issue brings together a diverse group of scholars studying these topics to spark much needed structural change through providing: 1) additional terminology describing nuances of identity taxation; 2) empirical insights about identity taxation for groups not previously examined; and 3) recommendations for resistance and advocacy to change inequitable practices.

Introduction

Ethnic and racial studies special issue

The violent acts of racism that caused the deaths of George Floyd, Breonna Taylor, Ahmaud Arbery, and countless others in 2020 were heartbreaking and tragic, and sadly, all too familiar. These acts catalyzed a reinvigoration of the Black Lives Matter movement and activism against anti-black police brutality in the United States. In the aftermath, protests ensued across the country and around the world as concerned citizens, politicians, and corporations began to challenge the entrenched status quo of white supremacy and anti-black systemic racism that has plagued the United States for centuries. At the same time, the COVID pandemic swept through the United States and the world, infecting, and ultimately causing the deaths of, millions of people – particularly the most marginalized and vulnerable. Former US President Trump's stigmatization of COVID as the "Chinese flu" also contributed to a rise in anti-Asian rhetoric, sentiment, and hate crimes in the United States. As the nation (and world), mobilized to respond to these acts and the COVID pandemic raged on, institutions of higher education also took action. Many stated institutional commitments to creating inclusive environments for all community members and increasing diversity through the admission or hiring of more Black, Latinx, Indigenous, and Asian American students, staff, and faculty. Others organized various virtual meetings, presentations, and rallies in support of addressing racism and racial inequality within their institutions and the broader communities. Unfortunately, and again expectedly, much of the labour associated with overhauling racist and problematic structural, curricular, and programmatic systems in these institutions has too often fallen upon community members of colour, particularly Black, Latinx, and Indigenous people. Given the impact of longstanding racial discrimination towards these groups, these labour expectations occurred at the very time that they themselves were often personally experiencing greater loss and trauma than their peers due to COVID and the racial violence of 2020. However, the extra "diversity-related labour," asked of underrepresented faculty during the 2020 pandemic and calls for racial justice is not new.[1] In 1994, scholar Amado Padilla coined the term "cultural taxation" to describe the expectation placed on faculty of colour to address diversity-related departmental and institutional affairs. In our 2011 *Ethnic and Racial Studies* article entitled "Why Don't You Get Somebody New to Do It: Race and Cultural Taxation in the Academy," we expanded Padilla's definition of cultural taxation to include extra burdens that stem from faculty of colour's commitment to campus diversity issues and the lack of legitimacy they experience from colleagues challenging their existence in the academy. The following year, we proposed further expansion of the concept and adoption of the term "identity taxation" to include and emphasize the extra labour performed by members of a variety of different marginalized groups because of their intersectional *identities* (Hirshfield and Joseph 2012). These articles have been cited extensively and scholarship about these concepts (or related ones) has proliferated since they were published. Taken together, this scholarship demonstrates how the pervasiveness of systemic racism and entrenched patriarchy in academia in the United States have served to perpetuate, rather than ameliorate, ethnoracial, gender, and other forms of social inequality.

Unfortunately, the years since 2020 have not been significantly easier for people of colour in the US or worldwide. Despite, or perhaps in reaction to, the increase in anti-racist social movements in the US, there have been widespread attacks on scholars of and pedagogy using Critical Race Theory (Hatziponagos 2021; Kolhatkar 2022). The US has also seen a national rollback of legislation designed to protect the rights of marginalized people, especially related to voting rights, gun control, immigration, and reproduction (Leonhardt 2022). These shifts in government and the loss of protected civil rights have important implications for everyone, but especially for Black, Latinx, and Indigenous Americans. As such, this is an important socio-historical moment for revisiting the concepts of cultural and identity taxation. Both have relevance for addressing systemic racism and improving the experiences of marginalized people in academia.

The aim of this special issue was to bring together a diverse group of scholars from a variety of racial, cultural, disciplinary, and professional backgrounds who have published work in this area to learn from their experiences, insights, and significant research regarding cultural and identity taxation in various contexts. With these six articles we hope to accomplish three main goals. First, we bring cultural and identity taxation into critical conversation with scholarship using other similar terms (i.e., cultural tax credit, inclusion tax, racialized equity labour, institutional penalty) that describe the extra burdens academics experience due to their underrepresented social identities (Lerma, Hamilton, and Nielson 2020; Melaku 2019; Rosales et al. 2022; Zambrana, Carvajal, and Townsend 2023). Second, we broaden the scope of research on the topic by empirically assessing the ways that cultural and identity taxation affect a variety of academic stakeholders, including students and staff, rather than the faculty members that were the primary focus of previous work. Finally, the articles in this special issue provide a unique opportunity for reflection about the consequences that this type of work has on the careers of marginalized academics at a moment when institutions and the broader society are ripe for transformation in disrupting structural racism.

First, we aim to explore and synthesize the wide range of terms that have been used to describe cultural and identity taxation in recent scholarship on this topic. Amado Padilla, the originator of the term "cultural taxation" among faculty of colour, is joined by three junior colleagues in an article exploring how cultural taxation plays out among graduate students of colour (Rosales et al. 2022).[2] Padilla and his colleagues argue that differences in pre-graduate school socioeconomic status (SES) and other privileged identities (i.e., gender) may allow certain graduate students of colour to benefit from participating in diversity-related labour compared to students of colour with less privileged social identities. Padilla and his colleagues refer to this benefit as a "cultural tax credit." Next, Ruth Zambrana and co-authors use nationally representative survey data to explore how the burdens of mentoring, service, and perceived discrimination differentially affect the career pathways of Latino faculty of different ethnicities (Zambrana, Carvajal, and Townsend 2023). The authors argue that these burdens contribute to an "institutional penalty" for Mexican American and Puerto Rican faculty, where the institution extracts identity-based service from and enacts penalties on marginalized groups that negatively affect their careers and health. They deliberately use this language to shift the responsibility for the burden of work from the individual to the structures that cause them. Finally, Melaku and Beeman (2022) argue that the "inclusion tax" – various types of labour, especially presentational labour, that people of colour exert to be included in their predominantly White workplaces – increased Black women faculty's marginalization during the pandemics of COVID-19 and police racial violence against Black Americans in 2020.

Moving beyond discussions of terminology, the next two articles are empirical studies highlighting experiences of underrepresented academics from various professions, racial and ethnic backgrounds, and academic ranks. Using recent data, these articles provide additional evidence of the immense and pervasive nature of cultural and identity taxation on university campuses. First, Ebony McGee and co-authors use the concepts of identity taxation and stereotype management to qualitatively explore the ways that women of colour engineering faculty differ in their approaches to addressing racialized and gendered salary disparities in their departments and institutions (McGee et al. 2023). Next, Laura Hamilton and colleagues extend their previous work on "racialized equity labour," which they define as uncompensated efforts for people of colour to address systematic racism and racial marginalization within their organizations (Lerma, Hamilton, and Nielson 2020). Their article explores how different organizational logics of race such as "diversity" (identity-focused infrastructure) and "equity" (infrastructure addressing systemic racism) shape the experience of racialized equity labour for university employees – both people of colour and White allies – on two college campuses (Hamilton, Nielsen, and Lerma 2022).

As a conclusion to this extensive empirical overview of racism, sexism, and identity taxation in academia, the special issue ends with recommendations for reducing the burden of identity taxation for marginalized faculty. Caroline Sotello Viernes Turner (2022) draws from her vast experience as a faculty member and administrator to share her insights about the vital role of departmental and institutional commitments in developing a diverse faculty, alleviating identity taxation among underrepresented faculty, and creating authentically inclusive environments for their community members.

This special issue is being published nearly 15 years after we were first invited as graduate students to work on a qualitative research project examining how professors recognized for excellent teaching deal with difficult moments in the classroom and their respective departments at a large midwestern research intensive public university. Those difficult moments usually addressed topics of race, diversity, and inequality within various university settings. We joined the team in part because of our research interests and desire to develop our qualitative research skills. Tiffany racially identifies as Black and ethnically identifies as an African American cisgender and heterosexual woman; much of her graduate research focused on race and racism in the US and Brazil. Laura is a White, Ashkenazi Jewish cisgender, heterosexual woman whose research background mainly focused on gender and sexuality. Both of us aimed to pursue academic careers.

For me (Tiffany), working on the project was an eye-opening and at times traumatic look into what my future as a Black woman in the academy might hold. The accounts of explicit racial discrimination and challenges that faculty of colour endured from students and colleagues gave me pause about entering the professoriate. At the same time, this work also prepared me for the road ahead. I learned early on the importance of being strategic about my time, became empowered about strategically saying no to extra service obligations, and understanding the academic structure so I could better navigate it amid the structural disadvantages I would encounter due to my intersectional identities. Working on this project and the papers we published from it was similarly eye-opening for me (Laura) – it taught me terms to describe the challenges I had heard about from my professors and peers who were members of marginalized groups. As a white (cis heterosexual) woman, I also knew that I had the immense privilege of likely not facing the identity taxation that Tiffany (and others) faced. Yet I have been struck by how universal our findings are for women faculty. Though our work on identity taxation focused on women faculty in departments where they were minorities (e.g., Science, Technology, Engineering, and Math departments), gendered labour seems to be taken up by women faculty across the disciplinary spectrum (including sociology and my new professional context, medicine).

Indeed, we have consistently noticed how ubiquitous this extra work is for people of colour, for women, and for other marginalized people. However, the terminology that has been used to describe this labour is extremely varied. As a result, scholars struggle to find the right way to talk about the challenges marginalized academics face. What we have learned over the years since we first published our work in this area, and especially over the course of working on this special issue, is that these various terms are useful for highlighting the different features of this labour. The additional terminology introduced by scholars in this special issue provide more precision in recognizing the multifaceted ways that diversity-related labour influences the experiences of marginalized faculty, staff, and students. In doing so, institutional community members ranging from administrators to students can use this language to better assess and improve institutional cultures and climates that have for so long excluded, extracted substantial service from, and penalized marginalized populations.

Fortunately, as terminology for this type of extra work has become more precise, knowledge about the labour that is being asked of marginalized academics has also become more widespread. In response to increasing awareness of systemic racism after the events of 2020, institutions are increasingly prioritizing the hiring of administrators whose focus is on diversity, equity, and inclusion (DEI) and promoting and developing programmes that support the recruitment and retention of faculty and students of colour (Scanlon, Zupsansky, and Sawicki 2022). Yet, as the articles in this special issue show, there still is so much further that the academy needs to go. Before and in the aftermath of 2020, the burden of identity taxation among faculty, staff, and students of colour led to negative health consequences and immense emotional labour and feelings of guilt. More importantly, even as institutions shifted their emphasis to engage in more DEI labour, high profile cases of promotion being denied to academics of colour who study racism highlight that identity taxation is still a major barrier faced by academics (Flaherty 2022; Mochkofsky 2021; Weissman 2020).

Working on this special issue a decade later, we are both now tenured professors at our respective universities. We have worked at two institutions each, and both have appointments in Sociology and in an interdisciplinary field (International Affairs for Tiffany, Medical Education for Laura). However, the number of faculty of colour at our past and present institutions remains low. Tiffany is also the first and still only tenured Black faculty member in her department. Both of us are in service leadership roles and have noted that the majority of those in similar positions (i.e., heavy workloads, low prestige) are also women. Aside from our personal observations, previous scholarship and the research highlighted in this special issue indicates that even as institutions state that they value having diverse communities, they must also acknowledge and value the hidden, informal racialized and gendered equity labour that disproportionately falls upon marginalized community members. The intensity of such labour often reduces the research productivity of those faculty, which is still the currency of the (White, male-dominated) academy. Despite the physical, emotional, mental, and productivity toll this labour extracts, it still is not considered relevant in tenure and promotion cases. Additionally, faculty who engage in research on race- or equity-related topics are still viewed as less legitimate scholars. Thus, until the structural inequality within academia is addressed to effectively acknowledge and ameliorate this uneven playing field, DEI efforts will remain futile and systemic racism and the burden of identity taxation among underrepresented faculty, staff, and students will persist. We hope this special issue will be a catalyst to spark much needed structural change by providing academic administrators, scholars, staff, and students with: 1) additional terminology to describe the nuances of identity taxation; 2) empirical insights about the experience of identity taxation for groups that have previously not been examined; and 3) recommendations for resistance and advocacy to change current inequitable practices and structures. We also hope that it may be used as a guide to transform and effectively counter racism and sexism within academia, as well as the identity taxation that has developed as a consequence.

Notes

1. We interchangeably use the terms "underrepresented" and "marginalized" to refer to individuals whose social groups have been and remain underrepresented relative to majority faculty, staff, and students based on race, ethnicity, gender, and sexual orientation. When discussing "cultural taxation," these terms apply to faculty, staff, and students of colour.
2. For this paper and several others, we have named the senior authors due to their well-known work in the area and their role in development of the theoretical frameworks that undergird the papers in this special issue. We are sensitive to "the Matthew Effect," however, and want to highlight the important contributions of all authors of these papers (Merton 1968).

Acknowledgements

We thank the editors and staff of the *Journal of Ethnic and Racial Studies* for accepting and navigating us through the publication of this special issue on a topic that has shaped our careers in unanticipated ways. We also wish to acknowledge the contributors to this special issue for their patience, persistence, and dedication throughout the revision and production process. This special issue could not have come together without the reviewers who closely read and provided feedback to contributing authors and we thank you for the time you devoted to this process. Lastly, thank you to Alford Young Jr., and Mark Chesler, who were the primary investigators of the research team that generated the data for our two earlier articles on cultural and identity taxation. We so appreciate your mentorship and generosity in allowing us to be part of the team.

ORCID

Tiffany D. Joseph http://orcid.org/0000-0003-3351-1678
Laura E. Hirshfield http://orcid.org/0000-0003-0894-2994

References

Flaherty, Colleen. 2022. "Tenure: The Black Box." *Inside Higher Education*, May 19. " https://www.insidehighered.com/news/2022/05/19/recent-tenure-denial-cases-raise-questions.

Hamilton, Laura, Kelly Nielsen, and Veronica Lerma. 2022. "Diversity Is a Corporate Plan: Racialized Equity Labor among University Employees." *Ethnic and Racial Studies*. doi:10.1080/01419870.2022.2089049.

Hatziponagos, Rachel. 2021. "What the Founders of Critical Race Theory Have to Say about Conservative Attacks." Washington Post, July 22. https://www.washingtonpost.com/nation/2021/07/22/critical-race-theory-founders/.

Hirshfield, Laura, and Tiffany Joseph. 2012. "'We Need a Woman, We Need a Black Woman': Gender, Race, and Identity Taxation in the Academy." *Gender and Education* 24: 213–227.

Joseph, Tiffany, and Laura Hirshfield. 2011. "'Why Don't You Get Somebody New to Do It?' Race and Cultural Taxation in the Academy." *Ethnic and Racial Studies* 34: 121–141.

Kolhatkar, Sonali. 2022. "How Scholars Are Countering Well-Funded Attacks on Critical Race Theory." Yes! Magazine, January 11 . https://www.yesmagazine.org/social-justice/2022/01/11/critical-race-theory-scholars-counter-funded-attacks.

Leonhardt, David. 2022. "What's Next for the Supreme Court." *The New York Times*, June 27. https://www.nytimes.com/2022/06/27/briefing/supreme-court-abortion.html.

Lerma, Veronica, Laura Hamilton, and Kelly Nielson. 2020. "Racialized Equity Labor, University Appropriation and Student Resistance." *Social Problems* 67: 286–303.

McGee, Ebony E., Devin T. White, Joyce B. Main, Monica F. Cox, and Lynette Parker. 2023. "How Women of Color Engineering Faculty Respond to Wage Disparities." *Ethnic and Racial Studies*. doi:10.1080/01419870.2022.2159474.

Melaku, Tsedale. 2019. *You Don't Look Like A Lawyer: Black Women and Systemic Gendered Racism*. Lanham, MD: Rowman & Littlefield.

Melaku, Tsedale, and Angie Beeman. 2022. "Black Women in White Academe: A Qualitative Analysis of Heightened Inclusion Tax." *Ethnic and Racial Studies*. doi:10.1080/01419870.2022.2149273.

Merton, Robert. 1968. "The Matthew Effect in Science." *Science* 159: 56–63.

Mochkofsky, Graciela. 2021. "Why Lorgia Garcia Pena Was Denied Tenure at Harvard." *The New Yorker*, July 27, https://www.newyorker.com/news/annals-of-education/why-lorgia-garcia-pena-was-denied-tenure-at-harvard.

Padilla, Amado. 1994. "Ethnic Minority Scholars, Research, and Mentoring: Current and Future Issues." *Educational Researcher* 23: 24–7.

Rosales, Oswaldo, Amado Padilla, Emily Petruzelli, and Clarissa Gutierrez. 2022. "Cultural Taxation or 'Tax Credit'? Understanding the Nuances of Ethnoracially Minoritized Student Labor in Higher Education." *Ethnic and Racial Studies*. doi:10.1080/01419870.2022.2143717.

Scanlon, Scott, Dale Zupsansky, and Stephen Sawicki. 2022. "The Rise of the Higher Education Chief Diversity Officer." Hunt Scanlon Media, April 13. https://huntscanlon.com/the-rise-of-the-higher-education-chief-diversity-officer/.

Turner, Caroline. 2022. "On Marginality, Socialization and Lessons Learned for the Future of Faculty Diversity." *Ethnic and Racial Studies*. doi:10.1080/01419870.2022.2115308.

Weissman, Sara. 2020. "Faculty of Color Confront Extra Obstacles on the Road to Tenure." *Diverse Issues in Higher Education*, July 1. https://www.diverseeducation.com/demographics/african-american/article/15107221/faculty-of-color-confront-extra-obstacles-on-the-road-to-tenure.

Zambrana, Ruth, Diana Carvajal, and Jalah Townsend. 2023. "Institutional Penalty: Mentoring, Service, Perceived Discrimination and its Impacts on the Health and Academic Careers of Latino Faculty." *Ethnic and Racial Studies*. doi:10.1080/01419870.2022.2160651.

Cultural taxation or "tax credit"? Understanding the nuances of ethnoracially minoritized student labour in higher education

Oswaldo Rosales [ID], Emily P. Schell, Clarissa Gutierrez and Amado Padilla

ABSTRACT
In this conceptual paper, we use an intersectional approach to understand the divergent outcomes stemming from ethnoracially minoritized students' labour to improve diversity on U.S. campuses. Research shows that attempts to leverage the perspectives of ethnoracially minoritized faculty in diversity work has levied a burden, known as cultural taxation (Padilla 1994), on the professional advancement of this group. While the literature on cultural taxation on faculty is well-developed, the impacts of taxation on students is less understood. We argue that, when ethnoracially minoritized students are asked to perform diversity-related labour, they can experience a similar tax on their academic and professional progress. However, we expand on this discussion to introduce the concept of a "cultural tax credit," whereby some students may benefit in a meaningful way from this diversity-related labour based on intersections of their other identities. We provide recommendations to both mitigate taxation and increase credits for students.

As demand for greater equity and inclusion in the U.S. academy grows, universities[1] have struggled to demonstrate how they are meeting the needs of a diverse student body (Oliha-Donaldson 2021). Often these efforts begin with the institution developing a mission statement that emphasizes their commitment to diversity[2] and the inclusion of all community members. In addition, it is common practice today for students to write application essays that describe the diversity (e.g. race/ethnicity, socioeconomic status (SES), gender) they will bring to campus. Presumably, such diversity, equity, and inclusion (DEI) statements enable university administrators to better understand the range of diversity among their student body. However, we take the position that these diversity statements represent a clear example of the potential labour that ethnoracially minoritized students[3] may be asked to engage in at their chosen institutions. Since universities began to ethnoracially diversify their student and faculty populations in the 1970s, there has been a troubling and persistent dichotomy between ethnoracially minoritized students and faculty who are expected to enrich a higher education institution's diversity and their white peers who are positioned as the beneficiaries of this newly "diverse" learning experience (Antonio et al. 2004).

This phenomenon, sometimes called *cultural taxation* (Padilla 1994), describes the distinct burden placed on ethnoracially minoritized people to fulfill the diversity-related needs of their universities and the price they pay to enter and succeed in these exclusionary spaces. Delving further into the reproduction of racial inequities in higher education institutions, Lerma and colleagues (2020) coined the term *racialized equity labour* to name the undercompensated efforts of ethnoracially minoritized people to address systemic racism within organizations, focusing on the labour of ethnoracially minoritized undergraduates (e.g. protests) to improve conditions for peers.

To date, the predominant focus in the literature on cultural taxation explores the negative impact of racialized equity labour on ethnoracially minoritized faculty, highlighting the toll of activities, such as mentorship, on their research productivity relative to their white peers (Faucett et al. 2022; Hamilton, Nielsen, and Lerma 2021; Hirshfield and Joseph 2012; Joseph and Hirshfield 2011; Padilla 1994). Although the impact of cultural taxation on ethnoracially minoritized faculty has been well-documented, the nuanced ways in which racialized equity labour impacts undergraduate and graduate students is not as well-understood.

While ethnoracial status is the main identity of interest for this conceptual paper, our goal is to elucidate how the intersections of other identities, namely socioeconomic and first-generation college-going status, combine to produce different outcomes from racialized equity labour. In particular, we argue that having other marginalized or privileged identities can produce a mix of *cultural taxation* or *cultural tax credits*, respectively, for ethnoracially minoritized students. We define a cultural tax credit as benefit(s) garnered from performing racialized equity labour, in contrast to cultural taxation, which results in cost(s) from this labour.

To reiterate, credits can occur when racialized equity labour does not burden but facilitates ethnoracially minoritized students' academic/professional paths. Ethnoracially minoritized students are not a monolithic group with uniform levels of privilege. As we further explain in our conceptual framework, students within this group who hold more privileged identities (e.g. high SES, college graduate parents) may be able to leverage their higher levels of dominant (or "Bourdieusian") social and cultural capital to extract benefits in academic contexts (Bourdieu 1986). Students who hold less privileged identities may find themselves unable to leverage similar levels of capital when performing racialized equity labour, which could levy a tax on their academic or professional trajectories in turn. Although less privileged ethnoracially minoritized students may possess "non-dominant" capital, as suggested by Yosso's (2005) *community cultural wealth*[4] model–which can serve as a protective factor–our argument here focuses on Bourdieusian capital because it aligns with the forms of capital valued in mainstream (predominantly white) U.S. universities (Bourdieu 1986; Bourdieu and Passeron 1990; Rios-Aguilar et al. 2011).[5]

Literature review

In the first publication delineating cultural taxation as a concept, Padilla (1994) shows how ethnoracially minoritized faculty's dedicated contributions to diversity-related efforts may go unrecognized/unrewarded within institutional reward systems that prioritize research. The combination of time committed to service at mostly white institutions, coupled with a lack of institutional recognition for such service, disproportionately hinders ethnoracially minoritized faculty from producing enough scholarship and accomplishing other professional achievements necessary to advance their careers. Joseph and Hirshfield (2011), and Hirshfield and Joseph (2012), call attention to the interaction of race and gender in faculty experiences, adopting *identity taxation* as a broadly encompassing term for the additional commitments delegated to faculty with minoritized identities linked to race, gender, and/or sexual orientation. Arguing that identity taxation can differentially affect faculty across intersectional identities (Crenshaw 1991), Hirshfield and Joseph (2012) highlight the additional labour that Black women faculty often endure in the academy. Furthermore, service by ethnoracially minoritized faculty may not be valued often. Rios-Aguilar and colleagues (2011) also call attention to the ways in which *funds of knowledge*[6] in Latinx communities are not perceived as legitimate forms of capital in dominant spaces, such as universities, contributing to barriers to advancement for Latinx faculty and students.

Although cultural and identity taxation have been documented among faculty, the impacts of diversity-related labour (i.e. racialized equity labour) among ethnoracially minoritized undergraduate and graduate students have not been investigated enough. One of the main early studies to investigate these impacts reveals how ethnoracially minoritized students are affected by structural racism and the burnout stemming from their labour to dismantle racist barriers (Lerma, Hamilton, and Nielsen 2020). However, a key distinction to draw is that, while all experiences of cultural taxation are examples of racialized equity labour, not all racialized equity labour embodies cultural taxation. We therefore aim to build on Lerma and colleagues' (2020) crucial work by investigating how the intersections of multiple identities, such as SES and college-going identities (Cabrera and Padilla 2004), contribute to outcomes ranging from cultural taxation to cultural tax credits for ethnoracially minoritized students. In doing so, we also expand on a budding line of scholarship in studies of ethnoracially minoritized faculty. Guillaume and Apodaca (2020) have begun to examine how some early-career faculty have learned to strategically manage cultural taxation and use these service experiences to their advantage in route to tenure.

However, before proceeding, we want to place the onus on universities to address these systemic inequalities, rather than on ethnoracially minoritized faculty or students navigating the often non-inclusive academy. In addition to setting forth the new idea of a cultural tax credit, our goal is to explore how universities can restructure their institutional reward systems in ways that better acknowledge and benefit all ethnoracially minoritized students for their racialized equity labour. This restructuring will be mutually beneficial.

Conceptual framework

In order to understand the ways in which racialized equity labour can contribute to disparate outcomes for ethnoracially minoritized students, we rely on three frameworks: Crenshaw's (1991) theory of intersectionality, Cabrera and Padilla's (2004) culture of college, and Jack's (2019) conception of the "privileged poor" and "doubly disadvantaged." These three frameworks shed light on how engaging in racialized equity labour, when considering a confluence of identities beyond ethnoracial status, can lead to cultural taxation, tax credits, or a mix of both.

Grounded in the tradition of critical race scholarship, *intersectionality* dictates that each person's combination of identities – including, but not limited to race, gender, SES, and college-going identity (e.g. a person who has a well-developed identity geared toward attending college) – intersect to create different degrees of privilege, or lack of it (Crenshaw 1991). Intersectionality rejects a singular focus on any one dimension of identity while also rejecting an analytical approach that views oppression as the sum of an individual's "parts." For example, a Black woman's experiences within universities are not merely an addition of the discrimination her Black male classmates face to the discrimination her white female peers face. Her experiences are unique due to her converging identities as a Black woman, among many other identities she holds, and how those identities interact with the sociohistorical context of the space she inhabits (Harris and Patton 2019). Intersectionality, in its most authentic form, is also a "radical vision for social justice" that is often diluted in higher education by administrators and scholars who reference the construct performatively, while remaining uncommitted to changing marginalizing structures within higher education (Harris and Patton 2019). Our focus is on ethnoracially minoritized students at both the undergraduate and graduate levels who perform racialized equity labour and the differential outcomes that follow from that work when we factor in identities such as SES and having a college-going identity.

We also utilize Cabrera and Padilla's *culture of college* framework to highlight "college-going" as a unique identity (i.e. potentially independent of SES) that is salient to students' experiences of cultural taxation. Cabrera and Padilla (2004) describe their culture of college as the process by which middle-class families with parent(s) having college experience relay information to their children about college-going norms and practices (i.e. dominant/Bourdieusian capital). This information can be procedural in scope, such as what classes to take and how to maintain a high grade point average (GPA) required for college admission, how to prepare for college entrance examinations (e.g. SATs), or how to apply to colleges and receive financial assistance. This information also extends to the often engrained and internalized mindsets and behaviours that college-educated parents, older siblings, peers, or even non-kin individuals such as teachers and counselors can convey when discussing college (Jack 2019; Stanton-Salazar 2011). In this way, the culture of college framework draws heavily on Bourdieu's (1986) concept of *habitus*: one's "schemata of perception, conception, and action" that is conditioned by one's position in a broader social structure. Students with this culture of college orientation are not only more likely to attend a university but are also likely to understand the unspoken yet omnipresent "rules of the game" once there (Bourdieu and Passeron 1990; Jack 2019). Such "rules" include self-advocacy, as exemplified by students attending office hours and building relationships with faculty (Jack 2019); and independence, as exemplified by students forging their own academic/extracurricular paths (Stephens et al. 2012). Put simply, students who have been socialized into a culture of college are more likely than students who have not been socialized to display mindsets and behaviours that align with the expectations universities have for their students.

While Cabrera and Padilla (2004) focus on how SES can be a conduit for college success, Jack (2019) calls attention to the ways in which these mindsets can be cultivated without a middle- or higher-income upbringing. Jack found that, although many of the ethnoracially minoritized students he interviewed were low-income, 50% received scholarships to attend elite preparatory high schools, making up a group he calls the *privileged poor*. Even if these privileged poor students were not socialized into the culture of college by their families, their elite schools helped them understand the rules critical to their success. Conversely, students who attended under-resourced schools or whose families lacked capital (i.e. the doubly disadvantaged) lacked similar exposure and struggled in college.

Together, these frameworks highlight a need for scholars to understand cultural taxation from a nuanced, intersectional perspective. Not all ethnoracially minoritized students will experience the same impact from their racialized equity labour. Based on the unique intersections of each student's identities, students who possess more privileged identities are more likely to gain an overall credit from their racialized equity labour, whereas students who possess less privileged identities may be more likely to experience an overall tax from their racialized equity labour (see Figure 1).[7]

Cultural tax credits can manifest as acknowledgment from faculty or administrators, which may yield mentoring relationships, letters of recommendation, or job opportunities that are important to academic and professional advancement. For example, an ethnoracially minoritized graduate student who is tapped to serve on a campus-wide DEI committee might still spend multiple hours on committee-related tasks for which that student may not ultimately receive compensation or ownership of their ideas. However, as a result, that student may gain a network of influential administrators, alum, or faculty members who can support that students' present and future development. But this depends, we argue, on a specific convergence of identities that will either result in an overall cultural tax or cultural tax credit for the ethnoracially minoritized student performing racialized equity labour. As we demonstrate below, such racialized equity labour often does not have such positive outcomes.

Why might some students experience the impacts of their racialized equity labour as a tax credit, whereas others experience these impacts as a tax? Which students might be more likely to receive this credit? Can students receive both a credit and a tax for their racialized equity labour? Are there overall taxes or credits for certain scholarly or professional pursuits? To begin to answer these questions, we juxtapose the experiences of two hypothetical male, cisgender, and ethnoracially minoritized graduate students, Joshua and Samuel, to stimulate discussion and consider different plausible outcomes. Utilizing composite storytelling based in Critical Race Theory (Solorzano and Yosso 2001), Joshua and Samuel are based on the authors' (of this paper) personal experiences as graduate students to illustrate how cultural taxation and cultural tax credits manifest across different contexts. Although many administrators are likely to perceive Joshua and

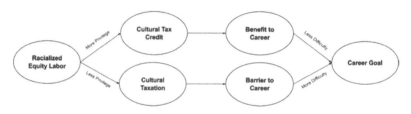

Figure 1. Cultural taxation and tax credits as pathways to careers.

Samuel as similar, analysis of their experiences through an intersectional framework reveals markedly different outcomes.[8]

Different outcomes from racialized equity labour: Joshua and Samuel's experiences

Joshua is a Latinx student who was raised in an upper middle-class home within walking distance to a major university in Cambridge, Massachusetts. He, his siblings, and both of his parents (of Mexican heritage) graduated from prestigious universities. Joshua was reared in a stable home and a safe community that offered many enrichment opportunities for him to develop his academic skills and interests. Joshua's parents also guided him into the culture of college by showing him how to take advantage of and maximize academic opportunities, such as applying for scholarships (Cabrera and Padilla 2004). Joshua attended a private high school, then a top private university, and upon graduation, was accepted into a highly ranked doctoral programme in psychology. Joshua's inculcation into the culture of college was a success.

Samuel is also from a minoritized Latinx background. His parents are blue-collar workers who lack a formal education beyond the U.S. equivalent of the 8th grade in Mexico. Samuel's family lives in a poor community in San Diego, California. Samuel was the only one in his family to attend and graduate from a large state university. Like Joshua, he was also admitted to the same doctoral programme. While Samuel was a relatively strong student, his parents were unable to provide guidance on developing study skills or navigating application processes because of their own limited educational and linguistic backgrounds. Samuel was also not one of the "privileged poor" students who could receive this guidance from non-kin peers or teachers at an elite high school (Jack 2019; Stanton-Salazar 2011). Samuel did not receive much guidance from either the counseling staff at his large public high school or state university. As a result, even through college, Samuel was not socialized as deeply into the culture of college as Joshua (Cabrera and Padilla 2004).[9] Nonetheless, through his hard work, persistence, occasional mentorship from experienced peers, and sources of knowledge, Samuel gained admission to the same competitive doctoral programme as Joshua.

While attending graduate school, university staff recruited both Joshua and Samuel to assist in a university-wide DEI initiative to create programmes for ethnoracially minoritized students. Joshua volunteered to co-create a collective for Black and Latinx undergraduate students, while Samuel volunteered to co-create a Black and Latinx first-generation college student group. Both Joshua and Samuel were honoured to have been selected to assist in creating these new programmes and volunteered their time. However, neither understood the magnitude of their undertaking: how much time would be necessary to complete this work and the subsequent impact on academic activities. Both students also felt implicit pressure or expectations from university administrators to take on this racialized equity labour. Consequently, both students had less time during the week to engage in research or related activities (e.g. conferences, coursework) that are essential to pursue their goal of securing a tenure-track faculty position. Despite the similar nature of Joshua and Samuel's work and time commitment, the outcomes for both students were quite different.

As a result of co-creating the ethnoracially minoritized students collective, Joshua further increased his visibility on campus. He was able to successfully use his dominant capital to network with other ethnoracially minoritized students and also with white students and faculty. These social activities were time-consuming and limited his focus on academics, but he was not impacted severely. Though Joshua had less time to devote to his research, he was able to find meaningful mentoring opportunities with non-minoritized and ethnoracially minoritized faculty that would ultimately help him advance his career goals. His grades suffered slightly but were inconsequential. Joshua's work to develop a student collective culminated in a positive environment for Black and Latinx students, and this development was viewed favourably by university leadership. Joshua was not paid for his labour; however, this was not a major concern for Joshua because his graduate stipend was adequate, and when necessary, could be supplemented by his family. Although Joshua navigates the world as an ethnoracially minoritized student, his high SES and strong orientation to the culture of college buffered the taxing effects of racialized equity labour on his academic and professional trajectory and allowed him to turn this work into an overall cultural tax credit.

Samuel did not have a similarly positive outcome as Joshua. Within half a year, Samuel began to feel that his volunteering was having a negative impact on time for studying and research. Though Samuel had increased visibility on campus from his collective's events, the process of event-planning and facilitation was time-consuming, which exacted a heavier toll on Samuel than on Joshua. Without the strong college preparation that Joshua's family and high school were able to provide, which offered an easier path to navigating college and graduate school, Samuel found himself needing more time to cultivate study strategies and identify academic supports–time and energy that were no longer available due to his racialized equity labour. Samuel grew increasingly stressed because he was falling behind his peers and not keeping up with his schoolwork. Although Samuel was at risk of academic probation at the end of two quarters of service, he continued to perform this racialized equity labour (alongside Joshua) due to his perception of administrator expectations and the enjoyment he felt from providing a supportive space for students like him. In addition to the cultural taxation that Samuel experienced due to his racialized equity labour, he also experienced economic hardship. Samuel's graduate stipend, while generous, often fell short of meeting all his financial needs. His family depended on him, so he took on other paid work (e.g. tutoring) to supplement his stipend in addition to his unpaid racialized equity labour. This further limited his ability to keep up with his studies compared to peers who were juggling fewer obligations. Though most graduate programmes prohibit working outside set hours, many students like Samuel seek work out of necessity.

Finally, although Joshua and Samuel both interfaced with the same influential campus leaders and faculty through their work, Samuel lacked the dominant capital to feel as comfortable as Joshua in professional networking. As a result, Samuel experienced more difficulties forming meaningful relationships that could have yielded mentorship, letters of recommendation, or other beneficial opportunities.

Another identity to consider is gender. Had Samuel been a woman, the taxation may have been worse. Some women do not take credit for the volunteer work they perform willingly making them vulnerable to external pressures to take on more work. One study by Haynes and Heilman (2013) showed that women were less likely to take credit for work done when engaged in similar work alongside men. Even more troublesome, due to social expectations of women to serve as caretakers, many may take on this additional labour without weighing the consequences or even perceive a need to request credit for such labour (Dean, Churchill, and Ruppanner 2022). In some cases, taxation may be worse for some women.

Joshua and Samuel both had less time for their graduate programme obligations because of their volunteer work, but Joshua experienced his racialized equity labour as a cultural tax credit, whereas Samuel experienced his respective duties as a cultural tax. In this hypothetical, yet plausible example, there are stark differences between these two students and how their levels of access to dominant capital shaped the outcomes of their racialized equity labour. Ethnoracial minoritization factored into why Joshua performed extra work, but it benefited him by offering the opportunity to build a network of faculty, administrators, and other students. His confidence, stemming from comfort navigating elite institutional spaces and male identity, allowed him to further enact and accumulate valuable dominant capital. Samuel had a less positive experience from his racialized equity labour. His unique intersection of identities made it more challenging for him to parlay this service into larger professional networks, mentorship, or other advancing opportunities.

We present the above hypotheticals, based on the authors' lived experience, with two caveats for further discussion. First, these hypotheticals focus on the graduate student experience with a career goal of a tenure-track faculty position, but the undergraduate context matters as well. Undergraduate ethnoracially minoritized students who engage in racialized equity labour can also be burdened by cultural taxation. It is not uncommon for these students to face negative consequences (e.g. academic probation) when balancing various uncompensated DEI efforts in addition to schoolwork (Lerma, Hamilton, and Nielsen 2020). In the context of pursuing academic careers, cultural taxation of undergraduate ethnoracially minoritized students can hinder their pipeline to graduate school, limiting diversity of campuses at the graduate level, and subsequently, at the faculty level. As such, this cultural taxation of undergraduate students ultimately presents a hidden institutional cost of its own for universities in the form of intellectual talent loss. In addition, non-academic careers can be taxed. Although the prevailing focus of the literature on cultural taxation is career advancement in academia, we also recognize that this taxation may impact undergraduate and graduate students pursuing non-academic careers by limiting the energy that could be devoted to bolstering resumes through career-enhancing opportunities.

Second, these hypotheticals highlight only a few identities an individual can hold such as ethnicity/race, first-generation college status, SES, gender, and college-going identity. It is essential to note the dynamic and multifaceted nature of intersectional identities, particularly as they relate to cultural taxation and cultural tax credits. Such phenomena do not exist as a simple binary, but rather on a continuum from less privilege to more privilege. In a similar way, there is a continuum with taxation on one extreme and tax credit at the other extreme.

Therefore, context matters. An ethnoracially minoritized student may experience taxation due to certain identities in one setting or situation, while receiving a tax credit in another. For example, a Black female student may experience cultural taxation fighting for more inclusive and supportive pedagogy in her school's computer science department but receive recognition for serving as president of her school's chapter of a Society of Black Engineers (where there may be financial support, a sense of belonging, and influential ethnoracial support network). The important point to consider is that, even though there is usually an ebb and flow of taxes and credits, students who are multiply marginalized likely have more sensitive tipping points than their more privileged peers–which has dire consequences for the future diversity of the professoriate and the knowledge it creates.

In the following section, we set forth three common examples of student racialized equity labour that manifests in either cultural tax credits or taxation to showcase how these gradations of support are working on many U.S. campuses. We also periodically refer to our hypothetical students, Joshua and Samuel, to highlight our position.

Examples of student labour: same goals, different support

It is important to emphasize that the focus of our critique lies in university structures that unfairly mete out advantages to certain students based on their arbitrary intersection of identities, rather than the individual students themselves. Students like Joshua who hold privileged identities (e.g. high SES, having a college-going identity, male, etc.) are not at fault for navigating institutions in ways that are beneficial. Ethnoracially minoritized students engage in many forms of racialized equity labour that might have the same goal (e.g. creating a more inclusive learning environment for similar students), but differ in levels of institutional support or acknowledgement. The following analysis focuses on three common forms of student labour: committee service, peer advising, and student organizing. Although, as discussed further in our implications section, there are certainly variations in individual students' experiences, we argue that committee service may likely provide a host of tax credits, advising may create either a credit or tax, and student organizing may likely present a tax.

Committee service

Responding to calls for greater institutional acknowledgement and accountability to inequities on campus, many universities have committees dedicated specifically to DEI issues. These committees are typically staffed by a select group of administrators, faculty, staff, undergraduates, and graduate students. Historically, these committees were often created performatively to give the impression of action on behalf of minoritized groups or to comply with social/legal pressures; as a result, these committees tended to have limited impact (Oliha-Donaldson 2021). However, given increasingly public calls from students and faculty alike for comprehensive racial justice plans, as opposed to mere solidarity statements (e.g. national attention to Pennsylvania State University's Black faculty organizing) (Anderson 2020), the status and impact of ethnoracially minoritized groups has likely been elevated in recent years. Furthermore, regardless of the effectiveness of these committees, the opportunity to interface with influential members of the campus community (e.g. school leaders) still yields a host of tax credits for the ethnoracially minoritized student representative, such as recommendations, demonstrated leadership, and extensive knowledge of a system's bureaucracy, which may prove helpful for navigating future employer or graduate school systems.

Given that these committees are composed of few members, student nominations or references from faculty or staff is a likely requirement for selection to these positions. To receive a nomination, students must either have a strong relationship with faculty and/or be a recognized leader. Like the hypothetical Joshua or the actual privileged poor that Jack (2019) discusses, some ethnoracially minoritized students socialized into a culture of college have less difficulty talking to faculty, attending office hours, or seeking individualized opportunities–steps essential to cultivating strong relationships (Jack 2019; Massey et al. 2006).

In addition to the selection processes serving as a barrier to ethnoracially minoritized students who might not have the necessary confluence of SES, culture of college, or gender-based privileges, the unpaid nature and timing of such committee service may present further barriers. As illustrated by the hypothetical experiences of Joshua and Samuel, unpaid labour presents different opportunity costs to students based on their pre-existing financial resources (Sawhill 2016). As a result, poor ethnoracially minoritized students may be left with a hard choice: take a paid position and forgo opportunities for long-term connections and professional advancement, forgo income in favour of committee service, or, as Samuel chose, take on an additional paid position. Even if an ethnoracially minoritized student chose one of the latter two options, the timing of meetings, which may be amenable to daytime work or class schedules of faculty and staff, may limit engagement from ethnoracially minoritized students who have part-time work or family obligations at those times. Accordingly, the combination of selection processes that value certain attributes, such as faculty relationships, in tandem with an unpaid compensation structure and logistics favouring a "traditional" work schedule bars committee service–a clear tax credit–from students who cannot enact dominant capital.

Peer advising or mentoring

Another form of racialized equity labour that can present a cultural tax credit for certain ethnoracially minoritized students is peer advising/mentoring programmes. Typically, peer advising is used to supplement four-year institutions' faculty or staff academic advising for first- or second-year undergraduates. Peer advisors can provide academic support (e.g. giving a student perspective on academic experiences) or broader socioemotional support (e.g. helping students navigate the challenges of this key life transition period) (Shiner 1999). Historically, peer advising has often taken place within a specific academic discipline where more experienced undergraduates support entering peers with an interest in that discipline. In light of concerns with academic advising lacking in cultural competence (Lee 2018), peer advising in ethnoracially minoritized communities has emerged (Mitchell, Wood, and Witherspoon 2010). One example is an undergraduate mentorship programme at our institution, which uses peer advisors to support incoming first-generation and/or low-income students with the goal of creating a sense of belonging (Sullivan 2017).

Similar to being on a campus-wide DEI committee, serving as a peer advisor can be parlayed into leadership experience or recommendations from administrators. Beyond the positive addition to one's resume, the opportunities for developing students' leadership skills and self-efficacy should not be overlooked. However, as with committee service, this opportunity has the potential of offering many forms of tax credits but is limited to a select group of ethnoracially minoritized students. The selection process for these peer advising programmes, particularly those with monetary compensation, is often rigorous, requiring letters of recommendations from faculty and demonstrated academic achievement. Some students, such as the hypothetical Samuel, may not meet one or both of those requirements because of co-existing work and family responsibilities, and limited relationships with faculty. Even before reaching the formal selection process, self-selection plays a prominent role. Students with a culture of college orientation, such as the hypothetical Joshua, are more likely to value the importance of seeking out and vying for leadership opportunities, such as peer mentoring. Other students who feel overwhelmed by schoolwork and necessary work to support themselves and/or family may feel less confident to seek out such positions. Ironically, it is this latter group of students – Samuel and like peers – who may have the most to offer incoming students, particularly first-generation and/or low-income ethnoracially minoritized students, because of their life-affirming first-hand experience navigating their university (Clark and Kalionzes 2011).

Unlike committee service, however, peer advising may not always be associated with a cultural tax credit. As discussed above, peer advising programmes for ethnoracially minoritized students arose because of persistent needs for greater institutional support of those populations (Lee 2018; Mitchell, Wood, and Witherspoon 2010). Consequently, even if a peer advisor receives compensation, in the absence of other institutional supports, these advising relationships may be undervalued by university staff. In addition, ethnoracially minoritized students (with other minoritized identities) in peer advising roles may feel a sense of indebtedness to help peers who are at an earlier stage of college. Piorkowski (1983) describes this phenomenon as *survivor's guilt*, focusing on the negative emotions that first-generation, low SES college students often experience based on perceptions of leaving family or friends "behind." Accordingly, as these aforementioned papers suggest and work by Hamilton and colleagues (2021) finds, due to inadequate institutional support, some peer advisors end up assuming unplanned and unpaid labour far beyond the initial terms of their peer advising relationship to mitigate their guilt and uplift similar peers: a clear example of taxation.

Additionally, in the absence of a peer advising programme entirely, some students, particularly those from first-generation college backgrounds, may feel obligated to create entirely informal networks of support. These informal advising or mentoring relationships likely mirror the institutionalized peer advising programmes discussed above, as these more advanced students may still provide advice on navigating their university (Gay 2004), identifying and building relationships with supportive faculty, or simply providing a friendly, supportive face in an otherwise unwelcoming, predominantly white space (Turner 1994). Despite the potentially identical nature of these informal advisors' work, in the absence of institutional recognition or compensation, this labour in service of their higher education institution presents an even more conspicuous cultural tax for ethnoracially minoritized students. Yet again, one sees how broader institutional decisions around the selectivity and compensation of certain peer advising programmes, investments in concurrent supports for ethnoracially minoritized students, and beliefs about the need for a formalized peer advising programme in the first place create different pathways to tax credits or taxation.

Student organizing

Student organizing at universities has a long history and may be triggered by external socio-political events, such as the Black Lives Matter movement, or internal events, such as the denial of tenure to a popular faculty member of colour or rejection of student calls to create a department of African and African American Studies (Retta 2021). Although student organizing is not usually institutionally sanctioned in the same way as committee service or peer advising, higher education leadership has typically embraced some student causes that were previously considered unpopular. Student organizing has tended to result in structural changes that have improved both the institution's standing among peer institutions and the lives of ethnoracially minoritized students (Lerma, Hamilton, and Nielsen 2020). However, students involved in making these campus changes are unlikely to see these improvements in their lifetime (Hamilton, Nielsen, and Lerma 2021). For example, a recent recommendation to departmentalize African and African American Studies at our institution – a decision the university is proud of (Leighton 2021) – came only after 50 years of dedicated student organizing (Retta 2021). Accordingly, the multi-generational costs to student organizers' academic and emotional well-being are another example of cultural taxation.

There are many elements of successful student organizing, including mobilizing multiple university constituencies (e.g. student allies, sympathetic faculty), disseminating relevant knowledge (e.g. flyers, teach-ins), and logistical organization for protests and other direct actions (e.g. contacting university security). Even in isolation, such tasks may require a full-time position at a university, like a diversity officer (in the case of teach-ins) or an event planner (in the case of logistical organization). Yet, unlike paid, full-time positions, individual or small groups of student organizers often juggle these unpaid tasks on top of their academic work and personal obligations. In addition to the lack of compensation or acknowledgement for students' efforts, student organizing is unlikely to produce a cultural tax credit for ethnoracially minoritized students.

Another essential element of student organizing – protests and direct action – helps explain why campus leadership, faculty, and staff are less likely to reward ethnoracially minoritized student organizers for this particular form of racialized equity labour. Protests draw attention to institutional failures, which puts student organizers at odds with administrators, faculty, or staff. These organizers do not typically engage with institutional agents with career advancement, recommendations, or mentorship in mind. Rather, as recent work from Gibson and Williams (2019) describes, they engage because they are angry and want to transform their institution for the better. Accordingly, student protestors' language (e.g. "no justice, no peace") and tactics (e.g. student "sit in" protests) may be alienating to administrators because of the negative publicity they bring to the institution (Murphy 2020). In turn, these students may be less likely to receive support from administrators, faculty, or staff in seeking opportunities, such as committee service, that might be more generative for students' academic or professional advancement.

It is also worth noting who makes up the bulk of student organizers on today's campuses. Although a comprehensive study of the characteristics of student protestors has not been attempted since the 1970s (e.g. Molm and Astin 1973), journalistic analyses of protest leaders (Anderson 2020) reveals that these organizers are more likely to be those most marginalized by their institution: first-generation/low SES, female, and/or disabled ethnoracially minoritized students. This finding is not entirely surprising: these students are most likely to be aware of inadequate institutional support for ethnoracially minoritized students, having suffered from inadequate support themselves. Unfortunately, student organizers who are juggling academic work, potential outside employment and/or familial responsibilities–in addition to the invisible and contentious labour involved in organizing–may be the very students who experience the most severe taxation while also being the least capable of weathering it.

Implications for higher education institutions

While our goal in drawing a distinction between cultural taxation and cultural tax credits is to acknowledge that ethnoracially minoritized students are not a monolithic group with uniform levels of privilege, it is critical to frame the deeper discussion around structural inequality and systemic racism. As higher education institutions seek to prioritize DEI and lasting cultural shifts in the academy, they must commit fully to dismantling pervasive systems of oppression and to the "radical vision for social justice" that Crenshaw (1991) and her contemporaries envisioned (Harris and Patton 2019). This pursuit involves eradicating the unfair load of labour placed on the shoulders of ethnoracially minoritized students (as well as faculty and staff). Accordingly, the question for administrators seeking to better support ethnoracially minoritized students must be: how can the institution be restructured so that these students no longer need to engage in racialized equity labour?

Nevertheless, in the immediate absence of such structural changes, we offer the following recommendations to higher education leaders and administrators seeking to more equitably distribute compensation and acknowledgement to all ethnoracially minoritized students engaged in this labour. Our recommendations are less concerned with changing or eliminating the three forms of racialized equity labour discussed above, as there is still need for DEI committees to share ideas with key university stakeholders, peer advising to provide culturally responsive advising to students of colour, and student organizing to hold universities accountable for contributing positively to the larger community. Rather, we want to encourage university leaders to change the institutional contexts in which this labour is situated–making changes to broader selection processes, compensation structures, and re-building trust with student of colour communities–so that student organizers (and others) may be just as likely to receive a tax credit from their work as students serving on committees.

Recommendation one: change selection processes

Our first recommendation is for administrators to think critically about the ethnoracially minoritized students they select for service or advising positions which, as we have shown above, can be a rich source of tax credits. Taking an intersectional approach to student selection from this diverse group is not only important from an equity and justice perspective, but for the efficacy of those committees or advising efforts. Although no one student can represent a group, it is more likely that the hypothetical Samuel may be able to speak to a wider range of ethnoracially minoritized student needs and demographics than the hypothetical Joshua, even if, as discussed above, Joshua is more likely to gain a coveted committee spot. The status quo yields committee recommendations that may not address the root concerns for many ethnoracially minoritized students, whereas an intersectional approach may be more likely to yield transformative change across multiple identities. In terms of advising, a peer advisor like Samuel, who struggled to navigate his university, may be better positioned to provide relevant support to a first-generation and/or low SES ethnoracially minoritized students who may be experiencing similar struggles.

Taking an intersectional approach to selective opportunities for ethnoracially minoritized students requires not only a critical eye from the selectors, but a fundamental restructuring of the process itself. What changes might begin to facilitate this restructuring? As discussed above, factors in both the committee and advising selection process (e.g. faculty references, high GPAs) may result in the self-selection of ethnoracially minoritized students with greater familiarity to a culture of college. Instead of indicators that focus on individual academic achievement, administrators might consider employing peer references that speak to the strength of students' community contributions, which may be more likely to draw out the community-oriented and derived funds of knowledge present in many low-income, ethnoracially minoritized communities (Rios-Aguilar et al. 2011; Vélez-Ibañez and Greenberg 1992). Administrators can also take into account students' academic growth and psychosocial adjustment throughout their time at their university, rather than simply GPA, and sensitivity to recognizing that students like Samuel have more obstacles to achieve a high level of academic success. Moreover, a time-intensive application process, even one that incorporates more inclusive elements, still may present too steep of an opportunity cost to some low-income students, and therefore is only an "ornamental," rather than actual, intersectional approach to selection (Harris and Patton 2019). Administrators should seek to reduce the time such application processes require, so that students are not forced to choose between applying to "creditable" opportunities and more pressing obligations. These changes might encourage engagement from a wider cross-section of ethnoracially minoritized students.

For these changes to work, however, non-traditional (e.g. first-generation) students must trust that their service to their higher education institution while potentially time consuming will be valuable and acknowledged. Where there is no trust, then no matter the selection process, students most able to help may not be willing to do so. Thankfully, the aforementioned changes to selection processes (e.g. valuing the importance of community contributions, rather than individual achievement; recognizing different opportunity costs to going through a selection process) will help reduce the distrust that ethnoracially minoritized students feel when their universities fail to recognize their non-dominant forms of capital (i.e. funds of knowledge) or the unique barriers they face in accessing higher education (Rios-Aguilar et al. 2011).

Recommendation two: expand access to cultural tax credits

Our second recommendation is to expand the number of "creditable" opportunities for ethnoracially minoritized students. As discussed above, student organizing is simultaneously a service to the university (although leadership may not perceive this) and a cultural tax for student organizers. How might administrators provide adequate support to student organizers to create cultural tax credits rather than cultural taxation? Such an answer likely varies by institution, so the following ideas should not be implemented without first centering the perspectives of ethnoracially minoritized student organizers on campus as well as considering the positive or negative attitudes of campus leadership, faculty, and staff towards this particular form of racialized equity labour. With this caveat in mind, we believe one option might be providing course credit for such efforts (e.g. a "Directed Reading in Social Action") to alleviate the double burden of necessary coursework and time devoted to organizing. Presumably, this approach would also reduce cultural taxation among ethnoracially minoritized faculty, who may informally mentor undergraduate/graduate students involved in organizing based on their personal sense of solidarity with students' causes; teaching such a course might reduce these faculty members' course loads while allowing them to receive their own version of a cultural tax credit for previously invisible labour. Another potential credit may be fellowship opportunities for student organizers that offer mentorship from notable representative community organizers, offsetting the need for low SES ethnoracially minoritized students to take on other jobs, while providing academic or professional enrichment.

Recommendation three: acknowledge the subjectivity of students' experiences

Our third recommendation is for administrators, faculty, and staff to acknowledge the subjectivity of ethnoracially minoritized students' experiences. Throughout this paper, we have complicated the idea of a monolithic ethnoracially minoritized student population by showing how, based on a convergence of identities, some ethnoracially minoritized students may experience more cultural tax credits in the form of academic or professional advantages, whereas others may experience more cultural taxation when in addition to race/ethnicity, other identities such as SES, college-going identity, and gender factor in, sometimes in powerful ways (including discouraging some students from pursuing an academic faculty position). However, academic and professional progress are only two elements of a students' higher educational experience: emotional and physical well-being also play essential roles. We hypothesize that ethnoracially minoritized students whose labour is taxing to their academic or professional progress likely experience concurrent declines in psychological and/or even physical well-being. A large body of literature supports this notion (e.g. Angner 2010; LeDoux et al. 2018) showing that a positive or negative subjective perception of one's experience has critical impacts on mental and physical well-being. Thus, even if an ethnoracially minoritized students' academic or professional progress is impeded by cultural taxation, a positive subjective perception of that task may mitigate the tax's negative impact by boosting a students' psychological or physical well-being. For example, the hypothetical Joshua may be more equipped to parlay his experience co-creating a student of colour collective into mentorship and recommendations; however, if Joshua feels tokenized by administrators' requests to help with this initiative, he may experience less of a cultural tax credit due to the negative impact of this task on his psychological well-being. A similar phenomenon may be observed among students who are asked to serve on DEI committees that are created to merely give the impression (i.e. virtue-signaling), rather than effect, of action on behalf of ethnoracially minoritized communities. On the flip side, if Samuel feels that his efforts on behalf of administrators' requests are appreciated or recognized, he may experience less of a cultural tax due to a potentially improved sense of well-being. Accordingly, it is important for administrators to not only expand access to cultural tax credits and replicate these credits in other contexts, but also to consistently "member check" with the recipients of these tax credits. Through consistent and well-compensated focus groups and interviews with a diverse cross-section of ethnoracially minoritized students, administrators can ensure that students' perceptions of their experience align with the tax credit that administrators hope to provide.

The above recommendations are centered around racialized equity labour carried out by ethnoracially minoritized students. Other minoritized student groups, such as women, LGBTQ, and disabled students are also engaged in similar labour to diversify their institutions. Additionally, although our paper focuses on both undergraduate and graduate students, undergraduate and graduate students are distinct populations that may respond differently to the same form of tax credits. For example, letters of recommendation may be a tax credit for both undergraduate and graduate students, but hourly pay may prove more beneficial to undergraduates than graduate students, as some graduate students also receive a stipend. Future scholarship should assess how these gradations of cultural taxation and potential shift to cultural tax credits may look in other minoritized student groups and between undergraduate and graduate students.

In conclusion, university leaders, faculty members, and staff, in conjunction with student leaders, can begin to foster more inclusive environments for ethnoracially minoritized students by critically evaluating and restructuring the institutional reward systems that perpetuate social inequality in minoritized students' career advancement and academic experience. Employing more equitable, sustainable reward practices that take a comprehensive range of cultural contexts and social identities into account may not only affirm students for their contributions to improve campus climate, but also help alleviate the burnout and imposter syndrome that minoritized students often endure when they are overworked, undercompensated, and undervalued (Ewing et al. 1996).

Notes

1. We will use university, college, and higher education institution interchangeably.
2. Our focus in this paper regarding diversity in higher education institutions pertains mostly to ethnoracial and socioeconomic diversity, but other identities, such as gender and sexual orientation are also important for universities to include.
3. Informed by Benitez's work (2010), we use the term "ethnoracially minoritized students," as opposed to minority students, to highlight the process of minoritization that historically underrepresented students (e.g., African American, Asian, Latinx) endure.
4. Yosso's (2005) model challenges dominant/Bourdieusian capital and suggests that marginalized communities of color have their own types of social and cultural capital, such as familial (e.g., commitment to family) and aspirational capital (e.g., having hope in the face of discrimination). She argues that such capital plays an essential role in achieving goals such as graduating from college.
5. This reality may be changing as universities increase the ethnoracial and socioeconomic diversity of their faculty and students.
6. Defined as knowledge based on personal experience within a given culture or smaller structure (e.g., family). For example, first-generation Latinx student translating/interpreting for Spanish-speaking immigrant parents.
7. Students with more privileged identities (e.g., upper middle-class) have more dominant capital due to having many resources (e.g., money, well-resourced schools, influential connections) versus less privileged students (e.g., low-income) who have less dominant capital because they lack resources.
8. Although Joshua and Samuel's stories may seem overly simplified, the successes and struggles these students faced are highly plausible and elucidate the racist and classist systems that impact ethnoracially minoritized students. Even if some students, such as Samuel, possess high non-dominant capital, these sources of knowledge are not as valued in mainstream U.S. universities as dominant Bourdieusian capital is. Accordingly, although highly flawed, the status quo at most U.S. universities is to perceive Joshua's capital through an asset-based framework, while perceiving Samuel's capital through a deficit-based framework.
9. Though Samuel likely had accumulated some dominant capital as he made his way to graduate school, differences in class status compared to Joshua suggest that Samuel did not have similar levels of dominant capital or the habitus to maximize the opportunity to turn his racialized equity labor into credits instead of taxation.

Disclosure statement

No potential conflict of interest was reported by the author(s).

ORCID

Oswaldo Rosales http://orcid.org/0000-0002-1606-5170

References

Anderson, G. (2020, November 9). "With us or Against us?" *Inside Higher Ed*. https://www.insidehighered.com/news/2020/11/09/students-color-haverford-college-continue-strike-racial-equity

Angner, E. 2010. "Subjective Well-Being." *The Journal of Socio-Economics* 39 (3): 361–368. doi:10.1016/j.socec.2009.12.001.

Antonio, A. L., M. J. Chang, K. Hakuta, D. A. Kenny, S. Levin, and J. F. Milem. 2004. "Effects of Racial Diversity on Complex Thinking in College Students." *Psychological Science* 15 (8): 507–510.

Benitez, M., Jr. 2010. "Resituating Culture Centers Within a Social Justice Framework: Is There Room for Examining Whiteness?" In *Culture Centers in Higher Education: Perspectives on Identity, Theory, and Practice*, edited by L. D. Patton, 119–134. Stylus.

Bourdieu, P. 1986. "The Forms of Capital." In *Handbook of Theory and Research for the Sociology of Education*, edited by J. Richardson, 241–258. Westport, CT: Greenwood.

Bourdieu, P., and J. C. Passeron. 1990. *Reproduction in Education, Society and Culture* (R. Nice, Trans. 2nd ed.). London, United Kingdom: Sage.

Cabrera, N. L., and A. M. Padilla. 2004. "Entering and Succeeding in the "Culture of College": The Story of Two Mexican Heritage Students." *Hispanic Journal of Behavioral Sciences* 26 (2): 152–170.

Clark, E., and J. Kalionzes. 2011. "Advising Students of Color and International Students." In *Academic Advising: A Comprehensive Handbook*, edited by V. N. Gordon, W. R. Habley, and T. J. Grites, 204–226. Jossey-Bass.

Crenshaw, K. 1991. "Mapping the Margins: Intersectionality, Identity Politics, and Violence Against Women of Color." *Stanford Law Review* 43 (6): 1241–1299.

Dean, L., B. Churchill, and L. Ruppanner. 2022. "The Mental Load: Building a Deeper Theoretical Understanding of How Cognitive and Emotional Labor Overload Women and Mothers." *Community, Work & Family* 25 (1): 13–29. doi:10.1080/13668803.2021.2002813.

Duckworth, A. L., C. Peterson, M. D. Matthews, and D. R. Kelly. 2007. "Grit: Perseverance and Passion for Long-Term Goals." *Journal of Personality and Social Psychology* 92 (6): 1087–1101.

Ewing, K. M., T. Q. Richardson, L. James-Myers, and R. K. Russell. 1996. "The Relationship Between Racial Identity Attitudes, Worldview, and African American Graduate Students' Experience of the Imposter Phenomenon." *Journal of Black Psychology* 22 (1): 53–66. doi:10.1177/00957984960221005.

Faucett, E. A., M. J. Brenner, D. M. Thompson, and V. A. Flanary. 2022. "Tackling the Minority Tax: A Roadmap to Redistributing Engagement in Diversity, Equity, and Inclusion Initiatives." *Otolaryngology–Head and Neck Surgery*, doi:10.1177/01945998221091696.

Gay, G. 2004. "Navigating Marginality en Route to the Professoriate: Graduate Students of Color Learning and Living in Academia." *International Journal of Qualitative Studies in Education* 17 (2): 265–288. doi:10.1080/09518390310001653907.

Gibson, C., and F. Williams. 2019. "Understanding the Impetus for Modern Student Activism for Justice at an HBCU: A Look at Personal Motivations." *The Urban Review* 52 (2): 263–276. doi:10.1007/s11256-019-00527-0.

Guillaume, R. O., and E. C. Apodaca. 2020. "Early Career Faculty of Color and Promotion and Tenure: The Intersection of Advancement in the Academy and Cultural Taxation." *Race Ethnicity and Education*, 1–18.

Hamilton, L. T., K. Nielsen, and V. Lerma. 2021. "Diversity is a Corporate Plan: Racialized Equity Labor Among University Employees." Manuscript in preparation. School of Social Sciences, Humanities and Arts, University of California, Merced & Extension, University of California, San Diego.

Harris, J. C., and L. D. Patton. 2019. "Un/Doing Intersectionality Through Higher Education Research." *The Journal of Higher Education* 90 (3): 347–372. doi:10.1080/00221546.2018.1536936.

Haynes, M. C., and M. E. Heilman. 2013. "It Had To Be You (Not Me)! Women's Attributional Rationalization of Their Contribution to Successful Joint Work Outcomes." *Personality and Social Psychology Bulletin* 39 (7): 956–969.

Hirshfield, L. E., and T. D. Joseph. 2012. "'We Need a Woman, We Need a Black Woman': Gender, Race, and Identity Taxation in the Academy." *Gender and Education* 24 (2): 213–227.

Jack, A. A. 2019. *The Privileged Poor: How Elite Colleges are Failing Disadvantaged Students*. Harvard University Press.

Joseph, T. D., and L. E. Hirshfield. 2011. "'Why Don't you get Somebody new to do it?' Race and Cultural Taxation in the Academy." *Ethnic and Racial Studies* 34 (1): 121–141.

LeDoux, J., R. Brown, D. Pine, and S. Hofmann. 2018. "Know Thyself: Well-Being and Subjective Experience." *Cerebrum: The Dana Forum on Brain Science* 2018: cer-01-18.

Lee, J. A. 2018. "Affirmation, Support, and Advocacy: Critical Race Theory and Academic Advising." *NACADA Journal* 38 (1): 77–87. doi:10.12930/NACADA-17-028.

Leighton, J. 2021, March 22. "Departmentalizing the African and African American Studies (AAAS) Program." *Stanford Today*. https://news.stanford.edu/today/2021/03/22/departmentalizing-african-african-american-studies-aaas-program/.

Lerma, V., L. T. Hamilton, and K. Nielsen. 2020. "Racialized Equity Labor, University Appropriation and Student Resistance." *Social Problems* 67 (2): 286–303.

Massey, D. S., C. Z. Charles, G. Lundy, and M. J. Fischer. 2006. *The Source of the River: The Social Origins of Freshmen at America's Selective Colleges and Universities*. Princeton University Press.

Mitchell, R. W., G. K. Wood, and N. Witherspoon. 2010. "Considering Race and Space: Mapping Developmental Approaches for Providing Culturally Responsive Advising." *Equity & Excellence in Education* 43 (3): 294–309. doi:10.1080/10665684.2010.496691.

Molm, L. D., and A. W. Astin. 1973. "Personal Characteristics and Attitude Changes of Student Protesters." *Journal of College Student Personnel*.

Murphy, K. 2020, June 3. "Hundreds Gather Peacefully on UNC Campus, Then March to Protest George Floyd Death." *The News & Observer*. https://www.newsobserver.com/news/local/article243238551.html.

Oliha-Donaldson, H. 2021. "A Genealogy of "Diversity:" From the 1960s to Problematic Diversity Agendas and Contemporary Activism." In *Confronting Equity and Inclusion Incidents on Campus: Lessons Learned and Emerging Practices*, edited by H. Oliha-Donaldson, 26–48. Routledge.

Padilla, A. M. 1994. "Research News and Comment: Ethnic Minority Scholars; Research, and Mentoring: Current and Future Issues." *Educational Researcher* 23 (4): 24–27.

Piorkowski, G. K. 1983. "Survivor Guilt in the University Setting." *The Personnel and Guidance Journal* 61 (10): 620–622. doi:10.1111/j.2164-4918.1983.tb00010.x.

Retta, M. 2021, March 16. "Stanford's African American Studies Department is the Result of Student Activism." *Teen Vogue*. https://www.teenvogue.com/story/stanford-african-american-studies-department.

Rios-Aguilar, C., J. M. Kiyama, M. Gravitt, and L. C. Moll. 2011. "Funds of Knowledge for the Poor and Forms of Capital for the Rich? A Capital Approach to Examining Funds of Knowledge." *Theory and Research in Education* 9 (2): 163–184. doi:10.1177/1477878511409776.

Sawhill, I. V. 2016, July 28. "Higher Education and the Opportunity Gap." *Brookings*. https://www.brookings.edu/research/higher-education-and-the-opportunity-gap/.

Shiner, M. 1999. "Defining Peer Education." *Journal of Adolescence* 22 (4): 555–566. doi:10.1006/jado.1999.0248.

Solorzano, Daniel G., and Tara J. Yosso. 2001. "Critical Race and LatCrit Theory and Method: Counter-Storytelling." *International Journal of Qualitative Studies in Education* 14 (4): 471–495. doi:10.1080/09518390110063365.

Stanton-Salazar, R. D. 2011. "A Social Capital Framework for the Study of Institutional Agents and Their Role in the Empowerment of Low-Status Students and Youth." *Youth & Society* 43 (3): 1066–1109.

Stephens, N. M., S. A. Fryberg, H. R. Markus, C. S. Johnson, and R. Covarrubias. 2012. "Unseen Disadvantage: How American Universities' Focus on Independence Undermines the Academic Performance of First-Generation College Students." *Journal of Personality and Social Psychology* 102 (6): 1178–1197. doi:10.1037/a0027143.

Sullivan, K. 2017, August 29. "Leland Scholars at Home on the Farm." *Stanford News*. https://news.stanford.edu/2017/08/24/leland-scholars-introduced-life-farm/.

Turner, C. S. V. 1994. "Guests in Someone Else's House: Students of Color." *The Review of Higher Education* 17 (4): 355–370. doi:10.1353/rhe.1994.0008.

Vélez-Ibañez, C., and J. Greenberg. 1992. "Formation and Transformation of Funds of Knowledge among U.S.-Mexican Households." *Anthropology & Education Quarterly* 23: 313–335.

Yosso, T. J. (2005). "Whose Culture has Capital? A Critical Race Theory Discussion of Community Cultural Wealth." *Race Ethnicity and Education* 8 (1): 69–91. https://doi.org/10.1080/1361332052000341006

Institutional penalty: mentoring, service, perceived discrimination, and its impacts on the health and academic careers of Latino faculty

Ruth Enid Zambrana, Diana Carvajal and Jalah Townsend

ABSTRACT
Institutional ethnoracial taxation increases work stress and reduces research productivity among Mexican American and Puerto Rican faculty. Latinos are a heterogenous group, yet little is known about differences in taxation, discrimination experiences and health by race, ethnicity, and nativity. This study explores three questions: Are there differences between URM (historically underrepresented) and non-URM Latinos in: 1) demographic factors, 2) taxation experiences and 3) physical and depressive symptoms and role overload? Survey respondents included 134 Mexican American, 76 Puerto Rican, and 108 non-URM Latino faculty. URM respondents are significantly less likely to report white race, more likely to report racial/ethnic discrimination, and more likely to report joint appointments compared to non-URM faculty. Almost 25% of respondents report clinical depressive symptoms. Disproportionate combinations of taxation from service, administrative demands and discrimination without institutional supports constitute an *"Institutional Penalty."* Reducing taxation demands requires institutional equity agendas to support research productivity, promotion, and retention.

Introduction

Latino[1] faculty constitute about 4.7% of faculty in postsecondary institutions in the US (US Department of Education NCES 2018). Latinos are composed of individuals with different histories, traditions, racial, ethnic, and class backgrounds. Additional differences include skin color, experiences of racism, and being perceived as "unfit" or of inferior intellectual ability. Mexican Americans and Puerto Ricans (hereinafter referred to as URM Latinos) are historically underrepresented minorities[2] (URM) and represent about 68% of the

US Latino population ("Hispanic Origin Groups in the U.S." 2019; Zong 2022). During the last three decades, URM Latinos have experienced a modest increase in their representation among faculty ranks in higher education with increases attributed to the inclusion of other Latinos (non-URM), about half of whom are foreign-born.[3] Although URM Latino faculty often experience ethnoracial taxation and discrimination, data on non-URM Latino faculty suggest they experience different forms of taxation, such as language barriers and feelings of loss of their home countries (Martinez, Chang, and Welton 2017). A significant body of work has identified different forms of taxation under multiple terms. Racial/ethnic, cultural, minority, identity and Black/Brown taxation are terms that have historic antecedents and refer to unrecognized and unrewarded academic labor not usually required of non-URM groups.

However, little is known about differences in work taxation and the resulting physical and mental health consequences of Latinos by race, ethnicity, and nativity. *Institutional Penalty* is coined here as a set of interrelated and overlapping structural, ethnoracial expectations in multiple work role areas (diversity, administrative or leadership service) that academic institutions impose on historically underrepresented faculty, often resulting in deleterious effects on health and well-being. This penalty is associated with three consequential realities on individual careers: (1) assigned roles proffer only symbolic institutional antiracist and equity measures but have limited benefit for the communities, students, and faculty members they purport to serve; (2) roles entail excessive, unrewarded academic service and administrative labor not valued in tenure and promotion; and (3) efforts rarely result in institutional investment in professional socialization, monetary compensation, or the meaningful, career-enhancing mentoring support by senior faculty needed for role efficacy and research productivity.

To our knowledge, the assessment of combined and multiple institutional demands on physical and depressive symptomology has not been quantitatively measured. Many studies have employed qualitative methods, tackled one or two ethnoracial expectations and have not had large enough sample sizes to test associations quantitatively (Casado Perez 2019; Guillaume and Apodaca 2022). The novel contribution of this paper is its examination of the physical and mental health consequences of the taxation penalty, namely the interactive effects of diversity service, leadership and administrative tasks combined with inadequate mentoring and discrimination, while interrogating the heterogeneity of Latinos by race, ethnicity and nativity. This study underscores the importance of Latinos as an untapped talent pool in higher education; the necessity of institutional equity to increase opportunity for upward mobility; and Latinos' pivotal role in training the next generation of students to ensure diverse representation.

Taxation in higher education is a persistent area of concern for URMs because it is institutionally inscribed in varied and (in)visible ways. A robust body of descriptive knowledge exists on the challenges experienced and the role of taxation among URM Latino faculty (Niemann et al. 2020; Rodríguez, Campbell, and Pololi 2015). Taxation is defined as "increased expectations that faculty of color should address diversity-related departmental and institutional affairs," and as such, these faculty often have additional responsibilities due to their commitment to this work (Joseph and Hirshfield 2011, 123). Ethnoracial taxation refers to *the unspoken* expectations placed on URM faculty to maintain the same workload as their non-URM peers while also disproportionally "[caring] for marginalized students, [being] overburdened with institutional service, and [having] obligations to teach colleagues about race and racism" based entirely on their racial/ethnic identities (Rideau 2021, 161). It decenters institutional responsibility for work taxation that often diminishes research productivity and, instead, places it on the individuals who serve the institutions' diversity mission.

This paper connects the consequences of taxation with suboptimal physical and depressive symptoms. It adds an important analysis to the literature on the sociology of work and race and ethnicity, which has generally aggregated Latinos into a monolithic, undifferentiated group. The majority of studies on Latino professionals, including faculty, have failed to assess the differential impacts of discrimination and taxation on Latinos by race, ethnicity and nativity. We argue that the cumulative effects of multiple service ethnoracial expectations combined with perceived discrimination and inadequate mentoring represent an institutional penalty that often adversely contributes to physical and depressive symptoms, role overload and career derailment. In this paper, we describe demographic differences between URM and non-URM Latinos, explore distinct experiences of taxation, and proffer fair and impartial practices to address the higher education inequities experienced by Latino subgroups.

Literature review

Ethnoracial taxation deserves critical attention in higher education systems because it intersects with historical identifiers of race and ethnicity, stereotypes of low intelligence, low socioeconomic status, perceived dangerousness/criminality, post-1980s diversity initiatives, and a platform of diversity representation rather than an investment in URM professional development. The construct of taxation has been present in multiple forms throughout the last three decades. Padilla (1994) eloquently defines "cultural taxation" in the following way:

> [...] the obligation to show good citizenship toward the institution by serving its needs for ethnic representation on committees, or to demonstrate knowledge and commitment to a cultural group, which may even bring accolades

> to the institution but which is not usually rewarded by the institution on whose behalf the service was performed. (26)

All forms of racial/ethnic/gender-based taxation constitute an unjust burden that can be defined as a penalty because these work responsibilities hamper career persistence and do not have academic value in promoting achievement of tenure or promotion to a higher rank. Taxation encompasses multiple experiences, including exclusion, pigeonholing faculty into teaching racial/ethnic classes regardless of their expertise, serving as department diversity officers and/or committee members, advising URM students combined with persistent questioning of competence and legitimacy of their research by students and peers (Chesler and Young 2015; Turner 2021; Pérez 2019; Trejo 2020; Robinson and Henriquez Aldana 2020).

Engagement in institutional diversity efforts often engender multiple disparities in exposure to racism and discrimination, social and professional isolation, inadequate mentorship, heavy clinical burdens, and promotion disparity – all of which negatively affect the health and career trajectory of URM Latino faculty (Salinas et al. 2020). These combined disparities, to the extent that non-URM faculty are not expected to perform them, exacerbate the institutional penalty that URM faculty experience. For example, the absence or inadequacy of mentoring for early career faculty is associated with fewer research collaborations and transmission of network capital (Bateman et al. 2021; O'Meara et al. 2020), which places URM faculty at a unique yet hidden disadvantage within the academic hierarchy (Kelly and McCann 2014). Taxation often presents as informal requests and is usually not linked with compensation, dossier recognition, or other rewards. In effect, institutions place the brunt of their diversity initiatives on a small group of URM Latino faculty who often engage in academic labor to promulgate institutional visibility, good will, and racial equity intentions. These service obligations penalize URM faculty because they represent barriers to research productivity, mentoring opportunities, and are often ignored for tenure and promotion (Guillaume and Apodaca 2022).

Among non-URM Latino faculty, studies describe workplace dissatisfaction as associated with barriers to information-seeking contributing to specific stressors, including completing and maintaining immigration paperwork, adjusting to different cultural values, coping with loneliness and isolation, navigating language barriers, and experiences with racism (Mamiseishvili and Lee 2018). Despite these barriers, non-URM Latino faculty report higher research productivity and spend less time on teaching, mentoring, and service compared to URM Latino faculty; they also report less career satisfaction (Kim et al. 2020). In contrast, taxation studies describing URM Latino experiences have yielded a modest body of literature regarding institutional service and teaching demands resulting in decreased productivity (Turner

2021; Salinas et al. 2020). Often overlooked is the connection between multiple work-associated taxation roles jointly with discrimination and inadequate mentoring and its impact on health and role overload. Acknowledging the heterogeneity among Latinos, we shed insight on the differences and similarities between URM and non-URM Latinos and describe how work-associated taxation experiences may adversely affect career trajectories and health.

The relationship between Latino faculty work stress and its impact on physical and depressive symptoms is an understudied area of inquiry and represents a major gap in knowledge. Contemporary population health knowledge is unveiling new understandings of the role of taxation, markers of institutional racism, on health conditions, early departures and lower promotion rates to full professor among URM faculty (Gumpertz et al. 2017; Pizarro and Kohli 2020; Stone and Carlisle 2019; Zambrana et al. 2020). For example, the harsh terrain of academia for URM faculty who experience role overload coupled with institutional racism requires management of emotions to avoid and/or not reinforce stereotypes of being "dangerous" (males) or "hysterical" (females) (Dade et al. 2015). Additionally, promotion and tenure processes, which heighten stress and anxiety for all faculty, can be particularly pernicious for URM faculty who may experience a discreditation of their research and an obligation to represent their race/ethnicity while also being labeled as affirmative action hires (Chancellor 2019).

These taxation experiences and the guarded responses that are manifestations of the institutional penalty for URM faculty often result in *racial battle fatigue* (RBF), which depletes emotional energy, erodes spirit, and strains intellectual resources – all of which detract from research productivity and career advancement (Haynes et al. 2020; Smith 2016). Physical manifestations of RBF include headaches, weakened immune systems and increased blood pressure, while emotional manifestations include "frustration, anger, exhaustion, physical avoidance, psychological or emotional withdrawal, escapism, and at times acceptance of racist attributions" as well as depression and isolation (Arnold, Crawford, and Khalifa 2016; Louis et al. 2018; Smith, Allen, and Danley 2007, 552; Williams 2019). URM faculty are often viewed as the champions and executors of diversity yet do not benefit from this work and such efforts usually fail to achieve promotion/tenure (Lawrence et al. 2021; Rodríguez, Campbell, and Pololi 2015). While diversity service associated with taxation experiences frequently contributes to adverse consequences, including frustration with inequitable institutional practices and perceived resistance to change, URM faculty often express a strong sense of responsibility, commitment, and pride in paying it forward (Joseph and Hirshfield 2011). The questions of who reaps the benefits and who is disadvantaged by the institutional penalty are central to the higher education equity discourse.

We draw upon an intersectional framework to contextualize the experiences of URM and non-URM Latino respondents at the intersections of history, race/ethnicity, power, and social status to examine patterns of unequal treatment in higher education institutions. The advantaging of one group over another in access to opportunity has deep roots in structural racism (Zambrana and Williams 2022). An intersectional lens drawing on critical race theory provides a solid theorizing foundation to examine the shared representational identities and intergenerational experiences of historic population groups. The analytic strength of the intersectional framework is its understanding of how historically underrepresented Latino groups (Mexican American and Puerto Rican) are connected to the power of social institutions and their complex inequalities and how structural inequities are shaped by historical incorporation, race, ethnicity, nativity and class identifiers (Collins 2019; Dill and Zambrana 2009; Zambrana and Hurtado 2015). Four critical assumptions guide our frame: a) racism is ordinary and not aberrational; b) US society is based on a "White-over-color ascendancy" that advances White supremacy; c) race and racism are social constructions; and d) storytelling "urges Black and Brown writers to recount their experiences with racism" (Delgado and Stefancic 2001, 7–9).

We position this study within the reality of racial inequity among the heterogenous group of Latinos in higher education. The academic work site is defined as a bastion of culturally driven organizational rules and norms that obscure "individual capacities for clarity and responsibility," especially in recognizing the covert nature of racialized processes (such as multiple institutional taxation demands) (Chesler and Crowfoot 2000, 437; Embrick, Domínguez, and Karsak 2017; Espino and Zambrana 2019; Feagin 2020). This study answers three questions: (1) Are there differences in demographic factors between URM and non-URM Latinos? 2) Are there differences in their taxation experiences? and 3) Are there differences in the relationship between their taxation experiences and physical and depressive symptoms and role overload?

Data and methods

The data are drawn from a larger national cross-sectional survey study of 616 faculty in research universities in the United States. For this paper, data were analysed for 318 respondents of which 210 were URM (Mexican American and Puerto Rican) and 108 were identified as non-URM Hispanic respondents who self-reported ancestry in Spanish-speaking Latin American countries and Spain. Data were collected via a self-administered web-based survey using 143 items from standardized instruments on demographic factors, family, and employment characteristics, perceived racial/ethnic discrimination, mentoring, administrative service and physical and depressive symptoms (See Zambrana 2018 for a full description of measures).

Sample criteria selection

Eligibility criteria included US-born men and women who self-identify as Mexican American, Puerto Rican or "Other Hispanic" (Other Hispanic included US or foreign-born respondents) and were tenure-track assistant or tenured associate professors at Carnegie-defined very high/high research-extensive universities (McCormick and Zhao 2005). Participants were identified through network sampling techniques using academic listservs, personal contacts, and respondent referrals to assure representation by racial, ethnic, and sex demographics as well as rank and geography. The study was approved according to IRB procedures at the University of Maryland College Park.

Measures of sociodemographic, family and employment characteristics

Sociodemographic data included age, nativity, parental education, house-hold net worth, race, ethnicity, sex, marital status, number of children, annual income, and home ownership. Employment characteristics included academic rank, primary academic discipline, estimated hours spent on research, teaching, university service, outside professional activities, joint and administrative appointments, and type of institution (public, private, other). Sociodemographic and employment characteristics provide an important context for understanding taxation in research universities. Employing US Census Bureau measures, self-reported race and ethnicity were ascertained by two questions: (1) "What is your race?" and (2) "Are you of Hispanic/Latino origin?" Sex was measured as: Are you (1) male, (2) female, or (3) other? Marital status was measured as: (1) never married, (2) married/living with spouse/living with partner/partnered, or (3) separated/divorced/widowed. The number of children was measured as (1) none, (2) one-two, or (3) three or more. Items to assess employment and educational characteristics were adapted from the National Science Foundation Survey of Earned Doctorates Study (National Center for Science and Engineering Statistics 2020).

Sample description

The study sample included 134 Mexican Americans (41.8%), 76 Puerto Ricans (24.2%) and 108 Other Hispanics (34%). Other Hispanic participants origi-nated from a total of 15 other Latin American countries or Spain, including Colombia ($n = 13$), Cuba ($n = 10$), Spain ($n = 10$), Argentina ($n = 9$), Brazil ($n = 7$), Peru ($n = 7$), Chile ($n = 5$), Ecuador ($n = 4$), and El Salvador ($n = 3$). Seventy-five percent of Other Hispanics were born outside of the US.

The average age of the sample was 43.2 years, with no significant differences by subgroup. About 60% of respondents reported female and about 40% reported male. Most of the sample was married, with approximately half reporting a household size of two. Most respondents had 1–2 children (55.6%), and about a third had no children (35.6%). Approximately 21% of the sample was geographically located in the Northeast, 18.6% in the Mid-Atlantic, 12.1% in the Southeast, 13.5% in the Midwest, and 34.9% in the Southwest/West. About 60% of all participants were employed in large public universities, while 40% were employed in private and other research universities. Respondents represented a variety of disciplines, with about one quarter in Arts and Humanities, 21.1% in the Social Sciences, and 16.7% in Professional Schools.[4]

Description of measures

Four measures were selected as indicators of the institutional penalty. These include: (1) the perceived impact of the adequacy of the mentoring relationship on career growth; (2) perceptions of race/ethnic bias or discrimination by a superior; (3) perceptions of being left out of opportunities for professional advancement based on race/ ethnicity; and (4) having a joint appointment.

Mentoring Scales: Mentorship of early-career faculty is an important socialization process to guide new hires to obtain information about institutional expectations, understand their role, and perceived identity affirmation (Bauer et al. 2007). One item measured whether respondents reported having a current mentor with a yes/no response option. Mentor's sex was measured as an individual item with male/female response option. Mentor's race/ethnicity was measured as an individual item with Non-Hispanic White, Non-Hispanic Black, Hispanic/Latino, or another race/ethnicity as response options. Mentoring as an institutional support variable for the participant was assessed using two scales from the National Faculty Survey (Robert Wood Johnson Foundation 1995). The *Mentor Facilitated Activities Scale* asked whether mentors facilitated mentee participation for six items with yes/no response options. Activities included invitations to conferences and opportunities for research collaborations on book chapters or article co-authorship. The *Mentorship Relationship Functions Scale* assessed respondents' perceived performance of their current faculty mentor. Five items asked about the frequency of the mentor's availability to critique the mentee's scholarly work, promote visibility outside the institution, prospectively advise about criteria for promotion, hold progress meetings about promotion criteria, and provide emotional support and inspiration concerning the mentee's academic career. Response options included never (1) to always (5). Total scores ranged from 5 to 25, with higher scores indicating more frequency of relationship functions. A final cognitive appraisal item asked, "Do you believe that inadequate mentoring has impeded your career growth?" The response options ranged from very significantly (1) to not at all (5).

Perceived Discrimination Scale: Multiple forms of discrimination manifest in the daily lives of Latino faculty and contribute to identity taxation, workplace stress, and physical and depressive symptoms. The 6-item *Perceived Gender, Race, Ethnicity and Class Bias or Discrimination in the Workplace* scale was adapted from the National Faculty Survey (Robert Wood Johnson Foundation 1995). Respondents were asked whether, in their professional career, they have ever encountered gender, racial/ethnic, and/or class discrimination by a superior or colleague and whether they were ever left out of opportunities for professional advancement based on their gender, race/ethnicity, and/or class. Response options were on a 4-point scale that ranged from never (1) to always (4).

Life event stress, role overload and physical and depressive symptoms scales

Taxation is often exacerbated by additional stressful life events, which may contribute to role overload due to personal loss or economic strain. In turn, multiple and simultaneous life stressors can exacerbate physical and depressive symptoms. A 12-item *life event* stress inventory measured the presence of life events over the past year. Examples of events include "spouse or partner death and major problems with money." Four response options included: No (1), Yes and it upset me not too much (2), Yes and it upset me moderately (3), and Yes, it upset me very much (4). We identified and compared the top five ranked life stressors that may compound the impacts on physical and depressive symptoms and role overload of study respondents.

Role Overload Scale measured the extent to which job demands exceeded resources (personal and workplace) and the extent to which an individual was able to accomplish workloads. The subscale included ten items ranging from rarely or never true (1) to true most of the time (5). Scores ranged from 10–50, with higher scores representing higher overload.

Physical symptoms were measured with the 18-item Physical Symptoms Index (PSI), which assesses physical and somatic health symptoms associated with psychological distress (Spector and Jex 1998). Each is a condition/state about which a person would likely be aware (e.g. headache and stomach). For each symptom, respondents were asked, "During the past 4 weeks, did you have any of the following symptoms? If you did have the symptoms, did you see the doctor about it?" Response options included: No; Yes, and I saw a doctor; and Yes, but I didn't see a doctor. We used the total symptom scores, ranging from 0 to 18, with higher scores indicating a higher prevalence of physical symptoms.

Depressive symptoms were measured with the 8-item Center for Epidemiologic Studies *Depression Scale* (CES-D) (Radloff 1977). The scale is widely used with women and racial/ethnic minority groups with adequate reliability. Scoring was based on a Likert-type scale using options ranging from rarely (0) to most days (3) and scores ranging from 0–24. Higher scores indicate higher levels of depressive symptoms. A score greater ≥ 7 suggests a clinically significant level of depression.

Analytic strategy

US Census race/ethnic categories, jointly with covariables (race, ethnicity and nativity), were used to examine Latino heterogeneity. To answer the first question regarding demographic differences (e.g. age, self-reported race, marital status) between URM (Mexican and Puerto Rican) and non-URM (Other Hispanics), univariate statistics (frequencies, means, standard deviations) were employed to describe characteristics for each of the three groups. Parental education was dichotomized as less than college completion (first-generation) and college completion (non-first-generation). One-way ANOVA tests were used to examine differences in taxation experiences (Question 2) for continuous variables (mentoring relationship functions, life event stress, role overload, and physical and depressive symptoms) between groups. Chi-square tests were conducted to assess group differences for categorical variables (race, age, rank, mentor characteristics and race/ethnic discrimination from superior and being left out of opportunities). Lastly, to assess differences in the associations of mentoring relationship functions, inadequate mentoring and perceived discrimination from a superior, hours of research, administrative and joint appointments, and being left out of opportunities based on perceived racial/ethnic discrimination with physical and depressive symptoms and role overload (Question 3), Pearson correlation coefficients and ANOVAs were employed to compare differences between groups. The significance level was set at .10 to reduce the chances of a Type II error (Hackshaw and Kirkwood 2011).

Study limitations

Several limitations include the non-probability cross-sectional study design, respondent self-selection, recall bias, and inadequate measurement of any undisclosed/undiagnosed disability (physical or mental) that may be associated with a successful career path. Findings may not be representative of the experiences of all Latino faculty in research universities, teaching colleges and minority-serving institutions. These data add to the growing body of scholarship regarding taxation as a significant contributor to premature morbidity among URM faculty, low retention and promotion rates, and fills a critical knowledge gap regarding the burdens of the institutional taxation penalty experienced by many URM Latino faculty and its impact on health and career persistence.

Results

Table 1 displays data on respondent demographic characteristics by URM (Mexican American and Puerto Rican) and non-URM (measured as Other Hispanic). These analyses highlight demographic (self-reported race,

Table 1. Demographic characteristics by URM and Other Hispanic (non-URM) respondents.

	Online Survey Sample ($n = 318$)			
	Total Sample $n = 318$ (%)	Mexican American $n = 134$ (41.8%)	Puerto Rican $n = 76$ (24.2%)	Other Hispanic $n = 108$ (34%)
Age M (SD)	43.17 (7.80)	43.22 (8.73)	42.95 (7.53)	43.20 (6.83)
Self-reported Race				
White****	133 (49.3)	39 (39.0)	22 (35.5)	72 (66.7)
African American/ Black	11 (4.1)	1 (1.0)	10 (16.1)	-
Some other race/ mixed race***	126 (46.7)	60 (60)	30 (48.4)	36 (33.3)
First Generation College**				
First Generation (<college completion)	122 (46.6)	60 (56.6)	24 (40)	38 (39.6)
Not First Generation (college completed)	140 (53.4)	46 (43.4)	36 (60)	58 (60.4)
Marital Status				
Never Married	37 (11.7)	19 (14.3)	7 (9.1)	11 (10.4)
Married/partnered	236 (74.7)	97 (72.9)	57 (74.0)	82 (77.4)
Separated/Widowed/ Divorced	43 (13.6)	17 (12.8)	13 (16.9)	13 (12.3)
Individual Annual Income				
>70,000	119 (37.5)	54 (41.6)	26 (35.2)	39 (36.4)
70,001–90,000	92 (29.0)	38 (29.2)	20 (27.0)	34 (31.8)
90,001–115,000	55 (17.4)	25 (19.2)	13 (17.6)	17 (15.9)
115,000+	42 (13.3)	13 (10.0)	15 (20.3)	14 (13.1)
Owns Home*				
Yes	225 (71.0)	88 (66.2)	52 (67.5)	85 (79.4)
Current Household Net Worth				
≥90,000	78 (25.2)	30 (26.1)	25 (35.2)	23 (24.0)
90,001–200,000	107 (34.6)	47 (40.9)	25 (35.2)	35 (36.5)
200,001 or more	97 (31.3)	38 (33.0)	21 (29.6)	38 (39.6)

*$p < .10$.
** $= p < .05$.
*** $= p < .01$.
**** $= p < .001$

generational status, income, and home ownership) differences in response to our first research question. Self-reported race shows that 49.3% of the total sample identified as White, 4.1% as African American/Black, and 46.7% as some other race/mixed race. Approximately 39% of Mexican Americans, 36% of Puerto Ricans, and 67% of Other Hispanic respondents identified as White. Mexican Americans were significantly more likely to have mothers with less than a college education (first-generation college status) compared to Puerto Ricans and Other Hispanics. Nearly three-quarters (71%) of the sample reported owning a home, with Other Hispanics significantly more likely to report homeownership (79.4%) compared to URM respondents. Almost 40% of the sample (37.5%) reported an individual annual income of $70,000 or less, while 17.4% reported an individual income of $90,000–115,000. Puerto Ricans were most likely to report a household net worth of under $90,000 (35.2%), and Other Hispanics were significantly more likely to report a household net worth of $201,000 or more (39.6%).

The second set of analyses compares taxation experiences by URM and non-URM respondents. Table 2 shows work characteristics including rank, service appointments, research hours per week, mentoring and discrimination experiences, and role overload. Over half of the sample was assistant professors (57.6%). Mexican Americans were most likely to be assistant professors (62.2%), and Other Hispanics were the most likely to be associate professors (46.7%).

Regarding administrative service, just over 20% of the sample reported having a joint appointment, with Puerto Ricans being the most likely (33.9%) and Other Hispanics being significantly less likely (14.3%) to report having a joint appointment. Nearly three-quarters (73%) of the sample served in an administrative position, with Other Hispanics being the least likely to hold administrative positions (69.7%). Although time invested in academic responsibilities did not differ significantly by subgroups, with 42.8% of all respondents engaged in research 21 + hours per week, a higher percentage of Other Hispanics (46.5%) dedicated time to research compared to about 40% of Mexican American and Puerto Rican respondents.

Just over half of the sample reported currently having a mentor.[5] Other Hispanics were significantly more likely to report having two mentors (41.9%), and Mexican Americans (37.3%) and Puerto Ricans (36.4%) were significantly more likely to report having 3 + mentors. Puerto Ricans (70.7%) and Other Hispanics (62.8%) were significantly more likely than Mexican Americans to have a male mentor, while Other Hispanics were significantly more likely to have a White mentor (72.1%) compared to Puerto Ricans (49.3%) and Mexican Americans (46.3%). Other Hispanics were significantly more likely to report opportunities for research collaboration and co-authoring articles/books/chapters as mentor facilitated activities, while Other Hispanics

Table 2. Work characteristics, taxation experiences and role overload by URM and Other Hispanic (non-URM) respondents.

	Total sample $n =$ 318 (%)	Mexican American $n = 133$ (41.8%)	Puerto Rican $n = 77$ (24.2%)	Other Hispanic $n = 108$ (34%)
Rank				
Assistant	174 (57.6)	79 (62.2)	39 (55.7)	56 (53.3)
Associate	128 (42.4)	48 (37.8)	31 (44.3)	49 (46.7)
Has a Joint Appointment**				
Yes	59 (21.1)	23 (20.4)	21 (33.9)	15 (14.3)
Has an Administrative Appointment				
Yes	206 (72.8)	85 (75.20)	46 (74.20)	75 (69.70)
Hours per Week: Research				
0–10	69 (25.5)	27 (24.5)	18 (30.0)	24 (23.8)
11–20	86 (31.7)	39 (35.5)	17 (28.3)	30 (29.7)
21+	116 (42.8)	44 (40.0)	25 (41.7)	47 (46.5)
Impact of Inadequate Mentoring on Career Growth				
Very significantly/ great deal	64 (21.1)	25 (19.5)	17 (22.7)	22 (21.8)
Somewhat	117 (38.5)	56 (43.0)	23 (32.0)	38 (37.6)
Hardly/not at all	123 (40.5)	48 (37.5)	34 (45.3)	41 (40.6)
Perceived Racial/Ethnic Discrimination by a Superior**				
Never/Rarely	187 (60.9)	78 (60.0)	38 (50.7)	71 (69.6)
Often/Always	120 (39.1)	52 (40)	37 (49.3)	31 (30.4)
Left out of Opportunities Based on Perceived Race/Ethnic Discrimination				
Never/Rarely	226 (73.9)	97 (74.6)	49 (67.1)	80 (77.7)
Often/Always	80 (26.1)	33 (25.4)	24 (32.8)	23 (22.3)
Role Overload (RO) Mean (SD)				
RO Score	33.83 (7.4)	33.53 (8.1)	33.98 (6.70)	34.07 (7.2)

$*p < .10$.
$** = p < .05$.
$*** = p < .01$.
$**** = p < .001$

and Puerto Ricans were significantly less likely than Mexican Americans to report annual career reviews as mentor-facilitated activities. The mentoring relationship functions scale showed significant differences, with Mexican Americans having the highest average mentoring relationship functions score while Other Hispanics report the lowest average mentoring relationship functions score. About one-fifth of all respondents reported that inadequate mentoring very significantly impacted their careers. About 40% of the sample reported that inadequate mentoring "somewhat" affected their career. Overall sixty percent (59.6%) of respondents reported an adverse impact of mentoring on their career trajectories.

Approximately 39.1% of the total sample reported often or always experiencing racial/ethnic discrimination, with Mexican Americans (40%) and Puerto Ricans (49.3%) significantly more likely than Other Hispanics (30.4%) to report racial/ethnic discrimination from a superior and more likely to report being left out of opportunities based on race/ethnicity. The *Role Overload* mean score was 33.83 (7.4 SD), with a range of scores of 1–50, suggesting high overload experiences for all respondents.

Lastly, we describe stressful life events associated with family and/or work life. About one-third of the sample reported stressful life events: "having a close friend/family member pass away or diagnosed with a serious illness" (35.3%), "having financial problems" (32.7%), and "having a major conflict with colleagues" (31.4%), while 20.4% reported job loss and almost 10% reported divorce or breakup. URM respondents were more likely to report "major money problems" and twice as likely to report divorce/breakup compared to Other Hispanics. About one-third of the total sample experienced conflict with colleagues, with Mexican Americans slightly less likely (28.8%) to experience conflict compared to Puerto Ricans (33.3%) and Other Hispanics (33%).

Associations among taxation experiences, physical and depressive symptoms and role overload

The third study question examines the associations among mentoring, perceived discrimination, appointments and physical and depressive symptoms and role overload. Statistically significant differences were observed among the three subgroups for mean physical health symptom score ($M = 4.45$), with Mexican Americans reporting the highest average physical symptom score ($M = 5.02$) while Other Hispanics ($M = 3.74$) reported the lowest average physical symptom score. The depression scale showed high overall rates of depressive symptoms across all groups, with 24.2% of the sample reporting clinically significant symptoms ($M = 4.12$) (not shown).

Table 3 displays the associations of mentoring relationship functions, impact of inadequate mentoring on career growth, impact of perceived discrimination by a superior, hours of research, administrative and joint appointments, and left out of opportunities based on perceived racial/ethnic discrimination with physical and depressive symptoms and role overload. Significant associations are observed by subgroup with notable differences. Puerto Ricans experience the highest number of significant associations, while Other Hispanics experience the lowest number of significant associations with physical and depressive symptoms and role overload. Inadequate mentoring was significantly associated with role overload and depressive symptoms for all respondents. For Mexican American respondents, being left out of opportunities based on perceived race/ethnic discrimination, fewer hours of research, and perceived racial/ethnic discrimination by a superior were all significantly associated with higher role overload and higher physical symptoms. For Puerto Rican respondents, three factors were most prominent: left out of opportunities based on perceived race/ethnic discrimination, joint appointment, and perceived racial/ethnic discrimination by a superior were associated with physical and depressive symptoms. Among Other Hispanics, being left out of opportunities based on perceived race/ethnic discrimination was significantly associated with

Table 3. Associations of adequacy of mentoring, perceived discriminations, hours of research, joint and administrative appointments with physical and depressive symptoms and role overload by URM and Other Hispanic (non-URM) respondents.

	Mexican American (n = 133)	Puerto Rican (n = 77)	Other Hispanic (n = 108)
Mentoring Relationship Functions Scale (r)			
Physical Symptoms	.092	.179	.097
Depressive Symptoms	−.004	.065	−.197*
Role Overload	−.108	−.057	−.045
Impact of Inadequate Mentoring on Career Growth(F)			
Physical Symptoms	0.819	2.024	0.676
Depressive Symptoms	2.466*	2.564*	4.397**
Role Overload	4.635**	4.522**	7.281***
Left out of Opportunities Based on Perceived Race/Ethnic Discrimination (F)			
Physical Symptoms	1.850	2.839*	0.797
Depressive Symptoms	1.586	3.867**	3.864**
Role Overload	5.372***	1.391	6.717***
Hours of Research (F)			
Physical Symptoms	2.391*	0.613	1.604
Depressive Symptoms	2.275	1.743	1.962
Role Overload	11.392****	0.555	1.143
Has an Administrative Appointment (F)			
Physical Symptoms	5.205**	0.732	0.089
Depressive Symptoms	0.001	1.702	0.022
Role Overload	0.484	0.010	0.109
Has a Joint Appointment (F)			
Physical Symptoms	0.761	4.970**	0.593
Depressive Symptoms	0.015	2.812*	0.175
Role Overload	0.898	0.177	0.438
Perceived Racial/Ethnic Discrimination by a Superior (F)			
Physical Symptoms	0.241	4.207**	1.435
Depressive Symptoms	1.275	5.233**	1.720
Role Overload	15.642****	1.970	26.417****

*$p < .10$.
**$p < .05$.
***$p < .01$.
****$p < .001$.

depressive symptoms and role overload, while perceived racial/ethnic discrimination by a superior was associated with role overload.

Discussion

The study findings draw attention to major differences within the heterogeneous category of Latinos (URM vs. non-URM) and the implications of the institutional penalty on academic careers. While similarities in taxation experiences are present between URM and non-URM Latinos, results are discussed with a focus on differences as posed in the study questions. The first question is: Are there differences in demographic factors between URM and non-URM Latinos? Two salient results include differences in racial identity and socioeconomic indicators. Non-URM Latinos were significantly more likely to report White race, have parents who are college graduates, have assets over $201,000 and report homeownership compared to URM Latinos. One's phenotype and race confer social advantages when identified by self and others as White in the predominantly white setting of academia (López and Hogan 2021). For non-URM Latinos, color and class privilege may facilitate access to White mentors and protect against chronic microaggressions and discrimination from superiors (Feagin 2020).

Deeply embedded within the academy is the institutional advantage that whiteness provides. As noted by Jones et al. (2008), Whiteness "is an asset in a race-conscious society. Attention to the ways in which opportunity is structured and the value assigned so that 'whiteness' is favored may suggest new levels for intervening in health disparities" (502). Conversely, *lack of whiteness* eliminates a protective cloak and leaves many URMs vulnerable to inequity in service obligations, research and mentoring opportunities, role overload and subsequent physical and depressive symptoms. Racialization and colorism, jointly with less available financial assets, can exacerbate the institutional penalty and stressful life events among those not perceived as White and negatively impact their career trajectories (Niemann et al. 2020; Salinas et al. 2020). For many URM Latinos who do not identify as or present as White, the burden of institutional diversity representation often exacerbates role overload and invokes manifestations of institutional racism.

National socioeconomic indicators for non-URM Latinos are consistent with extant data, which show that non-URM Latinos are more likely to have parents with a college education, almost twice as likely to complete college degrees compared to Mexican American and Puerto Rican groups and have higher rates of homeownership and generally lower rates of poverty (Flores 2017; Zong 2022). One study examined differences in assets between URM and White faculty showing that about 15% of URM Latino female faculty and about 25% of URM Latino male faculty had investment income, compared to over one-third of White men and women (Mora, Qubbaj, and Rodríguez 2018). Future studies are needed to assess these differences in assets between Latino groups by race, ethnicity, class and nativity. Given the protective life benefits of higher family education levels and economic capital conferred in the transmission of assets and wealth, non-URM Latinos may be at an advantage in achieving career advancement and may likely have additional resources to buffer stressful life events and work strain in response to the institutional penalties that they may experience.

The second question examined role obligations in the form of joint appointments, more frequently held by URM respondents. These appointments reflect the higher likelihood of URM faculty having interdisciplinary degrees, engaging in ethnoracial-driven projects and having a commitment to praxis. Due to the underrepresentation of Latino faculty at research universities, diversity leadership and joint appointments are more common experiences in these institutions for URM Latinos, which often increase discriminatory encounters with institutional administrators and peers and contribute to a decreased sense of belonging (Arnold, Crawford, and Khalifa 2016; Lewis et al. 2021). Yet, these same departments that share joint appointments are often under-resourced, with few senior faculty serving as mentors (Shavers, Butler, and Moore 2014). Institutional joint and leadership appointments among early career URM faculty increase their academic labor and constitute harm-inducing practices because they are involved in additional service work without developmental mentorship on institutional practices and leadership skills and adequate resources and/or compensation.

Moreover, these experiences rarely result in productive engagement in research collaborations, high-profile program development or sustainable equitable institutional change. All too often, these professional service efforts often result in discouragement and, at times, obliterate the *raison d'etre* for choosing an academic life and participating in diversity service. The disadvantages of engaging in these administrative roles and joint appointments in the early years of their careers reduce their opportunities to learn the institutional culture, jumpstart their research activities and acquire a solid social network and circle of support among their peers and senior faculty. These barriers to integration into their institutional culture promote an *Institutional Penalty* that is more likely to be experienced by URM than non-URM Latinos, and may result in debilitating consequences such as depletion of physical and emotional capabilities (*Racial Battle Fatigue),* less productivity and higher rates of physical and mental health conditions.

The third question assesses the relationships between taxation measures and physical and depressive symptoms and role overload. Serious, yet understudied, consequences of workplace stress caused by multiple forms of taxation include adverse physical and depressive symptoms, which are associated with lower retention and promotion rates (Gumpertz et al. 2017; Stone and Carlisle 2019). The relationships between high levels of workplace stress, reported as perceived race/ethnic discrimination, inadequate mentoring, and less collaborative research opportunities collectively represent a cluster of detrimental experiences that undergird role overload and the depletion of intellectual, physical and mental resources (Arnold, Crawford, and Khalifa 2016; Pizarro and Kohli 2020; Haynes et al. 2020).

URM respondents experienced a higher number of significant associations of taxation experiences with physical symptoms compared to non-URM faculty. Their physical health was deeply impacted by multiple service obligations with limited institutional supports in unwelcoming environments, often contributing to harmful physical health impacts (Williams, Lawrence, and Davis 2019). In contrast, non-URM respondents do not report health impacts associated with administrative roles, which may be related to higher likelihood of being tenured, more experience and mentorship by White male faculty. These three factors may confer more access to social networks that help non-URMs navigate institutions and may account for their lower rates of reporting discriminatory experiences and physical symptoms. In addition, the advantages of White racial privilege, more involvement in research collaborations, and increased access to economic assets may defer a need for additional salary-seeking and reduce institutional penalty experiences.

High rates of depressive symptoms (20–25%) were observed across all subgroups. When compared to national depression rates (19.6%), depressive symptoms are higher for study respondents (24.2%) (Budhwani, Hearld, and Chavez-Yenter 2015). Although inadequate mentoring was significantly associated with depressive symptoms for all respondents, higher rates of URM participation in administrative service combined with discrimination by superiors and reduced time in research adversely impacted depressive symptoms. Given the lower taxation burden of non-URM Latinos, depressive symptoms may derive from causes that are different than those of URM Latinos. Those born outside of the US may have significant difficulty adapting to new environments and being separated from family. This is exacerbated by the need to integrate into a contemporary professional society laden with historical oppression, colonization and domination not completely understood by them (Mamiseishvili and Lee 2018). In contrast, URM Latinos may experience depression in response to a melding of life stressors, workplace discrimination, and inequitable workload (Zambrana 2018). The disadvantages experienced by URM Latinos may be reflective of the systematic inequities established by and commonly applied in academia (Bonilla-Silva and Peoples 2022). These differences by race, nativity, class, and ethnicity, including the impact of discriminatory experiences on role overload, require further inquiry.

The unique insights gained by these findings are the prominent barriers that exist for URM Latinos to achieve role clarity and efficacious career performance and how both are manifestations of the institutional penalty. The absence of quality mentoring creates institutional socialization gaps that hinders research productivity, obscures access to social capital, informational sources, and social networks, and inhibits exposure to the "hidden curriculum" or informal rules about which many URM faculty are unaware (Mendez et al. 2020; Thorne et al. 2021; Zambrana et al. 2015). Although non-URM faculty report lower mentoring relationship support, inadequate mentoring may be less injurious for them as they are more likely to be tenured, report significantly less discrimination and have higher likelihood of mentorship by White faculty. The latter three factors may confer some protection from the adverse impacts of institutional racial/ethnic discrimination and enable access to other channels of information, effectively lessening their taxation and its impact on well-being.

Equity implications and inclusion recommendations for higher education institutions

Extant literature has focused on the intense relationship between underrepresentation and the nefarious taxation on URM and non-URM Latino faculty, who are often the "only one" or "a few in the midst of many" who are expected to champion diversity and represent institutional interests at the expense of their careers (Thomas 2019). Not unnoticed is the startling number of recommendations offered to reduce the institutional penalty. Yet limited progress and significant institutional resistance is observed in implementing prior equitable recommendations to reduce the multiple service demands on a small group of faculty, increase Latino faculty, and, most importantly, redistribute institutional diversity tasks to all faculty.

This study contributes to the growing body of knowledge that informs six central recommendations as priority actions to reduce the institutional penalty to enhance career outcomes for URM faculty, increase institutional supports to promote academic careers and decrease early departures from higher education. First, cluster hiring of URM Latino faculty at the assistant, associate, and full professor levels across multiple colleges and departments in traditional and non-traditional disciplines is an effective practice. It accomplishes multiple equity goals, including a demonstration of respect for the importance of varying theoretical perspectives in higher education, increasing representation, and decreasing taxation. Moreover, the presence of URM groups in higher education assures diverse experiences and role models for URM and non-URM students (Samuels 2020). A second recommendation is to develop affinity spaces where URM faculty can share their research ideas, seek collaboration, and expand their networks with interdisciplinary senior scholars. One innovative idea is an interdisciplinary "speed mentoring" event on faculty members' campuses and nearby campuses to increase social capital and research networks (Cook, Bahn, and Menaker 2010).

In addition, URM faculty may need different kinds of support and access to mentoring throughout the life course associated with race/class/ethnicity. The authors suggest affinity spaces could also provide access specifically to "career coaches." In this case, mentors for URMs could specifically function as career guides with a focus on educating URMs about how to succeed in academia. Previous work has noted that such coaches may be instrumental in cases where mentees' research mentors are unable to provide career advice due to differences in lived experiences (Williams, Thakore, and McGee 2016). Third, necessary for URM faculty advancement are equitable and competitive salary packages with research start-up funds and support by chairs to delay administrative positions until advancement to full professor. Fourth, an intentional mentoring approach for the purposes of role socialization to increase role efficacy and protect from taxation is a crucial institutional investment. This entails incentivizing and informing senior majority culture faculty regarding the unique obstacles that URM faculty confront in achieving professional advancement due to the *Institutional Penalty*. Fifth, as institutions encourage faculty to take on public-facing "diversity and equity" roles, they must ensure that resources, including time, compensation, mentorship, and decision-making power to decrease taxation accompany such roles and include all faculty in EI efforts (Holmes IV et al. 2022).

Lastly, to address the fact that such taxation roles often disadvantage URM faculty career success and benefit institutions, requirements for achieving promotion and tenure need to include a mandate of equity/inclusion (EI) work for all faculty. Institutions need to do the work of clearly and transparently defining equity and inclusion (EI) metrics and requirements for promotion. Diversity is plentiful in research institutions of higher learning. What is less discernable is the representation of URMs in higher education. Institutions must provide clarity about the value of each EI-associated metric. For example, chairing a committee should carry more weight than simply being a committee member (O'Meara et al. 2020). These recommendations urge an institutional culture shift so that equity and inclusion values are endorsed and upheld by the leadership, but not at the expense of the careers of URM faculty.

Conclusions

Our findings confirm both the heterogeneity among Latinos and the adverse consequences of academic work experiences or institutional penalties on their health and well-being. Institutions are called upon to reassess their practices and understanding of the unique positionalities of URM and non-URM Latinos. Taxation research among URMs is abundant and reflective of institutional racism, which has grave career and health consequences. Diversity as a clarion call is not enough and, in effect, may mask racism as it fails to confront equity and inclusion. Academic institutions have a clear mandate to dismantle pervasive racism by recognizing and addressing the inequitable *Institutional Penalty* often carried by URM faculty. Leaders must be held accountable for increased equity and inclusion among URM Latinos, African-Americans, and American Indian/Native American groups. Currently, the proportion of existing Latino faculty illustrates a disproportionate underrepresentation of two historically underrepresented groups – Mexican Americans and Puerto Ricans. Transparent research of implementation strategies is necessary not only to measure degrees of success but also to understand which groups benefit most from diversity efforts and how identity taxation affects the career persistence and well-being of URM and non-URM Latinos.

Notes

1. The term "Latino" includes individuals from about 20 countries who may be of mixed races including White, Black, Mestizo, or Indigenous (González Burchard et al. 2005). Despite being used by the Census Bureau, both "Hispanic" and "Latino" are disputed terms, because not all self-identified Latino persons have Spanish ancestry or experienced the historic colonial status and economic/social impacts due to their race or indigeneity. For consistency unless specifically noted, we use the term Latino regardless of gender.
2. Traditionally and historically underrepresented has many differing definitions. In this paper it refers to Latino groups who have been denied access and/or suffered past intergenerational institutional discrimination in the United States and includes Mexican American/Chicanos and Puerto Ricans.
3. "Other Hispanic" (either US or foreign-born) include those who report origination in South America, Central America, and the Caribbean excluding Puerto Rico. "Other Hispanic" was used in this study as the identifier of self-reported identity. Other Hispanic and non-URM Latino are used interchangeably.
4. Professional schools included business, social work, accounting, public policy, journalism, law, library science.
5. Mentoring data are not shown. These data are available upon request.

Disclosure statement

No potential conflict of interest was reported by the author(s).

Funding

This work was supported by University of Maryland Tier 1 seed grants, Division of Research, Faculty Incentive Program, and the Annie E. Casey Foundation: [Grant Number 214.0277]; Robert Wood Johnson Foundation: [Grant Number #68480].

References

Arnold, Noelle Witherspoon, Emily R. Crawford, and Muhammad Khalifa. 2016. "Psychological Heuristics and Faculty of Color: Racial Battle Fatigue and Tenure/ Promotion." *The Journal of Higher Education* 87 (6): 890–919. doi:10.1353/jhe. 2016.0033

Bateman, Lori Brand, Laura Heider, Selwyn M. Vickers, William A. Anderson, Anthony C. Hood, Evelyn Jones, Corilyn Ott, Sequoya Eady, and Mona N. Fouad. 2021. "Barriers to Advancement in Academic Medicine: The Perception gap Between Majority men and Other Faculty." *Journal of General Internal Medicine* 36 (7): 1937–1943. doi:10. 1007/s11606-020-06515-5

Bauer, Talya N., Todd Bodner, Berrin Erdogan, Donald M. Truxillo, and Jennifer S. Tucker. 2007. "Newcomer Adjustment During Organizational Socialization: A Meta-Analytic Review of Antecedents, Outcomes, and Methods." *Journal of Applied Psychology* 92 (3): 707–721. doi:10.1037/0021-9010.92.3.707

Bonilla-Silva, Eduardo, and Crystal E. Peoples. 2022. "Historically White Colleges and Universities: The Unbearable Whiteness of (Most) Colleges and Universities in

America." *American Behavioral Scientist* 66 (11): 1490–1504. doi:10.1177/00027642211066047

Budhwani, Henna, Kristine Ria Hearld, and Daniel Chavez-Yenter. 2015. "Depression in Racial and Ethnic Minorities: The Impact of Nativity and Discrimination." *Journal of Racial and Ethnic Health Disparities* 2 (1): 34–42. doi:10.1007/s40615-014-0045-z

Casado Pérez, Javier F. 2019. "Everyday Resistance Strategies by Minoritized Faculty." *Journal of Diversity in Higher Education* 12 (2): 170–179. doi:10.1037/dhe0000090

Chancellor, Renate L. 2019. "Racial Battle Fatigue: The Unspoken Burden of Black Women Faculty in LIS." *Journal of Education for Library and Information Science* 60 (3): 182–189. doi:10.3138/jelis.2019-0007

Chesler, Mark A., and James Crowfoot. 2000. "An Organizational Analysis of Racism in Higher Education." In *Organization and Governance in Higher Education*. 5, edited by Christopher M. Brown, 436–469. Boston, MA: Pearson Custom Pub.

Chesler, Mark A., and Alford A. Young Jr. 2015. *Faculty Identities and the Challenge of Diversity: Reflections on Teaching in Higher Education*. New York: Routledge.

Collins, Patricia Hill. 2019. *Intersectionality as Critical Social Theory*. Durham: Duke University Press.

Cook, David A., Rebecca S. Bahn, and Ronald Menaker. 2010. "Speed Mentoring: An Innovative Method to Facilitate Mentoring Relationships." *Medical Teacher* 32 (8): 692–694. doi:10.3109/01421591003686278

Dade, Karen, Carlie Tartakov, Connie Hargrave, and Patricia Leigh. 2015. "Assessing the Impact of Racism on Black Faculty in White Academe: A Collective Case Study of African American Female Faculty." *Western Journal of Black Studies* 39 (2): 134–146.

Delgado, Richard, and Jean Stefancic. 2001. *Critical Race Theory: An Introduction*. New York: New York University Press.

Dill, Bonnie Thornton, and Ruth Enid Zambrana. 2009. "'Critical Thinking About Inequality: An Emerging Lens.' Chap. 1." In *Emerging Intersections: Race, Class, and Gender in Theory, Policy, and Practice*, edited by B. T. Dill, and R. E. Zambrana, 1–21. New Brunswick, N.J.: Rutgers University Press.

Embrick, David G., Silvia Domínguez, and Baran Karsak. 2017. "More Than Just Insults: Rethinking Sociology's Contribution to Scholarship on Racial Microaggressions." *Sociological Inquiry* 87 (2): 193–206. doi:10.1111/soin.12184

Espino, Michelle M., and Ruth E. Zambrana. 2019. "'How Do You Advance Here? How do You Survive?' An Exploration of Under-Represented Minority Faculty Perceptions of Mentoring Modalities." *The Review of Higher Education* 42 (2): 457–484. doi:10.1353/rhe.2019.0003

Feagin, Joe R. 2020. *The White Racial Frame: Centuries of Racial Framing and Counter-Framing*. New York: Routledge.

Flores, Antonio. 2017. "2015, Hispanic Population in the United States Statistical Portrait." Pew Research Center's Hispanic Trends Project. Pew Research Center, May 31, 2020. https://www.pewresearch.org/hispanic/2017/09/18/2015-statistical-information-on-hispanics-in-united-states/.

González Burchard, Esteban, Luisa N. Borrell, Shweta Choudhry, Mariam Naqvi, Hui-Ju Tsai, Jose R. Rodriguez-Santana, Rocio Chapela, et al. 2005. "Latino Populations: A Unique Opportunity for the Study of Race, Genetics, and Social Environment in Epidemiological Research." *American Journal of Public Health* 95 (12): 2161–2168. doi:10.2105/AJPH.2005.068668

Guillaume, Rene O., and Elizabeth C. Apodaca. 2022. "Early Career Faculty of Color and Promotion and Tenure: The Intersection of Advancement in the Academy and

Cultural Taxation." *Race Ethnicity and Education* 25 (4): 546–563. doi:10.1080/13613324.2020.1718084

Gumpertz, Marcia, Raifu Durodoye, Emily Griffith, and Alyson Wilson. 2017. "Retention and Promotion of Women and Underrepresented Minority Faculty in Science and Engineering at Four Large Land Grant Institutions." *PloS One* 12 (11): 1–17. doi:10.1371/journal.pone.0187285

Hackshaw, Allan, and Amy Kirkwood. 2011. "Interpreting and Reporting Clinical Trials with Results of Borderline Significance." *Bmj* 343: 1–5. doi:10.1136/bmj.d3340

Haynes, Chayla, Leonard Taylor, Steve D. Mobley Jr, and Jasmine Haywood. 2020. "Existing and Resisting: The Pedagogical Realities of Black, Critical Men and Women Faculty." *The Journal of Higher Education* 91 (5): 698–721. doi:10.1080/00221546.2020.1731263

"Hispanic Origin Groups in the U.S." 2019. Pew Research Center. Pew Research Center, September 9, 2021. https://www.pewresearch.org/ft_21-09-01_keyfactslatinos_origin_table_final1/.

Holmes IV, Oscar, Alexis Nicole Smith, Denise Lewin Loyd, and Angélica S. Gutiérrez. 2022. "Scholars of Color Explore Bias in Academe: Calling in Allies and Sharing Affirmations for us by us." *Organizational Behavior and Human Decision Processes* 173: 1–7. doi:10.1016/j.obhdp.2022.104204

Jones, Camara Phyllis, Benedict I. Truman, Laurie D. Elam-Evans, Camille A. Jones, Clara Y. Jones, Ruth Jiles, Susan F. Rumisha, and Geraldine S. Perry. 2008. "Using "Socially Assigned Race" to Probe White Advantages in Health Status." *Ethnicity & Disease* 18 (4): 496–504.

Joseph, Tiffany D., and Laura E. Hirshfield. 2011. "'Why Don't you get Somebody new to do it?' Race and Cultural Taxation in the Academy." *Ethnic and Racial Studies* 34 (1): 121–141. doi:10.1080/01419870.2010.496489

Kelly, Bridget Turner, and Kristin I. McCann. 2014. "Women Faculty of Color: Stories Behind the Statistics." *The Urban Review* 46 (4): 681–702. doi:10.1007/s11256-014-0275-8

Kim, Dongbin, Susan B. Twombly, Lisa Wolf-Wendel, and Angie A. Belin. 2020. "Understanding Career Mobility of Professors: Does Foreign-Born Status Matter?" *Innovative Higher Education* 45 (6): 471–488. doi:10.1007/s10755-020-09513-x

Lawrence, Jourdyn A., Brigette A. Davis, Thea Corbette, Emorcia V. Hill, David R. Williams, and Joan Y. Reede. 2021. "Racial/Ethnic Differences in Burnout: A Systematic Review." *Journal of Racial and Ethnic Health Disparities* 9: 1–13. doi:10.1007/s40615-020-00950-0

Lewis, Jioni A., Ruby Mendenhall, Ashley Ojiemwen, Merin Thomas, Cameron Riopelle, Stacy Anne Harwood, and Margaret Browne Huntt. 2021. "Racial Microaggressions and Sense of Belonging at a Historically White University." *American Behavioral Scientist* 65 (8): 1049–1071. doi:10.1177/0002764219859613

López, Nancy, and Howard Hogan. 2021. "What's Your Street Race? The Urgency of Critical Race Theory and Intersectionality as Lenses for Revising the US Office of Management and Budget Guidelines, Census and Administrative Data in Latinx Communities and Beyond." *Genealogy* 5 (75): 1–23. doi:10.3390/genealogy5030075

Louis, Dave A., Scott D. Michel, Jennifer E. Deranek, and Sarah L. Louis. 2018. "Reflection, Realization, and Reaffirmation: Voices of Black and White Faculty Members Engaged in Cross-Racial Mentoring." *Multicultural Perspectives* 20 (4): 205–215. doi:10.1080/15210960.2018.1527151

Mamiseishvili, Ketevan, and Donghun Lee. 2018. "International Faculty Perceptions of Departmental Climate and Workplace Satisfaction." *Innovative Higher Education* 43 (5): 323–338. doi:10.1007/s10755-018-9432-4

Martinez, Melissa A., Aurora Chang, and Anjalé D. Welton. 2017. "Assistant Professors of Color Confront the Inequitable Terrain of Academia: A Community Cultural Wealth Perspective." *Race Ethnicity and Education* 20 (5): 696–710. doi:10.1080/13613324.2016.1150826

McCormick, Alexander C., and Chun-Mei Zhao. 2005. "Rethinking and Reframing the Carnegie Classification." *Change: The Magazine of Higher Learning* 37 (5): 51–57. doi:10.3200/CHNG.37.5.51-57

Mendez, Sylvia, Jennifer A. Tygret, Valerie Martin Conley, Comas Haynes, and Rosario Gerhardt. 2020. "Exploring the Mentoring Needs of Early-and Mid-Career URM Engineering Faculty: A Phenomenological Study." *Qualitative Report* 25 (4): 891–908. doi:10.46743/2160-3715/2020.4159

Mora, M. T., A. R. Qubbaj, and H. Rodríguez. 2018. "Advancing Latinas and Other Women in STEM Through Dual Career Hiring." In *Advancing Women in Academic STEM Fields Through Dual Career Policies and Practices*, edited by M. R. McMahon, M. Mora, and A. R. Qubbaj, 97–114. Charlotte, NC: Information Age Publishing.

National Center for Science and Engineering Statistics, National Science Foundation. 2020. *Doctorate Recipients from U.S. Universities: 2019*. Alexandria, VA: NSF 21-308. https://ncses.nsf.gov/pubs/nsf21308/.

Niemann, Yolanda Flores, Gabriella Gutiérrez y Muhs, Carmen González, and Angela Harris. 2020. *Presumed Incompetent II: Race, Class, Power, and Resistance of Women in Academia*. University Press of Colorado; Imprint Series: Utah State University Press.

O'Meara, KerryAnn, Liana Sayer, Gudrun Nyunt, and Courtney Lennartz. 2020. "Stressed, Interrupted, and Under-Estimated: Experiences of Women and URM Faculty During One Workday." *The Journal of the Professoriate* 11 (1): 106–137.

Padilla, Amado M. 1994. "Research News and Comment: Ethnic Minority Scholars; Research, and Mentoring: Current and Future Issues." *Educational Researcher* 23 (4): 24–27. doi:10.3102/0013189X023004024

Pérez, Patricia A. 2019. *The Tenure-Track Process for Chicana and Latina Faculty: Experiences of Resisting and Persisting in the Academy*. New York: Routledge.

Pizarro, Marcos, and Rita Kohli. 2020. ""I Stopped Sleeping": Teachers of Color and the Impact of Racial Battle Fatigue." *Urban Education* 55 (7): 967–991. doi:10.1177/0042085918805788

Radloff, Lenore Sawyer. 1977. "The CES-D Scale." *Applied Psychological Measurement* 1 (3): 385–401. doi:10.1177/014662167700100306

Rideau, Ryan. 2021. ""We're Just not Acknowledged": An Examination of the Identity Taxation of Full-Time non-Tenure-Track Women of Color Faculty Members." *Journal of Diversity in Higher Education* 14 (2): 161–173. doi:10.1037/dhe0000139

Robert Wood Johnson Foundation. 1995. *National Faculty Survey*. Princeton, NJ: Robert Wood Johnson Foundation.

Robinson, Petra A., and Julie J. Henriquez Aldana. 2020. "Making Lemonade from the Lemon of Cultural Taxation: Developing Global Citizens Who Think Critically and Who Promote Diversity and Social Justice." *In Handbook of Research on Diversity and Social Justice in Higher Education*, 1–18. IGI Global.

Rodríguez, José E., Kendall M. Campbell, and Linda H. Pololi. 2015. "Cross-Comparison of MRCGP & MRCP(UK) in a Database Linkage Study of 2,284 Candidates Taking Both Examinations: Assessment of Validity and Differential Performance by Ethnicity." *BMC Medical Education* 15 (1): 1–5. doi:10.1186/s12909-014-0281-2

Salinas Jr, Cristobal, Patrick Riley, Lazaro Camacho Jr, and Deborah L. Floyd. 2020. "Mentoring Experiences and Perceptions of Latino Male Faculty in Higher

Education." *Hispanic Journal of Behavioral Sciences* 42 (1): 117–140. doi:10.1177/0739986319900026

Samuels, Elias M. 2020. "Evaluating the Implementation and Impact of A Cluster-Hiring Initiative at a Research University: How Causal Mechanisms Link Programmatic Activities and Outcomes." *Performance Improvement Quarterly* 32 (4): 401–426. doi:10.1002/piq.21304

Shavers, Marjorie C., J.Y. Butler, and James L. Moore. 2014. "Cultural Taxation and the Over-Commitment of Service at Predominantly White Institutions." In *Black Faculty in the Academy: Narratives for Negotiating Identity and Achieving Career Success*, edited by Fred A Bonner, 41–51. New York: Routledge.

Smith, M. D. 2016. "Walking the Tightrope of Academe with no Net." In *Beyond Retention: Cultivating Spaces of Equity, Justice, and Fairness for Women of Color in US Higher Education*, edited by B. L. H. Marina, and S. N. Ross, 25–45. Charlotte, NC: Information Age Publishing.

Smith, William A., Walter R. Allen, and Lynette L. Danley. 2007. "Assume the Position … You Fit the Description." *American Behavioral Scientist* 51 (4): 551–578. doi:10.1177/0002764207307742

Spector, Paul E., and Steve M. Jex. 1998. "Development of Four Self-Report Measures of Job Stressors and Strain: Interpersonal Conflict at Work Scale, Organizational Constraints Scale, Quantitative Workload Inventory, and Physical Symptoms Inventory." *Journal of Occupational Health Psychology* 3 (4): 356–367. doi:10.1037/1076-8998.3.4.356

Stone, Andrea L., and Shauna Elbers Carlisle. 2019. "Examining Race/Ethnicity Differences in the Association Between the Experience of Workplace Racial Discrimination and Depression or Negative Emotions." *Journal of Racial and Ethnic Health Disparities* 6 (5): 874–882. doi:10.1007/s40615-018-0524-8

Thomas, Najmah. 2019. "In the Service of Social Equity: Leveraging the Experiences of African American Women Professors." *Journal of Public Affairs Education* 25 (2): 185–206. doi:10.1080/15236803.2018.1565041

Thorne, Kelsie M., Martinque K. Jones, Tangier M. Davis, and Isis H. Settles. 2021. "The Significance of Race in Cross-Racial Mentoring of Faculty of Color." *Translational Issues in Psychological Science* 7 (4): 462–472. doi:10.1037/tps0000286

Trejo, JoAnn. 2020. "The Burden of Service for Faculty of Color to Achieve Diversity and Inclusion: The Minority tax." *Molecular Biology of the Cell* 31 (25): 2752–2754. doi:10.1091/mbc.E20-08-0567

Turner, Caroline Sotello Viernes. 2021. "On Diversity, Identity and Socialization: Inequality of Educational Outcomes." *Education Policy Analysis Archives* 29 (41): 1–22. doi:10.14507/epaa.29.5329

US Department of Education, National Center for Education Statistics, Integrated Postsecondary Education Data System (IPEDS). 2018. The Condition of Education (NCES 2017-144), Characteristics of Postsecondary Faculty.

Williams, Monnica T. 2019. "Adverse Racial Climates in Academia: Conceptualization, Interventions, and Call to Action." *New Ideas in Psychology* 55: 58–67. doi:10.1016/j.newideapsych.2019.05.002

Williams, David R., Jourdyn A. Lawrence, and Brigette A. Davis. 2019. "Racism and Health: Evidence and Needed Research." *Annual Review of Public Health* 40: 105–125. doi:10.1146/annurev-publhealth-040218-043750

Williams, Simon N., Bhoomi K. Thakore, and Richard McGee. 2016. "Career Coaches as A Source of Vicarious Learning for Racial and Ethnic Minority PhD Students in the Biomedical Sciences: A Qualitative Study." *PLoS One* 11 (7): 1–19. doi:10.1371/journal.pone.0160038

Zambrana, Ruth Enid. 2018. *In Toxic Ivory Towers*. New Brunswick, New Jersey: Rutgers University Press.

Zambrana, Ruth Enid, Anita Allen, Eve Higginbotham, JoAnn Mitchell, Debra J. Perez, and Antonia Villarruel. 2020. "Equity and Inclusion Effective Practices and Responsive Strategies: A Guidebook for College and University Leaders." http://crge.umd.edu/wp-content/uploads/2020/07/SummitGuidebookFinal-June-8-2020.pdf.

Zambrana, Ruth Enid, and Sylvia Hurtado. 2015. "An Intersectional Lens: Theorizing an Educational Paradigm of Success." In *The Magic Key: The Educational Journey of Mexican Americans from K-12 to College and Beyond*, edited by Ruth Enid Zambrana, and Sylvia Hurtado, 77–99. Austin: University of Texas Press.

Zambrana, Ruth Enid, Rashawn Ray, Michelle M. Espino, Corinne Castro, Beth Douthirt Cohen, and Jennifer Eliason. 2015. "Don't Leave Us Behind." *American Educational Research Journal* 52 (1): 40–72. doi:10.3102/0002831214563063

Zambrana, Ruth Enid, and David R. Williams. 2022. "The Intellectual Roots Of Current Knowledge On Racism And Health: Relevance To Policy And The National Equity Discourse." *Health Affairs* 41 (2): 163–170. doi:10.1377/hlthaff.2021.01439

Zong, Jie. "A Mosaic, Not a Monolith: A Profile of the U.S. Latino Population, 2000-2020." Latino Policy & Politics Institute, October 27, 2022. https://latino.ucla.edu/research/latino-population-2000-2020/?mc_cid = f588ff5963&mc_eid = 6cafb18dfc.

Black women in white academe: a qualitative analysis of heightened inclusion tax

Tsedale M. Melaku ⬤ and Angie Beeman

ABSTRACT
This article explores how existing issues of systemic racism in academia were heightened for Black women faculty during COVID-19 which coincided with high-profile killings of Black people in 2020. Several theories of cultural taxation have created space to discuss the nuanced experiences of marginalized groups in white spaces. In reflecting on academia, this article highlights "the inclusion tax" – the various labours exerted to be included in white spaces and resist and/or adhere to white social norms. While the 2020 pandemics reveal the deeply entrenched nature of systemic racism, they did not create the inequities Black women faced but worsened and exposed them. Using data from an exploratory, online open-ended survey of sixteen ($n = 16$) Black women faculty, we demonstrate how the inclusion tax heightened during that time. We argue that the inclusion tax negatively impacts Black women, adding significant invisible labour that further perpetuates racial and gender inequality.

Numerous scholars have theorized how historically marginalized group members experience various forms of *taxation* in academia and other white institutional spaces (Padilla 1994; Joseph and Hirshfield 2011; Hirshfield and Joseph 2012; Rodríguez, Campbell, and Pololi 2015; Dnika, Thorpe-Moscon, and McCluney 2016; Melaku 2019a). The ubiquity of systemic racism and discrimination in organizations of various kinds continue to be reflected in how Black, Indigenous, and other People of Color (BIPOC) navigate white spaces (Beeman 2015a, 2015b; Wingfield 2019b; Wingfield and Chavez 2020; Ray 2019; Melaku 2019a). The events of 2020, including the global Coronavirus (COVID-19) pandemic and racial violence (Coleman 2020), reignited a national and global movement to combat systemic racism and redirected attention to the deep entrenchment of white supremacy and systemic racism in various American institutions that dispro-portionately affect BIPOC (Feagin 2006; Bonilla-Silva 1997, 2014; Moore 2008).

Amid the racial reckoning of the summer of 2020, there have been many public statements and commitments to social and racial justice, signalling an intentional shift towards creating substantive change in various institutions, including academia. BIPOC who are already managing a significant level of invisible labour are frequently asked to lead these efforts. Historically, Black women have done much of this labour and been pushed to the margins of transformational work because they experience intersectional racial and gender oppression (Ladner 1971; Collins 1986, 2000; Essed 1991; Crenshaw 1991; Brewer 2003; Simien 2006). The global pandemics of COVID-19 and racial violence presented a critical moment to assess how Black women aca-demics experience invisible labour and navigate various challenges in their professional and personal lives (Melaku 2019a; Wingfield 2019a).

In this article, we advance the *"inclusion tax"*, a theoretical concept devel-oped outside of academia (Melaku 2019a), defined as the resources spent – time, money, emotional and cognitive labour exerted by marginalized groups, and specifically BIPOC – to navigate white spaces and adhere to or resist white norms (Melaku 2019a, 2019b, 2021). Using data from an explora-tory, qualitative, online, open-ended question survey of sixteen ($n = 16$) Black women faculty in higher education, we demonstrate how the inclusion tax heightened amid the 2020 racial reckoning. Specifically, we discuss the nega-tive impact of the invisible labour stemming from navigating workplace racism on these women and highlight the nuanced ways this labour reflects the colour-blind racist ideology in white institutional spaces. This work contributes to cultural taxation scholarship by engaging a concept that focuses on the *costs* Black women faculty spend to be included. Black women faculty are not just doing "diversity work"[1]; they are constantly engaging in impression manage-ment, strategic maneuvring, taking calculated risks, and much more to gain access to necessary resources and support for advancing their careers. The inclusion tax, which manifests in uncompensated and unrecognized labour, is also prevalent for various other marginalized groups in any predominantly white and male workplaces where the organizational structure upholds sys-temic racist and sexist practices. To illustrate the impact of the inclusion tax on Black women, this article examines the following research question: *How have COVID-19 and racial violence in 2020 influenced the professional and per-sonal lives of Black women faculty who work in predominantly white institutions?*

Literature review

Black faculty in educational institutions have historically faced harsh realities navigating white academe. They are significantly underrepresented in faculty and leadership positions: out of 836,597 full-time faculty in degree-granting postsecondary institutions, only 47,477 (5.7%) were Black, of which 27,571 (3.3%) were Black women and 19,906 (2.4%) Black men (NCES 2022). Moreover, the representation across various career ranks seems to point at challenges in navigating advancement in academia, specifically, issues related to visibility, professional development, isolation, relationship building, overuse in diversity affairs, work/life balance issues, student interactions, negative evaluations from students and colleagues, overly burdened with service and teaching, and lack of tenure and promotion (Padilla and Chávez 1995; Gutiérrez y Muhs et al. 2012; Bowen 2012; Beeman 2015a, 2015b, 2021).

Numerous studies evidence the ways that women of colour in faculty and administrative positions are forced to navigate racist and sexist discriminatory practices and policies that hinder their access to growth and success (Stanley 2006; Gutiérrez y Muhs et al. 2012; Essed 2010; Williams 1991). The numerous barriers facing Black women in academic institutions often lead to high attrition rates or significant lateral moves that hinder their career trajectories relative to their white counterparts (Awe 2006; Fries-Britt and Kelly 2005; Jayakumar et al. 2009). In addition to recruitment, significant attention should be paid to the retention of Black faculty, an issue that needs more consideration and focus to understand why so few Black faculty remain in academia after securing positions (Awe 2006; Jayakumar et al. 2009, Fries-Britt and Kelly 2005; Kelly, Gayles, and Williams 2017).

Various forms of taxation in white academe: pay the tax

Scholars have examined the impact of race, ethnicity, gender, and other marginalized identities on BIPOC faculty experiences, calling attention to the existence of cultural (Padilla 1994) and identity taxation (Joseph and Hirshfield 2011; Hirshfield and Joseph 2012), as well as a minority tax (Rodríguez, Campbell, and Pololi 2015) that BIPOC faculty must pay in academic institutions. Padilla defined cultural taxation as the higher burden faculty endure taking on significant diversity-related projects within the institution at the behest of their administration and department because of their racial and ethnic identities (Padilla 1994). Further expanding upon Padilla's cultural taxation, Hirshfield and Joseph (2012) developed the concept of "identity taxation" to address how having multiple marginalizing identities, like race, gender, and sexual orientation, influence the service commitments of women and women of colour faculty. They argue that women faculty of colour are often called upon to do institutional diversity work and asked to advocate for marginalized groups[2] regardless of whether they are a member of that group or not. Identity taxation culminates in the expenditure of mental, emotional, and physical labours that faculty with marginalized identities must exert within their institution.

Rodríguez, Campbell, and Pololi (2015) developed a similar concept, the "minority tax", to describe the experiences of faculty of colour in academic medicine. The minority tax consists of the numerous responsibilities placed on faculty of colour to achieve institutional diversity and contributes to racial inequities in academic medicine. Experiences of racism and isolation alongside the minority tax perpetuate promotion disparities in their career trajectories (Rodríguez, Campbell, and Pololi 2015, 2–3).

The "inclusion tax", a concept developed through the analysis of the qualitative experiences of Black women lawyers in elite corporate law firms (Melaku 2019a), provides insights into how Black women and other marginalized groups navigate white institutional spaces. The inclusion tax is the additional resources "spent", including money, time, emotional, and mental energies expended to be *included* in white spaces and the labour spent adhering to or resisting white norms. Melaku (2019a) argues that there is an *invisible labor clause* that exists in the employment contract of marginalized groups, which conditions employment based on uncompensated and unrecognized work required to navigate white institutional spaces (Melaku 2019a, 16–18), including negotiating and navigating daily racial and gender aggressions (Sue, Capodilupo, and Holder 2008).

Unlike previous work on cultural taxation (Padilla 1994; Joseph and Hirshfield 2011; Hirshfield and Joseph 2012; Rodríguez, Campbell, and Pololi 2015), which primarily emphasized isolation and added labour related to DEI work, the *inclusion tax* emphasizes the invisible labour marginalized group members expend to negotiate and navigate their inclusion in white/dominant spaces. As such the goal of this article is to forefront the emotional, cognitive, and legitimacy work that is being done. For example, to mitigate being mistaken for non-professionals, Melaku (2019a) found that Black women lawyers must maintain an uber-professional appearance to dispel stereotypes about Black inferiority, perceived ability, and incompetence. Black women are fighting against white normative standards of beauty (St. Jean and Feagin 1998; Bryant 2013, 383) that out of hand disadvantage them in comparison to their white counterparts. In addition, the amount of financial resources placed into maintaining their hair, clothes, and other appearance-related necessities to be included in white spaces is costly for Black women (Melaku 2019a).

Beeman (2007, 2021) argues that these conditions can perpetuate what she calls "emotional segregation", an institutionalized process through which people of colour are not viewed as "emotional equals" or as "capable of sharing the same human emotions and experiences" (687). Consequently, the research and experiences of faculty of colour can be disrespected and devalued, viewed as not "real" research. Beeman (2021) notes that such emotional segregating practices are also exemplified when white progressives expect people of colour to be their sounding boards as they work through their own struggles understanding racism and anti-racism work.

Overall, the extra burdens and expectations placed on individuals because of their marginalized social identities in white institutional spaces is incredibly taxing. The structure of academe negatively disadvantages Black women faculty in their quest for professional development, inclusivity, and advancement opportunities. Cultural taxation, identity taxation, and the minority tax have significantly enhanced theoretical understandings of the additional work that faculty of colour must do in predominantly white academic institutions. The inclusion tax, however, articulates the ways in which invisible labour (emotional, cognitive, financial, and relational) manifests for marginalized groups in professional and social spaces. For Black women faculty during COVID-19 and racial violence, they are forced to pay a steeper inclusion tax navigating academia.

Method

Black feminist thought as methodological practice

We ground our qualitative understanding of the experiences of Black women in white spaces by utilizing Black feminist thought as methodological practice. Black feminist theory acknowledges the complex and rich insights made by Black women's work, intellectual contributions, knowledge production, and activism. Sociologist Patricia Hill Collins (1986) articulates the unique perspectives and experiences of Black women faculty in white academic spaces as "outsiders within". This results from the rooted nature of interlocking systems of oppression, embedded within the intersections of race, gender, and class, thereby producing "a special standpoint on self, family, and society for Afro-American women" (Collins 1986, S14). Collins theorizes that Black women utilize this marginality to produce Black feminist thought that is reflective of their distinctive standpoint.

Therefore, we intentionally use Black feminist thought to ground our qualitative understanding of Black women faculty's experiences in academe by drawing on an intersectional approach to amplify how their experiences are rooted in their distinct social location in society (Collins 1986, 2000), and driven by systemic racist practices embedded within white institutions. Intersectionality is a key methodological component of Black feminist thought. Intersectionality is essential to recognizing how various identities, social and biological categories, intersect, overlap, and combine in multiple and often simultaneous ways to create systemic inequality, oppression, and discrimination (Collins 1986, 2000; Crenshaw 1991; Essed 1991). We employ this Black feminist and intersectional lens to understand the inclusion tax Black women are forced to pay in white academe and the level of emotional segregation they encounter. In approaching this research from a Black feminist thought perspective, we recognize that

> [a]s outsiders within, Black feminist scholars may be one of many distinct groups of marginal intellectuals whose standpoints promise to enrich contemporary sociological discourse. Bringing this group – as well as others who share an outsider within status vis-a-vis sociology – into the center of analysis may reveal aspects of reality obscured by more orthodox approaches. (Collins 1986, S15)

The usage of Black feminist thought as a methodological practice is a political stance (Clemons 2019). As women of colour in academe, specifically Black women and Asian women, conducting research on Black women faculty experiences, we recognize our positionality. We actively work to address the privilege and oppression that are intricately connected to how we make meaning of the findings in this study, as well as how we interpret its value and importance within the larger sociological and historical context of the work targeting Black women in the workplace. By decentring whiteness, elevating Black women's voices, and challenging the status quo, we use Black feminist thought as a methodological practice to address racial inequality, with a strong commitment to working towards social change (Clemons 2019). The data presented comes directly from the lived experiences of Black women faculty and the perspective they have based on their standpoint in academe. We are reflective about our positionality as the researchers and the lens that we bring in this work, as praxis and method. We are intentional about how our positionality influences the way we see the data. Giving voice to Black women through our subjectivity is needed and must be included in knowledge production.

In *Black Feminist Thought: Knowledge, Consciousness, and the Politics Empowerment* (2000), Patricia H. Collins foregrounds Black women's intellectual tradition, rooted within discourses of self-definition, empowerment, and knowledge by examining the embeddedness of identity politics and its direct impact on their lived experiences. Collins goes beyond the simplistic analysis of social identities, emphasizing the critical importance of examining various social and biological constructs (i.e. gender, race, and class) as combining, intersecting, and overlapping to create a "matrix of domination" (Collins 2000). Therefore, we situate our work within a Black feminist thought framework to create a space where Black women faculty can share their experiences and contributions as activists and educators. In so doing, we emphasize the fact that they are producers of knowledge derived from their lived experiences. To analyze the data, we apply a Black feminist thought perspective to this study.

Research design

The purpose of this study is to examine how Black women faculty in academe are challenged by COVID-19 and racial violence, and how it has impacted their experiences in the workplace. We employed a qualitative online survey with open-ended questions (see Appendix) conducted via Qualtrics. Surveys were conducted between May and July 2021. Institutional Review Board of The City University of New York (IRB) approval was received prior to the start of this study (*institution blinded for review*, IRB File #2020-0809).

We utilized several methods to recruit participants, including reaching out to organization listservs, directly accessing university websites for potential candidates and snowball sampling methods. We drafted emails directly to the leadership of various academic organizations such as writing groups, and listservs that have Black faculty and staff membership. Furthermore, we reviewed random university departmental websites for potential participants that we perceived as Black women faculty. We acknowledge that this method potentially excludes mixed-race women who appear ambiguous but identify as Black. The survey requested that each participant recommend additional potential participants for the study. These various recruitment strategies were necessary to obtain the research sample. We received a total of seventy-seven (77) survey attempts, of which thirty-one (31) were completed. Given the nature of this study, we removed an additional fifteen (15) completed surveys from the final sample since they were from non-Black female faculty members. The final sample consisted of sixteen (16) completed survey responses from Black women faculty[3] in four-year public and private colleges/universities to discuss the experiences of Black women (see Table 1).

All respondents identified as female and Black, one of which also indicated that they are bi-racial. One (1) of the participants identified as Hispanic/Latino, while two (2) did not provide a response related to their ethnicity. All participants hold full-time employment at their respective institutions across the following ranks: Assistant Professors (7), Associate Professors (4), Lecturer/Instructor (2), and Postdoctoral Fellows (3).

The questions on the qualitative online survey focus on participants' perceptions of their experiences as they relate to racial violence, the impact of COVID-19, and political polarization because of the 2020 election. Questions also directly asked about institutional responses and commitments to racial and social justice resulting from racial violence, as well as responses to the COVID-19 pandemic. We asked about participants' emotional and cognitive well-being as they navigated multiple pandemics, and whether there were impacts to their career trajectories and experiences. The survey also requested participant demographic information including gender, race, ethnicity, age, occupation, and employment status. We chose online surveys,

Table 1. Demographic information of survey respondents ($n = 16$).

Characteristic	Frequency	Percent
Gender		
Female	16	100
Race		
Black	16	100
Bi-Racial	1	6.25
Ethnicity		
Non-Hispanic/Non-Latino	13	81.25
Hispanic/Latino	1	6.25
No response	2	12.5
Age		
21–34	4	25
35–44	7	43.75
45–54	2	12.5
55–64	1	6.25
65+	1	6.25
No response	1	6.25
Position		
Full professor	0	0
Associate professor	4	25
Assistant professor	7	43.75
Lecturer/Instructor	2	12.5
Postdoctoral fellow	3	18.75
Employment status		
Full-time	16	100
Part-time	0	0
Type of institution		
Four-year public	12	75
Four-year private	4	25
Region		
Midwest	1	6.25
Northeast	12	75
South	2	12.5
Canada	1	6.25

rather than face-to-face interviews and focus groups, because they provide a greater sense of anonymity and give respondents time to think through their experiences, which may be traumatic or sensitive, before formulating written responses. For the most part, we found participants' survey responses to be forthcoming, detailed, and direct.

To analyze the data, we created an excel worksheet of the de-identified responses to all survey questions. We deployed an open coding method to analyze the data. This practice requires a line-by-line assessment of analyzing raw data in order to "embed[ded] phenomena, patterns, concepts, and themes" (Price 2010, 156). We then read through the responses independently, coding for emerging themes related to challenges respondents faced in their workplaces, and in general, since the pandemic and in connection to recent cases of racial violence. We systematically reviewed participant responses in order to detect patterns and emerging themes to answer the research question (see Table 2). We paid particular attention to the terms respondents used to describe their work, perceptions of their work, and

Table 2. Frequencies of mentions of emergent themes ($n = 16$).

Themes	Mentions	Means	SDs
Anti-racism discourse	63	3.94	1.69
Performative allyship	52	3.25	1.61
Feeling unsafe/unprotected	31	1.94	1.53
Other	62	3.88	2.63
Total	208		

their emotional responses. We subsequently met to compare our findings and the themes participants noted as most significant (Mills, Bonner, and Francis 2006). Through this discussion, we identified common themes of feeling devalued, overworked, and unsafe in the responses. By deploying a Black feminist thought approach (Collins 1986, 2000), we consistently reflected upon the lived experiences of Black women as presented in the data, and as articulated by the respondents. We present our findings based on the emerging themes and patterns (Mills, Bonner, and Francis 2006) that developed from our analysis and utilize pseudonyms to identify respondents.

Findings

The following sections detail the experiences of Black women faculty in this study as they related to navigating anti-racism discourse and managing institutional performative allyship and feeling unsafe and unprotected. These findings complicate and are detrimental to Black women's overall experiences as they are forced to engage in strategic maneuvring requiring intentional self-care practices to manage their emotional and psychological well-being in this time of racial reckoning in white academe.

Navigating anti-racism discourse

Respondents in our study felt devalued from navigating anti-racism discourses. This theme was most common; we identified 63 mentions in our analysis across all responses (see Table 2). Throughout 2020 and into 2021, the discourse on race and racism has been front and centre compelling institutions in all industries to engage in public commitments and internal measures to address inequality. In academia, in particular, statements of racial and social justice produced by leadership and within departments signalled a recognition for change. The impact of this new drive to discuss and engage in racial equity projects created a push for BIPOC faculty, students, and staff to do this work (Ahmed 2012). Unfortunately, many institutions did not account for the added invisible labour that comes with doing diversity work. This is work that does not translate into recognition and compensation that would lead to tangible rewards with respect to promotion and advancement. Ironically, as institutions issued statements claiming a concern for diversity, equity, and inclusion, Black women felt *less* supported as they engaged in additional labour and felt less protected.

Janet, an Assistant Professor at a four-year public university in the Northeast, articulated how she was impacted by having to pick up additional diversity work to support students, saying: "I have to deal with and respond to unique needs along with the mental needs of my students while balancing my work and the mental needs of myself and family. The tangible work is not compensated or recognized" Likewise, Paula, an Associate Professor at a public university in the Northeast, stated:

> There was a statement after the murder of George Floyd which was pretty empty – embarrassingly so. I was also a bit shocked at the hollowness of the statement after murders of Asian women in Atlanta, but not surprised. At this point I have now come to expect these types of lackluster statements regarding racial and antisemitic violence from my institution. (Paula, Associate Professor, Public University in the Northeast)

Additionally, the Black women respondents express that they are experiencing added emotional and cognitive stress because of racial violence and the expectation of having to do anti-racist work at their institutions. Janet reveals:

> At the time of the protests last summer, I was under increased pressure to talk to people on campus about anti-Black racism and help craft institutional statements. It felt like I was working overtime during summer, a time when my white colleagues were free of responsibility. In light of the inability of our institution to follow up on these issues, I feel resentful towards individual colleagues and the institution itself. (Janet, Assistant Professor, Public University in the Northeast)

This directly speaks to the comparative experiences of faculty of colour, and particularly Black faculty and professionals that are expected to do diversity work because of their identities. This relates not only to cultural and identity taxation but also to the pressure Black women feel to engage in such work to ensure their own inclusion. As Paula states:

> I also work at a place where people tend to confuse people of color in public, which is also a sign of their lack of commitment. When they cannot even get our names right, even after we have just introduced ourselves, it demonstrates how they think about us. Finally, I have heard the ethnic studies departments referred to as "identity departments". Not only is this insulting and demonstrates yet again how thoroughly whiteness is normalized and viewed uncritically, it also reveals the levels of racism embedded throughout the institution even at its highest levels. (Paula, Associate Professor, Public University in the Northeast)

The inclusion tax highlights the nuanced labour that is involved in being in white spaces for Black women professionals. Regardless of field or institution, the inclusion tax concept provides a useful framework to engage how BIPOC and other marginalized groups must perform various types of invisible labour to be included in white/dominant spaces.

In responding to a question asking how their organization has reacted to the killing of Black people and racial violence, Theresa, an Assistant Professor at a four-year private university in the Northeast, emphasized how she was expected to engage in the additional labour of supporting students and faculty amidst the crisis. She noted that as a junior faculty member who also serves in an administrative role, she was expected to dedicate extra hours to sitting with students and counselling them, "working with Black faculty and student groups to enforce policy initiatives, where faculty of other races do not have to take on that burden". Theresa further stated, "My university put out a general statement and that's it. My school depended on me to lead the response and it was just too much of a load at the time with all that was happening personally" (Theresa). In this case, the inclusion tax is pronounced in the emotional, cognitive, and relational labour expended working on issues related to COVID-19 and racial violence. Navigating relationships with students and Black faculty to mitigate the impact of institutional policies in place to address inequities is taxing for Black women faculty in this study. Theresa's vantage point provides her with insights as both a Black faculty member and an administrator tasked with engaging students, faculty, and administrators.

Respondents also expressed how they are engaging in increased work managing institutional efforts to address COVID-19 and anti-racism, particularly in relation to the expectation of their time. For example, Rose, a Postdoctoral Fellow at a four-year public university in the Northeast, reported that she has seen an uptick in communications from the institution relating to online events addressing multiple pandemic concerns. Although she feels that this programming is positive, it also becomes consuming in negative ways due to existing pressures. Rose shares:

> COVID-19 saw an increase in online programming. My postdoc position was committed to promoting workshops and talks that dealt with our current pandemic moment as well as the larger issues facing an array of populations. My email inbox has been filled with invitations to all types of talks. On one end this was a great thing. On the other end it became overwhelming. It has [been] hard to keep up with so many things. Academia already requires you to consistently "be on". It operates like a machine that expects you to always be present and productive. I have had to learn to draw my own boundaries and protect my time. (Rose, Postdoctoral Fellow, Public University in the Northeast)

While the struggle to balance her time navigating institutional expectations and self-care has become increasingly pronounced because of the COVID-19 pandemic and racial violence, Rose speaks directly to the ways in which her identity as a Black woman created added pressure and expectations which she is required to manage in white institutional spaces. The inclusion tax rears its head in the cognitive and emotional maneuvring done to maintain a positive perception of her performance from the institution. Rose states,

> As a Black woman I am already expected to perform and always be on top of things. If I am not careful, I will be the one drained ... Living with chronic illness does shift my time and commitment. I have to be careful not to overwork because my body will and can shut down ... All Universities need to take into account the Spoon Theory. We are not machines. (Rose, Postdoctoral Fellow, Public University in the Northeast)

In addition, a lot of this invisible work also may not necessarily manifest into fundamental practices that would change the policy and culture of the institution. This leads to the sense of futility of BIPOC in white spaces exerting significant invisible labour doing work that is not valued by the institution. Paula, an Associate Professor, shares her feelings of being ineffective in getting the institution to recognize the need for diversity in this moment of racial awakening, and historically, saying: "Professionally, I feel that my lobbying efforts for increased diversity have been fruitless" (Paula). She continues by acknowledging the lack of institutional support: "Those who are in positions to make policy changes or approve new hires have been resistant to do so, instead claiming the lack of funds and bureaucratic hurdles above their position prevents them from doing so" (Paula). Paula shares the emotional and cognitive labour she is forced to engage in, attempting to gain traction with the proclaimed efforts of her institution, while figuring out ways to protect herself from doing work that is not valued. She notes: "I have taken a step back from some duties i.e. my institution can find someone else to speak during Black History Month" (Paula).

Performative allyship

The theme of performative allyship was the second most common with 52[4] mentions amongst all respondents referencing this theme. We defined performative allyship as the appearance of supporting BIPOC or other marginalized groups with no substantive change, though increased institutional communication was strewn across numerous responses of Black women professionals. Rose, Postdoctoral Fellow soon to be Assistant Professor, noted that even in her new position she was already being bombarded with communication regarding DEI events, saying:

> For the University I will be joining in the fall their efforts have been to focus on diverse hiring and online teaching/ programming. Although I have not officially started yet, I have definitely received so many emails. COVID-19 is being addressed but I think an additional effect is the idea that we can be reached all the time. (Rose, Postdoctoral Fellow, Public University in the Northeast)

These experiences also tie in with the debilitating aspect of being immersed within discourses, projects, and efforts that highlight Black trauma yet do not actually effect change. In this way, our findings indicate that recent statements in support of "diversity, equity, and inclusion" have only caused greater stress and frustration for women of colour. Yet Dana, another faculty at a four-year public institution in the Northeast, said that her institution increased communication efforts noting that "there were panels and a bevy of tepid emails of concerns for Black faculty" (Dana). However, she stated that these efforts were unnecessary in her opinion because "most of these forums are to educate people of European descent" (Dana). This statement is in line with findings in another recent study on women of colour (Melaku and Beeman 2022), where a Latina Professor Emeritus noted that DEI efforts were not only for the benefit of white people but that they were also deemed the experts on race and racism. Beeman (2022) argues that this process is tied to liberal white supremacist behaviours, where the ultimate goal is to position oneself as the better white person, rather than creating significant anti-racist change.

The inclusion tax works within racialized social structures (Bonilla-Silva 1997), racialized organizations (Ray 2019), and gendered organizations (Acker 1990), where the mechanisms of invisible labour are not explicit, yet they become evident through constant exposure forcing BIPOC to negotiate their presence in white spaces reproducing racial inequality to the benefit of white people, but specifically white men (Feagin and O'Brien 2003; Bonilla-Silva 2014; Feagin and Ducey 2017). As with Padilla's (1994) cultural taxation and Hirshfield and Joseph's (2012) identity taxation (2012), the expectation that BIPOC faculty take up invisible labour through diversity work in various forms in white spaces, also clearly suggests that the inclusion tax is persistent within their experiences navigating white academe. The uniqueness of the inclusion tax is its explication of different types of invisible labour that go beyond DEI work and is tangible in all areas where one is forced to navigate white space as a member of a marginalized group. Paula makes this clear when she states, "I feel I have to be present in order to represent the concerns of faculty and students of colour. You do not have a voice if you are not in the room". The inclusion tax offers an examination of the price paid by women of colour, Black women in particular, to be included in these spaces.

Feeling unsafe/unprotected

Another emerging theme amongst respondents dealt specifically with feeling unsafe in the workplace because of the violence perpetrated against Black people in America. There were a total of 31 mentions amongst the responses. This conveys the lack of confidence in institutional commitments to address racial inequality as professed in statements of solidarity. BIPOC professionals point to inadequate practices addressing racial inequities in the workplace. These feelings were triggered in various scenarios amongst participants. Sarah, an Assistant Professor from a four-year private university in the Midwest, reveals that she felt forced to go about business as usual when Black death and trauma were consistently on public display, not accounting for the impact it would have on her ability to process these events. She expresses anger at having to navigate these experiences saying:

> It is enraging having to work after news/video of yet another Black person being murdered, and then holding space for students and making something so personal a learning experience before I've even had the time to catch my breath or grieve. It's also upsetting to see such deadly white supremacy go unchecked as states are focusing on banning critical race theory and institutions are forming book clubs and committees when radical anti-racist change/policy is needed to save lives. It really drives home that our lives are not a priority. (Sarah, Assistant Professor, Private University in the Northeast)

Many respondents shared the pain they felt and the expectation to continue showing up, despite their pain. For example, Karina states:

> I want to not see one more video. I want to not have to cry. I think I have the critical tools to recognize a lot of things about this moment but sometimes, I also just need to detach. So I didn't though. I probably showed up to more zoom meetings than I ever did in person not just because of access but because *I did not know how less engagement would be perceived* (emphasis ours). (Karina, Assistant Professor, Public University in the Northeast)

The expectation and pressure both of these respondents felt to hold space for everyone while not having time to process their own emotions, speaks to the inclusion tax – the additional labour they engage in to present themselves professionally despite the rage, sadness, and other emotions they are feeling.

Laura, another Assistant Professor at a private four-year institution in the Northeast, articulates her concern for "Black and Brown" students and other employees with respect to COVID-19 and the ensuing impact of racial violence manifested in different mediums. She notes:

> The obvious change is that we have transitioned to operating the activities of the college through online mediums. However, the leadership of the college has not done an effective job of assuring faculty and staff that day-to-day operations of the college will be clean and safe for the predominantly Black and Brown students and employees who comprise the college community.

According to my perception, the leadership also hasn't done an effective job in addressing how the pandemic has impacted our student population in distinctive ways. We serve students who come from communities who continue to be particularly ravaged by the virus and all of its economic, public health, and social fallout. (Laura, Assistant Professor, Private University in the Northeast)

These respondents' articulations continue to bolster the idea that Black faculty do not have confidence in institutional responses as it relates to the experiences and safety of BIPOC in academe. In predominantly white institutions, leaders are not likely to privilege the emotional experiences of faculty of colour, especially if they are not experts on race and racism or have not experienced racial hostility and targeting as do people of colour. In this way, institutional practices that downplay the significance of such complaints perpetuate emotional segregation (Beeman 2007). The added emotional and cognitive labour of negotiating how institutional responses do not address the basic safety of its BIPOC community creates distrust in the leadership and toward white faculty. Paula shares her frustration with white colleagues in this regard:

I really don't feel like dealing with my colleagues' overt bias and/or unconscious racism. I had the misfortune of having a conversation with a colleague that I have known for several years about how they moved out of the city because of calls to defund the police. As a result of this conversation, I will never have another conversation about politics and/or race with this individual again. (Paula, Associate Professor, Public University in the Northeast)

White faculty are likely not even aware of the extent to which Black women self-censor themselves to ensure their own survival, emotional safety, and inclusion in white-normed spaces. Black women manage these emotions and continue to show up in their professional spaces (e.g. for the book clubs and committees Sarah mentioned) without showing the anger, sadness, and frustration they are experiencing. This inclusion tax continues to pervade the experiences of Black women professionals in this study, regardless of position.

Laura's account also highlights the direct impact of COVID-19 on "Black and Brown" communities that have suffered immense setbacks, while still not protecting the very students and employees who hail from communities intimately touched by COVID's devastating blows. The level of work that is necessitated by having to worry about how the institution will respond to public acts of violence or COVID-19 devastation within communities that are closely impacted by the virus and its ensuing tentacles on other aspects of life, continues to evade institution leadership as they negotiate their performative responses. In the words of one of our respondents, Rose, "the machine" that "requires you to consistently 'be on'" maintains the status quo. All of this added invisible work to show up, present oneself, and "be on" culminates in a heightened inclusion tax for BIPOC navigating anti-racism discourses, action plans, and the absence of both within white academe and other workplaces. The burden continues to fall on BIPOC regardless of institution.

Discussion

Our data reveals that Black women faculty in this study experienced a heightened inclusion tax in white academe. The inclusion tax results in significant invisible labour navigating and negotiating racial discourse while maintaining professional decorum despite the myriad of emotions Black women experience in this time of multiple pandemics. We find that COVID-19 and racial violence exacerbated existing workplace challenges related to racial and gender aggressions that negatively impact the experiences of Black women faculty in this study in academia. Through an intersectional approach and Black feminist thought lens, we centre and ground the narratives of Black women faculty in this study which provides deep insight into their lived experiences and perspectives. In doing so, we can recognize the invisible labour that permeates their everyday lives in both professional and personal spaces. Collins (1989) notes that

> the unpaid and paid work that Black women perform, the types of communities in which they live, and the kinds of relationships they have with others suggest that African-American women, as a group, experience a different world than those who are not Black and female … these experiences stimulate a distinctive Black feminist consciousness concerning that material reality. (747)

The Black women in this study collectively articulate how they operate within white institutional spaces, neither being "passive victims of nor willing accomplices to their own domination" (747). They strategize utilizing everyday practices, expending cognitive, emotional, relational, and financial energies fighting against and resisting oppression.

The study points to how some Black women in academe have to manage increased invisible labour and emotional segregation navigating anti-racism and racial violence discourses, of which both have a silencing effect on Black women's experiences in white spaces. Several key findings in this article suggest that Black women faculty in this study face continued pressures to do work that is neither compensated, recognized, or valued in the institution. Like other prominent studies examining the experiences of faculty of colour in academe (Padilla 1994; Stanley 2006; Gutiérrez y Muhs et al. 2012; Hirshfield and Joseph 2012), respondents in our study consistently corroborate that unlike their white counterparts, they are tapped to take on diversity work in the service of the institution without material rewards or positive recognition that supports their promotion and tenure trajectories (Ahmed 2012).

In line with both cultural and identity taxation, Black women faculty in this study articulate that they engage in increased labour because of their membership in racially subordinated groups. Guised in the efforts of pushing DEI projects forward, institutions call upon BIPOC employees, and particularly Black people to do work of promoting, encouraging, disseminating, and engaging in equity work. This is work they feel pressured to engage in; to be included, and taxed, when called upon. Yet, through this work, there is an erasure of the experiences of Black women embedded within the DEI push to educate.

The silencing of their lived experiences and continued racial aggression imbued in doing "race work" is taxing and exacerbates various inequities that persist in the workplace. This also draws us to recognize how some Black women may rationalize their experiences and consider alternative ways that work for them to continue to operate in white spaces by muting their own experiences, in part to be viewed as professional and to ensure their own inclusion. Data shows that respondents need space and time to cope with the emotional and psychological trauma of witnessing and experiencing racism both in public displays and within their institutions. Interestingly, some of the shorter responses powerfully illustrated a deep level of devaluation in the workplace. For example, in response to whether she addressed political issues in the workplace, one respondent as noted previously simply stated, "I don't bother". These participants seemed to have reached a point of reluctance or pessimism. Some responses addressed self-care, which is an important part of resilience, but respondents' attention to self-care resulted from overwork. Part of that self-care included withdrawing from their meetings and other duties to protect their physical and mental health. These responses also showed an awareness of the "inclusion tax" and knowledge that showing up angry or depressed or lacking the wherewithal to manage their emotions in the professional space would elicit negative evaluations of them as Black women, as would not showing up at all. Therefore, they showed up, taking on the additional labour because as Karina expressed, Black women have to navigate how they are perceived.

The data also revealed another troubling pattern – almost all the respondents expressed reservations about raising these political issues in their workplaces. The reality our respondents point to is that the current DEI efforts have resulted in recentering whiteness, holding up white allies as experts, and wearing out BIPOC who are also afraid to speak out due to past and current racial hostility. As articulated by Sara Ahmed (2012), diversity and equality have become embedded in performance culture, where "equality can participate in concealing inequality (110)". If that is the case, then DEI efforts are more harmful than beneficial to Black women, who are most often the ones speaking back to racism within the institution. For these reasons, Beeman (2021; 2022) argues that institutions must adopt a *racism-*

centered, intersectional approach rather than relying on vague "diversity, equity, and inclusion" initiatives. Without this focus, DEI is defined so broadly that it whitewashes the specific needs and experiences of women of colour. Having to take on the role of DEI leader, nurturer and confidant for students, faculty, and staff, while simultaneously experiencing racial inequality, is extremely taxing and requires expending incredible amounts of emotional, cognitive, and relational labour – ultimately forcing Black women faculty in this study to pay a steep inclusion tax in white academe.

Limitations and implications for future research

While this study provides rich and nuanced data to support the experiences of Black women faculty in academe, there were several limitations. First, we recognize that the time commitment required to complete an online open-ended question survey at the end of the semester may have contributed to the response rate. Given the demands on Black women's time in general due to significant underrepresentation in white spaces, we acknowledge that these issues may challenge their ability to participate in studies. We also accept that the attempts in relation to the successful completion of the survey may be indicative of the time constraints, as well as the emotional and psychological exhaustion, Black women are confronting during COVID-19 and the coinciding racial reckoning.

Second, we recognize generalizability as a challenge to this qualitative study. However, our findings are comparable to the findings of past and current research on Black women in academia and other predominantly white institutions. Black women have also been sharing these experiences through public scholarship and articles in outlets, such as The Chronicle of Higher Education (Ahmad 2020; June and O'Leary 2021), Inside Higher Ed (Robertson 2020, 2022), and the Harvard Business Review (Cheeks 2018; Melaku and Beeman 2020; Phillips, Rothbard, and Dumas 2009) to name a few. We also note the importance of the results to provide a rich, nuanced understanding of the lived experiences of Black women faculty by examining their specific cases in this research.

Research implications of this study point to the need to continue to do research centring the lived experiences of Black professionals. This contributes to the nuanced articulations of the experiences of Black women in academe, and white spaces in general. Particularly as it relates to how public discourses centring race and racism impact how Black professionals are called upon to take up the task of doing DEI work that does not have substantial institutional buy-in to create material rewards that positively impact their ability to navigate promotion and advancement. This research builds a case for the use of the inclusion tax as a theoretical concept to explain the varying ways that Black women expend invisible labour in white institutional spaces. Future research should continue to interrogate how systemic racism perpetuates discriminatory practices that are discreet and silenced in the context of public discourses of race and racism in organizations. Future researchers might also analyze strategies Black women faculty utilize to thrive within predominantly white or white-normed institutions, generational differences in these strategies and experiences, and the policies or practices these institutions can implement to support them.

Conclusion

It cannot be disputed or denied that 2020 and 2021 were important years of reckoning for institutions across various industries because of multiple pandemics, including COVID-19, racial violence, and political polarization. The deeply entrenched nature of systemic racism (Feagin 2006) within American medical, legal, educational, economic, and social institutions was further amplified by the disproportionate negative impact on Black and Latinx communities. Institutions were forced to recognize that racial inequality penetrates and permeates across all facets of American life driving policies, structures, practices, and culture to the detriment of Black communities. The incredible loss of life suffered within the Black community by state-sanctioned violence and inequitable social conditions that pervade Black life was on full display (Pirtle 2020; Coleman 2020; Melaku 2020). Institutions of all kinds need to have honest internal conversations (Livingston 2021) amongst the leadership about the underlying issues related to systemic racism. Black women are underrepresented among tenure-track faculty in academia. Many of the experiences they share are in part related to their outsider-within status, where their work is often unrecognized, unrewarded, and ignored. As Melaku (2019a) argues, Black women in white institutional spaces are simultaneously invisible and hypervisible as a result of the interconnectedness of their identities that interact in multiple and often simultaneous ways to create systemic social inequality. Whether in law firms or the halls of academe, Black women continue to pay a steep inclusion tax in white spaces.

Notes

1. We problematize the term "diversity" here to acknowledge the vagueness and ineffectiveness of the term. In many ways the language institutions use to respond to racial violence and inequity (diversity, equity, and inclusion) are limiting and do not directly name the problem of racism within institutions (see Embrick 2011; Ahmed 2012; Beeman 2021; Hamilton and Nielsen 2021). Throughout the paper, we reference "diversity work" as vague initiatives that Black women are expected to take on with very little reward or results.

2. Marginalized groups refer to individuals with membership in groups that have been historically excluded from social, economic, political, and cultural involvement in mainstream society based on their identities, including race, gender, sexuality, disability, class, ethnicity and other identities.
3. The final sample included three (3) postdoctoral fellows who also hold visiting assistant professor positions or are transitioning to a tenure-track position.
4. This theme was the second most common aside from the responses we labelled as "other" (62 mentions). Responses labelled "other" included a mix of simple "yes" or "no" answers, "N/A", "I am unsure", descriptive statements with no evaluation on the matter (e.g., "The organization has put out statements about the killing of Black people and Racial Upheaval") and comments such as "I don't bother", which we address further in the discussion.

Disclosure statement

No potential conflict of interest was reported by the authors.

ORCID

Tsedale M. Melaku ⓘ http://orcid.org/0000-0003-1188-4991

References

Acker, J. 1990. "Hierarchies, Jobs, Bodies: A Theory of Gendered Organizations." *Gender & Society* 4 (2): 139–158. doi:10.1177/089124390004002002.

Ahmad, A. S. 2020. "A Survival Guide for Black, Indigenous, and Other Women of Color in Academe." The Chronicle of Higher Education. https://www.chronicle.com/article/a-survival-guide-for-black-indigenous-and-other-women-of-color-in-academe?cid=gen_sign_in.

Ahmed, S. 2012. *On Being Included: Racism and Diversity in Institutional Life*. Durham, NC: Duke University Press.

Awe, C. 2006. "Retention of African American Faculty in Research Universities." *African Americans: Struggle for Recognition in the Academy* 17 (2): 33–57.

Beeman, A. 2007. "Emotional Segregation: A Content Analysis of Institutional Racism in US Films, 1980–2001." *Ethnic and Racial Studies* 30 (5): 687–712. doi:10.1080/01419870701491648.

Beeman, A. 2015a. "Walk the Walk but Don't Talk the Talk: The Strategic Use of Color-Blind Ideology in an Interracial Social Movement Organization." *Sociological Forum* 30 (1): 127–147. doi:10.1111/socf.12148.

Beeman, A. 2015b. "Teaching to Convince, Teaching to Empower: Reflections on Student Resistance and Self-Defeat at Predominantly White vs. Racially Diverse Campuses." *Understanding & Dismantling Privilege* 5 (1): 13–33.

Beeman, A. 2021. "'If Only We Are Brave Enough to Be It': Demanding More from Diversity, Equity, and Inclusion Efforts to Support Women Faculty of Color." *Critical Sociology* 47 (7-8): 1099–1109. https://doi.org/10.1177/08969205211003316.

Beeman, A. 2022. *Liberal White Supremacy: How Progressive Silence Racial and Class Oppression*. Athens, GA: University of Georgia Press.

Bonilla-Silva, E. 1997. "Rethinking Racism: Toward a Structural Interpretation." *American Sociological Review* 62 (3): 465–480. doi:10.2307/2657316.

Bonilla-Silva, E. 2014. *Racism Without Racists: Color-Blind Racism and the Persistence of Racial Inequality in America*. 4th edition. Lanham, MD: Rowman & Littlefield.

Bowen, D. M. 2012. "Visibly Invisible: The Burden of Race and Gender for Female Students of Color Striving for an Academic Career in the Sciences." In *Presumed Incompetent: The Cheeksintersections of Race and Class for Women in Academia*, edited by G. Gutiérrez y Muhs, Y. F. Niemann, C. G. González, and A. P. Harris, 116–132. Logan, UT: Utah State University Press.

Brewer, R. 2003. "Black Radical Theory and Practice: Gender, Race, and Class." *Socialism and Democracy* 17 (1): 109–122. https://doi.org/10.1080/08854300308428344.

Bryant, S. L. 2013. "The Beauty Ideal: The Effects of European Standards of Beauty on Black Women." *Columbia Social Work Review* 6: 80–81.

Cheeks, M. 2018. "How Black Women Describe Navigating Race and Gender in the Workplace." *Harvard Business Review*. https://hbr.org/2018/03/how-black-women-describe-navigating-race-and-gender-in-the-workplace.

Clemons, K. M., ed. 2019. "Black Feminist Thought and Qualitative Research in Education." In *Oxford Research Encyclopedia of Education*. Oxford University Press. doi:10.1093/acrefore/9780190264093.013.1194.

Coleman, A. R. 2020. "Black Bodies Are Still Treated as Expendable." VOX. Accessed 5 June 2020. https://www.vox.com/2020/6/5/21277938/ahmaud-arbery-george-floyd-breonnataylorcovid [https://perma.cc/C4C5-3HZL].

Collins, P. H. 1986. "Learning from the Outsider Within: The Sociological Significance of Black Feminist Thought." *Social Problems* 33 (6): s14–s32. doi:10.2307/800672.

Collins, P. H. 1989. "The Social Construction of Black Feminist Thought." *Signs* 14 (4): 745–773. doi:10.1086/494543.

Collins, P. H. 2000. *Black Feminist Thought: Knowledge, Consciousness, and the Politics of Empowerment*. New York: Routledge.

Crenshaw, K. 1991. "Race, Gender, and Sexual Harassment." *S. Cal. l. Rev.* 65: 1467.

Dnika, J. T., J. Thorpe-Moscon, and C. McCluney. 2016. "Emotional Tax: How Black Women and Men Pay More at Work and How Leaders Can Take Action." In *Gender, Race, and Ethnicity in The Workplace*, 12. New York: Catalyst.

Embrick, D. G. 2011. "The Diversity Ideology in the Business World: A New Oppression for a New Age." *Critical Sociology* 37 (5): 541–556.

Essed, P. 1991. *Understanding Everyday Racism: An Interdisciplinary Approach*. London, England: Sage.

Essed, P. 2010. "Dilemmas in Leadership: Women of Colour in the Academy." *Ethnic and Racial Studies* 23 (5): 888–904. doi:10.1080/01419870050110959.

Feagin, J. R. 2006. *Systemic Racism: A Theory of Oppression*. New York: Routledge.

Feagin, J. R., and K. Ducey. 2017. *Elite White Men Ruling: Who, What, When, Where, and How*. New York: Routledge.

Feagin, J. R., and Elieen O'Brien. 2003. *White Men on Race: Power, Privilege, and the Shaping of Cultural Consciousness*. Boston: Beacon Press.

Fries-Britt, S., and B. T. Kelly. 2005. "Retaining Each Other: Narratives of Two African American Women in the Academy." *The Urban Review* 37: 221–242. doi:10.1007/s11256-005-0006-2.

Gutiérrez y Muhs, G., Y. F. Niemann, C. G. González, and A. P. Harris. 2012. *Presumed Incompetent: The Intersections of Race and Class for Women in Academia*. Logan, UT: Utah State University Press.

Hamilton, L. T., and K. Nielsen. 2021. *Broke: The Racial Consequences of Underfunding Public Universities*. University of Chicago Press.

Hirshfield, L. E., and T. D. Joseph. 2012. "'We Need a Woman, We Need a Black Woman': Gender, Race, and Identity Taxation in the Academy." *Gender and Education* 24 (2): 213–227. doi:10.1080/09540253.2011.606208.

Jayakumar, U. M., T. C. Howard, A. R. Walter, and J. C. Han. 2009. "Racial Privilege in the Professoriate: An Exploration of Campus Climate, Retention, and Satisfaction." *The Journal of Higher Education* 80 (5): 538–563. doi:10.1080/00221546.2009.11779031.

Joseph, T. D., and L. E. Hirshfield. 2011. "'Why Don't You Get Somebody New to Do It?' Race and Cultural Taxation in the Academy." *Journal of Ethnic and Racial Studies* 34 (1): 121–141. doi:10.1080/01419870.2010.496489.

June, A. W., and B. O'Leary. 2021. "How Many Black Women Have Tenure on Your Campus? Search Here." The Chronicle of Higher Education. https://www.chronicle.com/article/how-many-black-women-have-tenure-on-your-campus-search-here?cid2=gen_login_refresh&cid=gen_sign_in.

Kelly, B. T., J. G. Gayles, and C. D. Williams. 2017. "Recruitment without Retention: A Critical Case of Black Faculty Unrest." *The Journal of Negro Education* 86 (3): 305–317. doi:10.7709/jnegroeducation.86.3.0305.

Ladner, J. A. 1971. *Tomorrow's Tomorrow: The Black Woman*. Garden City, NY: Doubleday.

Livingston, R. 2021. *The Conversation: How Seeking and Speaking the Truth About Racism Can Radically Transform Individuals and Organizations*. New York: Penguin Random House.

Melaku, T. M. 2019a. *You Don't Look Like A Lawyer: Black Women and Systemic Gendered Racism*. Lanham, MD: Rowman & Littlefield.

Melaku, T. M. 2019b. "Why Women and People of Color in Law Still Hear 'You Don't Look Like a Lawyer'." Harvard Business Review. https://hbr.org/2019/08/why-women-and-people-of-color-in-law-still-hear-you-dont-look-like-a-lawyer.

Melaku, T. M. 2020. "Amy Cooper, White Privilege and the Murder of Black People." Fair Observer. https://www.fairobserver.com/region/north_america/tsedale-melaku-amy-cooper-white-privilege-abstract-liberalism-george-floyd-death-protests-us-news-15161/.

Melaku, T. M. 2021. "The Awakening: The Impact of COVID-19, Racial Upheaval, and Political Polarization on Black Women Lawyers." *Fordham Law Review* 89 (6): 2519.

Melaku, T. M., and A. Beeman. 2020. "Academia Isn't a Safe Haven for Conversations about Race and Racism." Harvard Business Review. https://hbr.org/2020/06/academia-isnt-a-safe-haven-for-conversations-about-race.

Melaku, T. M., and A. Beeman. 2022. "Navigating White Academe During Crisis: The Impact of COVID-19 and Racial Violence on Women of Color Professionals." *Gender, Work & Organization*. doi:10.1111/gwao.12823.

Mills, J., A. Bonner, and K. Francis. 2006. "The Development of Constructivist Grounded Theory." *International Journal of Qualitative Methods* 5 (1): 25–35. doi:10.1177/160940690600500103.

Moore, W. L. 2008. *Reproducing Racism: White Spaces, Elite Law Schools, and Racial Inequality*. Lanham, MD: Rowman & Littlefield.

National Center for Education Statistics. 2022. Characteristics of Postsecondary Faculty. *Condition of Education*. U.S. Department of Education, Institute of Education Sciences. Accessed 1 June 2022. https://nces.ed.gov/programs/coe/indicator/csc.

Padilla, A. M. 1994. "Ethnic Minority Scholars, Research, and Mentoring: Current and Future Issues." *Educational Researcher* 23 (4): 24–27.

Padilla, R. V., and R. C. Chávez. 1995. *The Leaning Ivory Tower: Latino Professors in American Universities*. Albany, NY: State University of New York Press.

Phillips, K. W., N. P. Rothbard, and T. L. Dumas. 2009. "To Disclose or not to Disclose? Status Distance and Self-Disclosure in Diverse Environments." *Academy of Management Review* 34 (4): 710–732.

Pirtle, W. N. L. 2020. "Racial Capitalism: A Fundamental Cause of Novel Coronavirus (COVID-19) Pandemic Inequities in the United States." *Health Education and Behavior* 47 (4): 504–508. doi:10.1177/1090198120922942.

Price, J. M. C. 2010. "Coding: Open Coding." In *Encyclopedia of Case Study Research*, edited by A. J. Mills, G. Durepos, and E. Wiebe, 155–157. Thousand Oaks: Sage.

Ray, V. 2019. "A Theory of Racialized Organizations." *American Sociological Review* 84 (1): 26–53. doi:10.1177/0003122418822335.

Robertson, B. K. 2020. "Black Women Staff and Administrators' Perceptions of Organizational Culture at a Highly Selective PWI." Doctoral dissertation. University of Pennsylvania.

Robertson, B. K. 2022. "Black Women Navigating the Workplace: A Few Strategies." Inside Higher Ed. https://www.insidehighered.com/advice/2022/04/29/career-strategies-black-women-staff-members-higher-ed-opinion.

Rodríguez, J. E., K. M. Campbell, and L. H. Pololi. 2015. "Addressing Disparities in Academic Medicine: What of the Minority tax?" *BMC Medical Education* 15 (6): 1–5.

Simien, E. 2006. *Black Feminist Voices in Politics*. Albany, NY: State University of New York Press.

Stanley, C. A. 2006. "Coloring the Academic Landscape: Faculty of Color Breaking the Silence in Predominately White Colleges and Universities." *American Educational Research Journal* 43 (4): 701–736. doi:10.3102/00028312043004701.

St. Jean, Y., and J. R. Feagin. 1998. *Double Burden: Black Women and Everyday Racism*. Amonk, NY: M. E. Sharpe.

Sue, D. W., C. M. Capodilupo, and A. M. B. Holder. 2008. "Racial Microaggressions in the Life Experience of Black Americans." *Professional Psychology: Research and Practice* 39 (3): 329–336. doi:10.1037/0735-7028.39.3.329.

Williams, P. J. 1991. *The Alchemy of Race and Rights: Diary of a Law Professor*. Cambridge, MA: Harvard University Press.

Wingfield, A. H. 2019a. "Does Sociology Silence Black Women?." Gender & Society. https://gendersociety.wordpress.com/2019/06/04/does-sociology-silence-black-women/.

Wingfield, A. H. 2019b. *Flatline: Race, Work and Healthcare*. Oakland, CA: University of California Press.

Wingfield, A. H., and K. Chavez. 2020. "Getting In, Getting Hired, Getting Sideways Looks: Organizational Hierarchy and Perceptions of Racial Discrimination." *American Sociological Review* 85 (1): 31–57. doi:10.1177/0003122419894335.

Appendix

Survey Questions

Experiences of Women of Color in The Workplace Development/Inclusivity.

1. To what extent does the organization demonstrate a commitment to diversity? How do you perceive and interpret the organization's efforts and commitment to diversity?
2. What changes have you noticed in relation to COVID-19 with respect to efforts to address your concerns?
3. What changes have you noticed in relation to Racial Upheaval with respect to efforts to address your concerns?

IMPACT OF COVID-19.

1. How has COVID-19 impacted you personally and professionally?
2. Has COVID-19 impacted your emotional and cognitive well-being? If so, how?
3. How has your organization responded to COVID-19? How do you feel about that?
4. Do you believe you engage in more uncompensated and unrecognized work since COVID-19, or less? Please provide examples.

IMPACT OF RACIAL UPHEAVAL.

1. How has Racial Upheaval impacted you personally and professionally?
2. How has your organization responded to the killings of Black people and Racial Upheaval? How do you feel about that?
3. Have you experienced stress, emotional or cognitive, since the Racial Upheaval in America? If so, in what ways has this stress manifested?
4. Is there anything else you would like to share about how COVID-19 and Racial upheaval have impacted your trajectory in the workplace? And your personal life?

IMPACT OF THE 2020 ELECTION.

1. How do you feel about discussing politics in the workplace?
2. How has the 2020 election impacted your experience in the workplace?

How women of colour engineering faculty respond to wage disparities

Ebony O. McGee, Devin T. White, Joyce B. Main, Monica F. Cox and Lynette Parker

ABSTRACT

Women of Color (WoC) engineering faculty in higher education differ in their approaches to coping with inequities and salary disparities. This study draws upon McGee's Stereotype Management [McGee, E. O. 2016. "Devalued Black and Latino Racial Identities: A By-Product of College STEM Culture?" *American Educational Research Journal* 53 (6): 1626–1662; McGee, E. O. 2020a. *Black, Brown, Bruised: How Racialized STEM Education Stifles Innovation*. Cambridge, MA: Harvard Education Press. https://www.hepg.org/hep-home/books/black,-brown,-bruised#] and Identity Taxation [Hirshfield, L. E., and T. D. Joseph. 2012. "'We Need a Woman, We Need a Black Woman': Gender, Race, and Identity Taxation in the Academy." *Gender and Education* 24 (2): 213–227] to understand how WoC in Engineering respond to race and gender-based salary disparity in engineering higher education. Results reveal that WoC contend with identity taxation that forces them to navigate gendered negotiation systems to achieve salary parity. The racial backgrounds of WoC appeared to influence how they managed the impacts of pay inequity. Stereotype management emerges as a form of identity taxation that WoC use to navigate their academic environments. Our research suggests that, rather than confronting their structural racism, institutions of higher education place the onus on scholars of colour to use strategies to protect themselves from the reality of race/gendered wage disparity.

It is an open secret that Women of Color (WoC) faculty in higher education make less than their white and male counterparts (American Association of University Professors 2020).[1] Yet little is known about the process by which WoC faculty navigate salary negotiations. Choosing to engage in salary negotiation as a WoC presents many risks, and the rewards associated with such negotiations tend to be fewer than among their white and male counterparts (Moss-Racusin and Rudman 2010). There continue to be pervasive stereotypes about women who negotiate, taking on different forms by race/ethnicity (Toosi et al. 2019; Rudman et al. 2012). To protect themselves from the potential backlash of engaging in salary negotiation, WoC must manage both racial and gender stereotypes (Main et al. 2022; Ong, Smith, and Ko 2018).

Our previous wage equity study examined how some WoC engineering faculty actively and directly advocated for equitable salary increases (McGee et al., under review). However, a subset of WoC engineering faculty in the study did not self-advocate for a more equitable salary, even though they qualified for a higher salary. This paper examines this subset of WoC engineering faculty using qualitative data. It explores the following research questions concerning women engineering faculty whose salary was lower than that of their counterparts. RQ1: *Why did WoC engineering faculty decide not to advocate for race and gender pay equity or salary increases?* RQ2: *How did women in this sample rationalize their choice not to self-advocate, and are there differences by race?* We examine these questions through the lens of identity taxation, defined as shouldering physical, mental, or emotional labour due to membership in a historically marginalized group (Hirshfield and Joseph 2012), manifested through race and gender stereotype management (defined below). We extend these frameworks to examine the experiences of WoC engineering faculty in relation to negotiating wage disparities.

Understanding why some women engineering faculty did not negotiate higher salaries could reveal more about the faculty gender and race wage gap. Salaries for full-time women faculty members are approximately 81.2 per cent of men's, with women earning $79,368 and men earning $97,738 on average (American Association of University Professors 2020). Our research findings also provide insight into engineering chairs and Deans. We consider the risks of negotiating while being a WoC engineering faculty member. Our research may suggest ways to facilitate more equitable wages within engineering departments.

Despite expectations in the academy that faculty will engage in salary negotiations (Säve-Söderbergh 2019), findings suggest that such negotiations pose significant risks for WoC engineering faculty. Institutions have not created a space where women feel safe to negotiate; in response, some women either avoid or disengage from negotiations or reframe the issue. While our sample size is small, most qualitative studies aim not to generalize but to provide a rich, contextualized understanding of some aspect of the human experience. The low numbers of WoC in this sample reflect their underrepresentation within the engineering discipline and the understudied dimensions of their experience. Our paper begins to explore why WoC feel they must settle for less as a basis for future studies to investigate further wage disparity issues that may corroborate and extend our findings.

Literature review

Women faculty navigating the salary gap

Recent gender wage gap studies found that women of all races and ethnicities earned significantly lower wages than white men (Michelmore and Sassler 2016; Pew Research Center 2018). The National Women's Law Center calculated the total cost of the gender wage gap over a woman's career. If today's wage gap persists, in the course of a 40-year career, the average woman loses $407,760 compared to a man's earnings over that same period. For Black women, the total career losses rise to $941,600; for Latinas, the career losses can amount to nearly $1,121,440 (National Women's Law Center [NWLC] 2020). Depending on geographic location, these numbers can increase. For example, a Black woman in the District of Columbia may lose up to $1.98 million over her career (NWLC 2020).

In academia, Black women STEM faculty earn about 87 per cent of white women's salaries and about 62 per cent of white men's salaries; Latinas earn about 85 per cent of white women's salaries and about 61 per cent of white men's (Pew Research Center 2018). Despite growing numbers of women faculty in STEM academia, Calka (2020) discusses how the gender pay gap still exists in higher education settings; further, the gender disparity widens as faculty achieve higher ranks. For example, the average woman faculty member "will earn $14,618 or 12 per cent less than a male professor in the same rank" (Calka 2020, 3). In private institutions, this gap is larger, with women faculty earning $17,584 or 13.3 per cent less than their male counterparts (Calka 2020; Ginder, Kelly-Reid, and Mann 2017).

Women engineering faculty are disproportionately underpaid, promoted more slowly, receive fewer honours, and advance to fewer leadership positions than their male counterparts (Judson, Ross, and Glassmeyer 2019). Calka (2020) explains how the overall lack of women negatively affects their salaries. According to the College and University Professional Association for Human Resources (CUPA-HR) "the median pay ratio for women faculty in engineering is $0.89 in comparison with white men" (Calka 2020, 22). Even when controlling for faculty rank in science and engineering disciplines, the gender wage gap persists at all three faculty ranks (Johnson and Taylor 2019), "with the largest gap being at the full professor level of an average $10,379.57" (Calka 2020, 7).

Salary negotiation in higher education and backlash

Women are often held solely responsible for securing an equitable wage in a system that penalizes them for merely asking for a higher salary (Toosi et al. 2019). Llorens et al. (2021) highlight how effective negotiating correlates with "better starting salaries and start-up packages; salary increases; better work conditions; and increased allocation of personnel, lab space, and other resources" (2061), potentially kickstarting a successful faculty career. Further, the researchers note that men tend to initiate negotiations significantly more often than women (Llorens et al. 2021). However, when women engage in negotiations, they are less likely than men to be successful and may receive backlash for engaging in them (Hernandez et al. 2019; Mazei et al. 2015).

Researchers have noted initiating negotiations and negotiating assertively are perceived as more congruent with male gender roles (Llorens et al. 2021; Toosi et al. 2019; Toosi et al. 2020). For example, Llorens et al. (2021) explain that "expressions of emotions commonly associated with leadership characteristics, such as anger and pride (Brescoll 2016), are more widely tolerated and even appreciated when they emanate from men compared to women (Brescoll and Uhlmann 2008)" (2062). Women often report a reasonable fear of backlash if they strive beyond others' expectations or push back on additional workplace requests (Hsieh and Nguyen 2021). Negotiation may damage others' perceptions of how hirable they are, their opportunities for promotion, or their professional relationships with their peers (Bowles and Babcock 2013).

WoC experience these hierarchies differently from men and white women due to their specific race-gendered identities. Purushothaman et al. (2022) discuss how WoC broadly report "feeling the instinct to stay silent and be grateful for what they have" (para. 2). However, the researchers also noted racial differences in how WoC navigated backlash explaining:

> Black women found that revealing ambitious intentions and a healthy self-esteem caused them to be misinterpreted as angry, difficult, or aggressive. Many Asian cultures teach a reverence for authority that creates expectations with themselves and others that they should conform. Many immigrant Latinas are cautioned based on family experience not to rock the boat and are taught to keep their heads down. (Purushothaman et al. 2022, para. 4)

The backlash that WoC negotiators face functions to preserve the status differences across groups (Rudman et al. 2012).

Hernandez et al. (2019) explored what it means to perform salary negotiations while Black. Their regression analysis found that more racially biased job evaluators expected Black job seekers to be less likely to negotiate than comparable white job seekers. When Black job seekers violate these "race-stereotypic expectancies" during actual negotiations, the job evaluators are less willing to make concessions and assign significantly lower starting salaries than their white counterparts. Black women face a unique combination of racist and sexist biases. For example: Engaging in salary negotiations violates gender and racial stereotypes and generates backlash against them (Hightower 2019). Berdahl and Min (2012) found that Asian women who displayed dominant behaviours were more likely to experience backlash in the form of racial harassment due to their violation of prescriptive stereotypes that portray them as docile and quiet.

Unfortunately, there are potentially career-long, compounding consequences for not engaging in salary negotiations, particularly at the start of one's career. In academia, raises at tenure and promotion depend on the new hire's starting salary. A low starting salary creates a disparity that extends throughout an academic career (Cundiff et al. 2018). As Marks and Harold (2011) explain, "[given] a 5 per cent pay increase each year over a 40-year career, a twenty-five-year-old employee that starts at $50,000 would earn $634,198 less than an employee starting at $55,000 by the time s/he reached the age of 65" (371). Researchers suggest women who show less assertiveness by using more verbal disclaimers, asking for less, or not negotiating at all, obtain lower salaries and may even be seen as less competent (Kray, Kennedy, and Van Zant 2014).

The impact of women's underrepresentation in engineering

Casad et al. (2021) describe three factors that influence gender inequalities and often lead to the departure of women from STEM faculty roles: (1) numeric underrepresentation and stereotypes, (2) lack of supportive social networks, and (3) chilly academic climates. The National Center for Science and Engineering Statistics publishes data on engineering faculty demographics broken out by race and gender. The most recent data shows that WoC are underrepresented compared to white women in the engineering field (Table 1 and Table 2).

Women STEM faculty experience an unwelcoming and threatening academic climate. For example, some STEM department cultures encourage faculty to remain child-free to achieve tenure (Stromquist 2015). Women describe their departments as hostile and uncomfortable due to sexual harassment and discrimination (McGee, Frierson & Reinhart, in preparation; Casad et al. 2021). McGee and colleagues (2020) previously argued that investigating

> the discrimination, racialized pressure to succeed at all costs, and isolation experienced by WOC in higher education acknowledges that these issues

Table 1. Percentage of all engineering faculty by race.

All engineering faculty	All	Full	Associate	Assistant
White Women	16.50%	5.80%	11.32%	13.38%
Black Women	0.07%	0.73%	0.63%	0.63%
Asian Women	5.15%	4.38%	4.40%	6.73%
Latinas	0.84%	0.73%	0.63%	0.64%

Note. NSF, NCSES 2021.

Table 2. Percentage of women engineering faculty by race.

Women engineering faculty	All	Full	Associate	Assistant
White Women	58%	50%	66.6%	63.3%
Black Women	4.2%	6.25%	3.7%	3%
Asian Women	31%	37.5%	25.93%	30.3%
Latinas	5.04%	6.25%	3.7%	3%

Note. NSF, NCSES 2021.

> inadvertently reveal the role of intersectionality, since the intersectional identities of WOC can affect their raced and gendered interactions in White-male-normed STEM environments. (Eastman, Miles, and Yerrick 2019, 59)

WoC also experience the "pet-to-threat" syndrome – where WoC are praised for their work and service to the academy until they become viewed as professional threats (Thomas et al. 2013; Johnson, Thomas, and Brown 2017).

Asian women engineering faculty face racial challenges like other WoC; further, they are underrepresented in full professor ranks and academic leadership roles (McGee et al. 2020). Similarly, Misra et al. (2021) note that Asian-American women's perceptions of faculty workload fairness resemble those of Black and Indigenous women and Latinas. As recently as 2018, 91 per cent of over 300 engineering departments in the U.S. still did not have a single Black woman on their faculty (American Society for Engineering Education 2020). McGee (2020a) expands upon how this double bind had an additional impact on Black women in STEM as they seek to navigate pejorative stereotypes about Black motherhood. The research shows that Latinas are underrepresented at every stage of the engineering professoriate. Muñoz and Villanueva (2022) highlight that many Latina faculty experience a sense of isolation resulting from being the only Latina in their department. The authors explain that the reality that non-Latino white men dominate STEM fields impacts the recruitment and retention of Latinas and exacerbates the isolation of existing Latina faculty (Mora et al. 2018).

Theoretical framework: cultural taxation to identity taxation and stereotype management

In 2008, Harley exposed how Black women faculty were viewed as the "maids of academe" because of their disproportionate teaching loads and service burdens. Harley asserts that historically white institutions use the presence of minoritized women faculty to demonstrate their alleged inclusivity, a form of tokenism that is another variety of cultural taxation as this labour goes beyond typical (white) faculty expectations, "ultimately affecting a [minority] faculty member's academic productivity and social integration within an academic department or institution" (Hirshfield and Joseph 2012, 214). Expanding on Padilla's (1994) notion of cultural taxation, Hirshfield and

Joseph (2012) coined *identity taxation* to include other historically marginalized social identities, such as gender and sexual orientation alongside race. This taxation occurs when faculty members, particularly Black women and WoC, function as the "maids of academe," shouldering physical, mental, or emotional labour due to their membership in a historically marginalized group (Chambers and Sulé 2022).

Rideau (2021) explained that WoC faculty experience identity taxation in three ways: they "care for marginalized students" and are "overburdened with institutional service and obligations to teach colleagues about race and racism" (161). WoC faculty in STEM face challenges in teaching and service, tenure and promotion, and mentorship that negatively influence their career trajectory (Corneille et al. 2019):

- Teaching and Service: WoC faculty perform a disproportionate amount of teaching and diversity-related service with less access to resources and support such as lab equipment, graduate assistants, and financial assistance from their department or college (Furst-Holloway and Miner 2019).
- Tenure and Promotion: WoC STEM faculty perceive the tenure process to be unclear; they face bias in the criteria for establishing promotion and tenure and are penalized for devoting too much time to service (Liu, Brown, and Sabat 2019; Lisnic, Zajicek, and Morimoto 2019).
- Mentorship: Typical mentoring models are ineffective at meeting the needs of WoC, while sponsorship is effective at advancing WoC into leadership positions. Sponsors go beyond mentorship and use their power to advocate for the advancement of their mentees (Rodriguez, Jagsi, and Mangurian 2022).

McGee (2016) advanced the concept called stereotype management to explain the hidden cost of Black students' academic resilience and more recently adapted this framework to apply to faculty (2021). Stereotype management is a learned competency that enables Black students and faculty to recognize and negotiate stereotyped threats in ways that aid their academic achievement. Stereotype management helps individuals deflect stereotyping and racial microaggressions in STEM fields. However, stereotype management is also labour (or an identity tax) that people of color (PoC) must perform to deflect microaggressions. McGee notes that stereotype management is rooted in people of colours' own "developing understandings of racism and their developing senses of negotiations and assertions of what it means [to them] to be Black" (2011, 1349).

WoC students and faculty experience structural and race-related barriers as they navigate educational institutions that may damage their well-being and often drive them from the STEM arena, even after completing their doctorate. The stereotype management strategies Black STEM students and faculty have used to mitigate stressful racialized experiences often result in psychological effects, behavioural responses, and health consequences (McGee and Stovall 2015; McGee 2020b). How WoC faculty strategically anticipate a backlash when negotiating mirrors how Black STEM students manage stereotypes.

This paper draws upon stereotype management as a form of identity taxation to understand how WoC manage wage disparity issues. However, we have expanded the stereotype management framework to include engineering faculty, given they must function as university professors while managing stereotypes and identity taxation. Both stereotype management and identity taxation assume that racism is structural, embedded within systems, and not merely a matter of individual personalities or subjectivity. Our findings utilize participants' experiences to understand the systems they inhabit and navigate.

Data and methods

We draw our data from a sample of fifty-six WoC engineering faculty interviewed between 2016 and 2019 as part of a more extensive NSF funded study exploring how WoC engineering faculty persist in their academic careers. Given the extremely small numbers of WoC engineering faculty, we have anonymized some institution and rank data to protect participants. As participants described their experiences at their institutions, more than half of the women ($n = 36$) mentioned wage disparities. In another paper, we reported on twenty of the thirty-six women engineering faculty who negotiated and advocated for pay parity (McGee et al., under review). In the present paper, we focus on the sixteen women from the original study who did not negotiate for wage increases at their respective institutions, thirteen of whom self-identified as WoC. Table 3 describes the demographic characteristics of this sample.

Data collection

The authors conducted qualitative interviews and collected data at 30 institutions from 2016 to 2018. While we conducted mostly in-person interviews, we performed seven interviews via phone. Most of the interviews were audio recorded and lasted from 25 min to 1 h and 17 min. The interviews were professionally transcribed and analyzed in NVivo, a computer-assisted qualitative data analysis platform. The participants were recruited from the American Society for Engineering Education Membership database and compensated with a $50 gift card. We assigned participants pseudonyms that reflected their racial or ethnic identity. We honoured their identities while acknowledging that ethnic names are a source of discrimination

Table 3. Participant's demographic data.

Pseudonym	Race	Academic rank	Institution/Carnegie classification	Discipline
Dr Margot	Asian	Full Professor	Public Research/R1	Mechanical Engineering
Dr Huan Shi	Asian	Full Professor	Public Research/R1	Computer Engineering
Dr Jocelyn	white	Associate Professor	Private/R3	Software Engineering
Dr Sylvia	Asian	Instructor	Public Research/R1	Computer Science
Dr Jasmine	Asian	Associate Professor	Public Research/R2	Mechanical Engineering
Dr Donna	Black	Assistant Professor	Private/R3	Computer Engineering
Dr Josie	white	Instructor	Public Research/R1	Computer Engineering
Dr Debbie	Black	Associate Professor	Private Research/R1	Mechanical Engineering
Dr Tori	Black	Full Professor	Private/M2	Biological Engineering
Dr Raven	Latina	Full Professor	Public Research/R1	Chemical Engineering
Dr Caroline	Black	Full Professor	Public Research/R1	Biological Engineering
Dr Janelle	Asian	Assistant Professor	Public Research/R1	Electrical Engineering
Dr Katherine	white	Assistant Professor	Private Research/M2	Aerospace Engineering
Dr Phoebe	Asian	Assistant Professor	Public University/M1	Mechanical Engineering
Dr Morgan	white	Associate Professor	Public Research/R1	Electrical Engineering
Dr Jayda	Black	Assistant Professor	Public Research/R1	Biological Engineering

(Rubinstein and Brenner 2014). The semi-structured interview format included fourteen open-ended questions related to the women's experiences and eleven questions soliciting demographic information. The nature of the questions enabled participants to provide rich descriptions of their faculty experiences and speak directly about their wages and the issue of wage disparities.

Although the study focused on the experiences of WoC, we interviewed four women who identified as white to compare their experiences with the WoC in this study. The women engineering faculty in this study represented all academic ranks and multiple disciplines in the engineering field and hailed from all types of institutions. Some were from Hispanic-Serving Institutions (HSIs) and Historically Black Colleges and Universities (HBCUs). Overall, there were seven Asian women (all of whom were foreign-born, and five of whom were naturalized U.S. citizens), four white women, five Black women (all U.S. citizens), and one Latina (foreign-born).

Data analysis

The research and analysis team included four WoC, three of whom are faculty members and one man of colour. We wrote field notes following each interview to capture our immediate impressions and reviewed transcripts to ensure their accuracy. We expanded the coding architecture concerning wage disparities in our earlier research to explore the complexity of how WoC managed these disparities (McGee and Bentley 2017). We added new codes with our theoretical frameworks in mind as new themes emerged. Table 4 outlines the coding architecture that emerged from examining the experiences of women engineering faculty's rationalizations for avoiding salary negotiation. Our theoretical frameworks highlight that avoidance may be used as a legitimate tactic to preserve one's mental and physical health. For example, Hirshfield and Joseph (2012) suggested that researchers consider "what are some ways that people avoid being taxed?" Similarly, McGee and Martin (2011) detailed how students used avoidance as a tactic to "circumvent racialized beliefs that were prevalent in their majority white school environments" (1370). When coding responses, we examined both the participant's actions in response to wage disparities and the underlying beliefs behind their actions. Findings explore some of the quotes that led to these categorizations while foregrounding the contexts that these women must navigate.

Findings

Our findings reveal the varied ways that women engineering faculty relied on avoidance to navigate the wage disparities in their departments. Most WoC engineering faculty believed they received lower salaries and raises than their counterparts. While all the women in this sample avoided negotiating higher salaries, many situated their decision to avoid negotiations as a response to the structural inequalities surrounding women's experiences in the academy and the broader labour market. In the following sections, we outline the type of aversion that women engineering faculty employed to

Table 4. Coding architecture.

Code: Type of aversion response (Action)	Description: The way participants avoided engaging with the issue of wage disparities in their department
Avoidance	The participant intentionally does not engage with knowledge or information about wage disparities in their department.
Reframe	The participant is aware of the data but highlights other factors that they believe ease the impact of wage inequality.
Disengage	The participant is aware of the data but disengages to manage the impact of the data on them.
Code: Aversion Rationale (Belief)	Description: The underlying reason informing the participant's decision to avoid engaging with wage disparities.
Self-preservation	The participant does not engage in salary negotiation to preserve their mental and physical health.
Not impacted	The participant does not engage in salary negotiation because they believe they are not impacted in a significant way.
Determined futile	The participant does not engage in salary negotiation because they believe efforts will not produce results.

avoid engaging with the issue of gender wage disparities in their department and their aversion rationale, i.e. the underlying reason that informed the participant's decision to avoid engaging with wage disparities. Table 5 below presents how we classified each participant's advocacy aversion response (avoidance, disengaging, reframing) and a summary code of their rationale for taking that strategy (self-preservation, not impacted, determined futile).

This study sought to understand *why WoC engineering faculty decided not to advocate for race and gender pay equity or salary increases* and *how women in this sample rationalized their choice not to self-advocate*. These research questions addressed different aversion responses and the rationales behind those responses. The racial differences in how our participants responded to the wage disparity issue became evident when examining both the action and the belief behind it. We also found that faculty responded in racially specific ways, especially those who chose to reframe the salary issue.

Avoidance as a response to salary disparities in higher education

Researchers describe information avoidance as "any behaviour intended to prevent or delay the acquisition of available but potentially unwanted information" (Sweeny et al. 2010, 341). Some of our participants demonstrated avoidance by choosing not to seek out information on the salary disparities at their institutions.

For example, Dr Janelle, an Asian Assistant Professor in electrical engineering, described her disinterest in the publicly available faculty salary information. When asked about the nature of wage disparities at her institution, she responded, "I actually don't know. Because I worked at a public school, I think that information is available online. I never really wanted to look at it. I tell myself I'm not interested in knowing what other people make."

Table 5. Participant's aversion response and rationale.

Pseudonym	Race	Type of aversion response (Action)	Aversion rationale (Belief)
Dr Margot	Asian	Avoidance	Self-preservation
Dr Huan Shi	Asian	Reframe	Not impacted/Determined Futile
Dr Josie	White	Reframe	Not impacted
Dr Debbie	Black	Disengage	Determined Futile
Dr Jocelyn	white	Reframe	Not impacted
Dr Sylvia	Asian	Reframe	Not impacted
Dr Jasmine	Asian	Disengage	Determined futile
Dr Donna	Black	Reframe	Not impacted
Dr Tori	Black	Disengage	Self-preservation
Dr Raven	Latina	Disengage	Determined futile
Dr Caroline	Black	Disengage	Self-preservation
Dr Janelle	Asian	Avoidance	Self-preservation
Dr Katherine	white	Disengage/Reframe	Not impacted
Dr Phoebe	Asian	Reframe	Not impacted
Dr Morgan	white	Reframe	Not impacted
Dr Jayda	Black	Reframe	Self-preservation

Research shows that avoidance results when knowledge of specific information may require a change in deeply held beliefs, force an undesired action, cause an unpleasant emotion, or reduce happiness (Sweeny et al. 2010). While Dr Janelle's utterance "I tell myself" reveals she is aware of the wage disparities but actively and consciously preserves her health and well-being by managing her exposure to the information, one of the sacrifice strategies outlined in stereotype management (McGee 2016, 2020a).

Similarly, Dr Margot, an Asian electrical engineering full professor, knew that salary information was publicly available but chose not to view it. Dr Margot discussed how her avoidance was self-preservation, i.e. intended to protect her emotional well-being:

> Well, our salaries are officially public, so if you want to go to the website, you can look at it. I don't. I know I sound funny when I say that, but I don't [think] anything I'm going to see on the website … [is] going to make me happy.

Dr Margot's decision to avoid looking at the salary data seems to rest on protecting a fragile sense of contentment with her faculty job.

Both Dr Janelle and Dr Margot acknowledged the public availability of salary data, highlighting some transparency in their institutions. However, in cases where salary information is public, there may be undisclosed forms of compensation. For example, summer salary, bonuses, and favourable policies regarding start-up research funds are less likely to appear in publicly available sources. Whether compensation is or is not transparent at their institutions, both women work within systems where a defensive posture seems the best response to salary disparities. When the public availability of salary information merely confirms existing inequities and impacts the reader's self-perseveration, as Dr Margot says, it renders salary transparency moot. A policy of transparency without equity is self-canceling. It invites a response of avoidance by the people in the system who are most vulnerable to inequitable policies. This strategy allows wage disparities to continue to be business as usual.

Coping with wage disparities by disengaging from salary negotiations

Some women chose to disengage from the wage issue. Unlike avoidance, disengaging did not mean they did not seek to know the details. Instead, disengaging meant that the participant was aware of the wage disparities in their field; however, to protect their mental or physical health, they chose to disengage from the ongoing fight for parity. Women justified their disengagement as either an act of self-preservation of their mental health or they believed the effort futile. Dr Debbie, a Black mechanical and aerospace engineering associate professor, is an example of a participant who disengaged from wage disparities. She felt that negotiating for a higher salary was not warranted. Dr Debbie framed her position in terms of generational differences:

> I'm not of the generation that gets really mad about these things because it's sort of the way it is, and it seems to be that some of these things seems to be improving. It's kind of ridiculous, but it hasn't changed over these years. But I don't know that the root causes of these things are completely understood to be brutally honest, I never asked to be paid more when I was offered the job. I know a lot of male colleagues who did. So maybe if I had asked, I would have started off at a higher number. [...] I think women don't look as good when they negotiate for more money.

Dr Debbie is aware of the stereotypes surrounding women and salary negotiations. She explains that since nothing has changed over the years, she will refrain from negotiating for a higher salary. She frames individuals protesting race-gendered salary discrepancies as possibly exhibiting hostility or immaturity. An alternative would be to frame the race-gendered inequity in the academy that creates salary disparities as the threat.

Disengaging from salary negotiation was also a way to preserve one's mental health, as seen in the response of Dr Caroline, a Black full professor of biological engineering. She recalls:

> I think that one can go crazy if you keep looking at where your salary is relative to your colleagues, for women and for women of color it's going to be lower. If [I] keep looking I know that that would make me sick. I'm at a public institution so I can see. It would just make me sick. If you look at that stuff, it will make you crazy. And I don't know, I tend not to look at it now because when I got to be associate Dean I got a large raise, and I didn't know that that was going to happen.

For Dr Caroline, disengagement reflected two different rationales. First, she insists that looking at wage information would make her angry; her disengagement is likely a protective mechanism, a means of self-preservation. Second, her surprise at the salary increase for her promotion to assistant Dean highlights how her disengagement from wage disparities affected her knowledge about promotion and raises. Dr Caroline knows that women's salaries, especially WoC, are not on par with their (white) male peers. The risk she cites is that of "going crazy" implying she sees that her mental health is at stake.

Our frameworks' structural view of race and gender helps us locate Dr Caroline's position in a system in which the truth about how her salary compares with her peers "makes [her] sick." This potential threat to her health is the antithesis of a transparent system that identifies and addresses unwarranted disparities. Stereotype management strategies often aim to protect one's mental or physical health and wellness. The race-gendered system she inhabits places her in a position where she feels the best response is to protect her mental health by disengaging. The emotional toll and burden of advocating against wage disparities represents another form of identity taxation for WoC.

Reframing the salary disparity issue

Some participants believe that the wage disparity issue is exaggerated. The women in our study who reframed the wage disparities did so by minimizing the issue. Some women considered wage disparities a small matter compared to other benefits. These frames included a reliance on alleged "race neutrality" and meritocracy. Below we discuss the racialized strategies that women engineering faculty employed to "reframe" the wage disparity issue.

White women faculty tended to favour a "reframing" strategy, often feeling "not impacted" by the wage disparity. Many admitted being content with the engineering work or noted that wages were unimportant. Some white women engineering faculty were not concerned about the difference in wages because of the relatively higher socioeconomic status associated with being faculty. Some white women utilized reframing by comparing their positions to those in industry or raised topics that they believed superseded money. For example, Dr Jocelyn, a white software engineering associate professor, felt wage disparities did not impact her. She reframes the issue, insisting that examining wage disparities only exaggerates them. Dr Jocelyn takes an allegedly "race-neutral" position, which we extend here to include a gender-neutral stance. As she explains,

> There is just one thing. I don't know if you're going to like it or not or if you're going to agree with me or not. I feel like we're overstating the issue. The more we talk about the differences, the more we emphasize them. I think it will be more natural if we just let things just move on and treat people as one. Close your eyes and it doesn't matter who you're looking at, man, woman, colored, non-colored, and just judge based on their merit. I think that will make sure things go much better.

This attempt at gender and race-neutral positioning was another way to reframe the issue of wage disparities. STEM's culture has a history of positioning these fields of study as neutral, objective, universal, and non-political, encouraging STEMmers to adopt a race-neutral ideology (McGee 2020b). Compared with the larger study, the WoC faculty who took a race/gender neutral stance as their dominant strategy for managing stereotypes were few (McGee et al., under review). Unfortunately, this reframing, in effect, reifies the race-gender hierarchies that leave Black women and Latinas as the lowest STEM earners because a race-neutral attitude implies a refusal to acknowledge race-based inequities.

Asian women engineering faculty tended to respond to the issue of wage disparities by disengaging from or reframing the issues. Their responses were divided between "determined futile" and "not impacted." Some responses crossed over and were coded under both themes because these participants determined that wage inequities did not impact their lives or opportunities. For example, Dr Huan Shi, an Asian full professor of computer engineering, reframed the salary issue by expressing her love for her work and the fact that she and her children were financially self-sufficient:

> We're running into the seventh year of tuition freeze or whatever, and just looking forward to another bickering about it. It's like 3.25 per cent raise, so this is all a joke. Financially, I have enough. On the other hand, I'm pretty sure I could be paid a lot more. But it's value choice, right? It's the overall package and all that. I think I'm lucky compared to most people. My kids are healthy. One of them already started working, so I'm doing fine. It could be a lot better, but I'm happy where it is.

Dr Huan Shi believes she is not affected by wage disparities; further, she thinks that advocating for what she suspects will be only a small raise is futile. On the other hand, Dr Sylvia, an Asian mechanical/aerospace engineering instructor, was able to use her industry experience and earnings to supplement her faculty appointment:

> I'm a master's degree person, and in academia they pay master's degree very low, so I'm not even close. But I said, in my case is that all the wealth that I accumulated from the industry is what's sustaining now. If I was to live by the salary that I get from what I am now, this is very difficult. […] I don't think academia folks should be complaining. I mean, you already have summer off, winter off, right? Then you have only a few days at school. That's all you're required. That's something that industry people don't have.

Dr Silvia reframes the issue of wage inequality by minimizing its impact on her due to her educational status (master's degree only) and her industry experience. She compares the benefits of the academy versus industry, focusing on the perks of time off and a favourable work schedule. Those in academia who might wish to address wage disparities exhibit what she positions as a "complaining" attitude. Because WoC are underrepresented, they are often told to be grateful for entering this elite space and are discouraged from standing up for themselves.

For the Black and Latina women in our sample, avoiding wage disparities may provide short-term self-preservation, although their defensive strategies may compound the existing race-gendered wage gap. These inequitable structures have been designed to operate unchecked. Thus, the onus of ensuring wage equity for minoritized women lies with higher education administrations, boards, and donors, which have the authority to create change and should be proactively addressing these issues.

Discussion

The women in our study who avoided advocating for a wage increase or wage parity found themselves entrenched in an environment that provided little to no support to protect WoC negotiators. This environment includes data demonstrating the persistent wage differences within STEM higher education. To navigate these racialized and gendered structures, these women chose not to negotiate their salaries because (1) they felt the need to preserve their well-being, (2) they felt raising the issue was futile, or (3) they felt unimpacted by the issue. Women in our study understood wage disparities, but they believed that addressing them could produce emotional and psychological ramifications. They acknowledged that knowing about the wage inequities would not change their status at their institutions and that uncovering them would be too upsetting. In managing these psychological and emotional ramifications, these women displayed three significant responses: (1) avoiding the issue, (2) disengaging from the issue, and (3) reframing the issue. However, we found that the rationales behind their responses to wage inequity differed among the racial groups in our sample. Avoiding advocating for wage parity as a practice of self-preservation looked different for Black women than for white and Asian women in our sample.

Self-preservation and managing the health impacts of salary disparities

While all the women in this study avoided advocating for wage equity, the Black and Latina faculty in our sample appeared to be more careful in their avoidance strategies. Avoidance includes intentionally preventing or skirting unwanted knowledge that could directly impact one's emotional well-being, force an unpleasant decision or action, or disrupt a deeply held belief system. For these women, avoidance was a stereotype management technique that emerged as a necessary and strategic response empowering them to navigate structural barriers and protect their health. Dr Janelle, Dr Caroline, and Dr Margot all discussed having emotional and physical reactions to the wage disparity data indicating that overexposure to this information could make them sick or seriously impact their happiness. Dr Janelle expressed that while data was available, she was not aware of other's faculty's salaries. She made an active effort to remain in the dark.

Risking backlash and utilizing privilege

The decision of Black women and the Latina in our sample to refrain from negotiating appeared to be related to stereotype management. Recent research on STEM has shown how "colorblind ideologies nurture and promote notions of unhealthy forms of resilience while our social, political, and education systems continue to abuse and neglect URM [underrepresented minoritized] bodies and minds" (McGee 2020a, 635). For the Black and Latina women faculty in our sample, engaging in salary negotiations posed potential health risks and backlash based on stereotypes concerning their race-gender identity. Research highlights that when Black women negotiate, they violate employers' stereotypical perceptions about Black people and women (Hernandez et al. 2019). The Black women in our study were more likely to discuss protecting their mental and physical health from the anticipated backlash from being a Black woman asking for a salary raise. Black women's avoidance functioned as a means of self-preservation, managing the possibility that they would lose their job or suffer some other unwanted consequence because they acted counter to prevailing stereotypes.

Like our Black participants, our white and Asian participants utilized stereotype management to avoid salary negotiation. While many white and Asian women were able to rationalize their aversion as not impacted, their salaries and potentially other aspects of their tenure and promotion continue to be affected. This aversion from the largest groups of women in engineering may impact other women's current and future salaries. For example: when Asian women chose not to address wage disparities, their silence amplified the stereotype of Asian women as submissive (Rosette et al. 2016). Thus, given the disparities in representation and compensation among racially diverse women engineers, we argue that white and Asian engineering faculty members should use forms of racial privilege when negotiating for higher salaries to serve as better advocates for their Black and Latina sisters.

Unfortunately, awareness is insufficient to stop the wage disparity cycle for WoC. The solutions must come from the institutional side in the form of increased transparency around hiring, promotion, and compensation. If wage disparities are made visible, leaders should be able to recognize this and quickly correct their course without placing the onus on WoC to address disparities. Finally, white and Asian men could advocate for women's pay equity. They would then become allies/co-conspirators who use their racial and gender privilege to support wage equity.

Limitations of the study

While our small sample size does not allow us to generalize our conclusions about the broader racial groups, this qualitative study highlights the researchers' analysis and understanding of the context. We believe that the findings produced from our sample could guide studies using larger data samples. We hope that our addition to the literature about WoC in higher education will allow future researchers to leverage our findings to create broader studies that will collect sufficient data to justify generalizable conclusions.

Conclusion

Advocating for wage parity presents a significant risk to WoC STEM faculty. These WoC found strategies to manage and cope with the systemic racism of wage inequities while still achieving success within the higher education system. These strategies or coping mechanisms will not address wage injustice in the university workplace. Still, we recognize that those who negotiate risk retaliation, punishment, unfair criticism, and other forms of backlash. It may be the case that some WoC engineering faculty justify not negotiating because they see no way to address wage inequities through institutional means. WoC must find a way to cope when there is seemingly no solution. The lives of women STEM faculty are varied and complex; risking backlash may not be worth the impact on their stability. Institutions have largely failed to build institutionalized policies and practices to encourage WoC to negotiate safely.

This study provides insight into how WoC STEM faculty experience and navigate wage disparities from the point of view of the women who did not negotiate. Identity taxation and stereotype management work synergistically to help us analyze the complexity of how WoC in STEM manage wage disparities, highlighting the difficulties they face concerning current negotiation practices. Further, these disparities can impact WoC's health, financial well-being, career, and wealth-building capacity. If we want WoC engineering faculty to thrive and not merely survive in these contexts, we must pay them for all they are worth!

Note

1. By WoC, we mean women who identify as Black/African American; Hispanic/Latina; Native American/Indigenous; Asian American/Asian, and Pacific Islander.

Acknowledgements

Thanks to Dr Meseret Hailu and Dr Monica Miles and research assistants Jordan Rhym and Ruth Boyajian. all of whom provided critical assistance with data collection and analysis. We must also thank Dr Tiffany Joseph and Dr Laura Hirshfield for their guidance and expertise in the writing of this manuscript.

Disclosure statement

No potential conflict of interest was reported by the author(s).

Funding

This material is based upon work supported by the National Science Foundation under Grant Numbers 1535327, 1535456, and 1712618. Any opinions, findings, and conclusions or recommendations expressed in this material are those of the authors and do not necessarily reflect the views of the National Science Foundation.

References

American Association of University Professors. 2020. *Data Snapshot: Full-Time Women Faculty and Faculty of Color*. https://www.aaup.org/news/data-snapshot-full-time-women-faculty-and-faculty-color#.YoAYOZPMJes.

American Society for Engineering Education. 2020. *Engineering and Engineering Technology by the Numbers 2019*. https://ira.asee.org/wp-content/uploads/2021/02/Engineering-by-the-Numbers-FINAL-2021.pdf.

Berdahl, J. L., and J. A. Min. 2012. "Prescriptive Stereotypes and Workplace Consequences for East Asians in North America." *Cultural Diversity & Ethnic Minority Psychology* 18: 141–152. doi:10.1037/a0027692.

Bowles, H. R., and L. Babcock. 2013. "How Can Women Escape the Compensation Negotiation Dilemma? Relational Accounts are one Answer." *Psychology of Women Quarterly* 37 (1): 80–96. doi:10.1177/0361684312455524.

Brescoll, V. L. 2016. "Leading with Their Hearts? How Gender Stereotypes of Emotion Lead to Biased Evaluations of Female Leaders." *The Leadership Quarterly* 27 (3): 415–428. doi:10.1016/j.leaqua.2016.02.005.

Brescoll, V., and E. Uhlmann. 2008. "Can An Angry Woman Get Ahead? Status Conferral, Gender, and Expression of Emotion in the Workplace." *Psychological Science* 19: 268–275.

Calka, A. 2020. *Why Do Female Faculty Members Still Earn Less? Gender Pay Gap in Higher Education in Science, Health and Engineering Fields*. PhD diss., Seton Hall University. https://www.proquest.com/openview/db2829f2449b681464fa21d31b3071ec/1?pq-origsite = gscholar&cbl = 18750&diss = y.

Casad, B. J., J. E. Franks, C. E. Garasky, M. M. Kittleman, A. C. Roesler, D. Y. Hall, and Z. W. Petzel. 2021. "Gender Inequality in Academia: Problems and Solutions for Women Faculty in STEM." *Journal of Neuroscience Research* 99 (1): 13–23. doi:10.1002/jnr.24631.

Chambers, C. R., and V. T. Sulé. 2022. "For Colored Girls who Have Considered Suicide When the Tenure Track got Too Rough." In *Building Mentorship Networks to Support Black Women*, 121–135. Routledge. https://www.taylorfrancis.com/chapters/edit/10.4324/9781003147183-11/colored-girls-considered-suicide-tenure-track-got-rough-crystal-chambers-thandi-sul%C3%A9.

Corneille, M., A. Lee, S. Allen, J. Cannady, and A. Guess. 2019. "Barriers to the Advancement of Women of Color Faculty in STEM: The Need for Promoting Equity Using an Intersectional Framework." *Equality, Diversity and Inclusion* 38 (3): 328–348. doi:10.1108/EDI-09-2017-0199.

Cundiff, J. L., C. L. Danube, M. J. Zawadzki, and S. A. Shields. 2018. "Testing an Intervention for Recognizing and Reporting Subtle Gender Bias in Promotion and Tenure Decisions." *The Journal of Higher Education* 89 (5): 611–636. doi:10.1080/00221546.2018.1437665

Eastman, M. G., M. L. Miles, and R. Yerrick. 2019. "Exploring the White and Male Culture: Investigating Individual Perspectives of Equity and Privilege in Engineering

Education." *Journal of Engineering Education* 108 (4): 459–480. doi:10.1002/jee.20290.

Furst-Holloway, S., and K. Miner. 2019. "ADVANCEing Women Faculty in STEM: Empirical Findings and Practical Recommendations from National Science Foundation ADVANCE Institutions." *Equality, Diversity and Inclusion* 38 (2): 122–130. doi:10.1108/EDI-03-2019-295.

Ginder, S. A., J. E. Kelly-Reid, and F. B. Mann. 2017. *Enrollment and Employees in Postsecondary Institutions, Fall 2016; and Financial Statistics and Academic Libraries, Fiscal Year 2016: First Look (Provisional Data) (NCES 2018-002)*. U.S. Department of Education, National Center for Education Statistics. http://nces.ed.gov/pubsearch.

Harley, D. A. 2008. "Maids of Academe: African American Women Faculty at Predominately White Institutions." *Journal of African American Studies* 12 (1): 19–36. doi:10.1007/s12111-007-9030-5.

Hernandez, M., D. R. Avery, S. D. Volpone, and C. R. Kaiser. 2019. "Bargaining While Black: The Role of Race in Salary Negotiations." *Journal of Applied Psychology* 104 (4): 581. doi:10.1037/apl0000363.

Hightower, C. D. 2019. *Exploring the Role of Gender and Race in Salary Negotiations* (Publication No. 4943). PhD diss., Louisiana State University. https://digitalcommons.lsu.edu/gradschool_theses/4943.

Hirshfield, L. E., and T. D. Joseph. 2012. "We Need a Woman, we Need a Black Woman': Gender, Race, and Identity Taxation in the Academy." *Gender and Education* 24 (2): 213–227. doi:10.1080/09540253.2011.606208.

Hsieh, B., and H. T. Nguyen. 2021. "Coalitional Resistance: Challenging Racialized and Gendered Oppression in Teacher Education." *Journal of Teacher Education* 72 (3): 355–367. doi:10.1177/0022487120960371

Johnson, J. A., and B. J. Taylor. 2019. "Academic Capitalism and the Faculty Salary Gap." *Innovative Higher Education* 44 (1): 21–35. doi:10.1007/s10755-018-9445-z.

Johnson, L., K. M. Thomas, and L. Brown. 2017. "Women of Color in the STEM Academic Workplace." In *Research on Women and Education. Women of Color in STEM: Navigating the Workforce*, edited by J. Ballenger, B. Polnick, and B. Irby, 39–56. Information Age Publishing.

Judson, E., L. Ross, and K. Glassmeyer. 2019. "How Research, Teaching, and Leadership Roles are Recommended to Male and Female Engineering Faculty Differently." *Research in Higher Education* 60 (7): 1025–1047. doi:10.1007/s11162-018-09542-8.

Kray, L. J., J. A. Kennedy, and A. B. Van Zant. 2014. "Not Competent Enough to Know the Difference? Gender Stereotypes About Women's Ease of Being Misled Predict Negotiator Deception." *Organizational Behavior and Human Decision Processes* 125 (2): 61–72. doi:10.1016/j.obhdp.2014.06.002.

Lisnic, R., A. Zajicek, and S. Morimoto. 2019. "Gender and Race Differences in Faculty Assessment of Tenure Clarity: The Influence of Departmental Relationships and Practices." *Sociology of Race and Ethnicity* 5 (2): 244–260. doi:10.1177/2332649218756137

Liu, S. N. C., S. E. Brown, and I. E. Sabat. 2019. "Patching the "Leaky Pipeline": Interventions for Women of Color Faculty in STEM Academia." *Archives of Scientific Psychology* 7 (1): 32. doi:10.1037/arc0000062.

Llorens, A., A. Tzovara, L. Bellier, I. Bhaya-Grossman, A. Bidet-Caulet, W. K. Chang, Z. R. Cross, … N. F. Dronkers. 2021. "Gender Bias in Academia: A Lifetime Problem That Needs Solutions." *Neuron* 109 (13): 2047–2074. doi:10.1016/j.neuron.2021.06.002.

Main, J. B., E. O. McGee, M. F. Cox, L. Tan, and C. G. P. Berdanier. 2022. "Trends in the Underrepresentation of Women of Color Faculty in Engineering (2005–2018)." *Journal of Diversity in Higher Education*, doi:10.1037/dhe0000426.

Marks, M., and C. Harold. 2011. "Who Asks and who Receives in Salary Negotiation?" *Journal of Organizational Behavior* 32 (3): 371–394. doi:10.1002/job.671.

Mazei, J., J. Hüffmeier, P. A. Freund, A. F. Stuhlmacher, L. Bilke, and G. Hertel. 2015. "A Meta-Analysis on Gender Differences in Negotiation Outcomes and Their Moderators." *Psychological Bulletin* 141 (1): 85. doi:10.1037/a0038184.

McGee, E. O. 2016. "Devalued Black and Latino Racial Identities: A By-Product of College STEM Culture?" *American Educational Research Journal* 53 (6): 1626–1662. doi:10.3102/0002831216676572.

McGee, E. O. 2020a. *Black, Brown, Bruised: How Racialized STEM Education Stifles Innovation*. Cambridge, MA: Harvard Education Press. https://www.hepg.org/hep-home/books/black,-brown,-bruised#.

McGee, E. O. 2020b. "Interrogating Structural Racism in STEM Higher Education." *Educational Researcher* 49 (9): 633–644. doi:10.3102/0013189X20972718.

McGee, E. O., and L. C. Bentley. 2017. "The Troubled Success of Black Women in STEM." *Cognition and Instruction* 35 (4): 265–289. doi:10.1080/07370008.2017. 1355211.

McGee, E. O., W. Frierson, and M. Reinhart. in preparation. "Sexual Harassment in STEM Higher Education." *TBD*.

McGee, E. O., J. B. Main, M. F. Cox, D. White, and L. Parker. under review. ""I'll still be here": Factors that Override or Excuse Wage Disparities for Women Engineering Faculty."

Mcgee, E. O., J. Main, M. L. Miles, and M. Cox. 2020. "An Intersectional Approach to Investigating Persistence Among Women of Color Tenure-Track Engineering Faculty." *Journal of Women and Minorities in Science and Engineering* 27 (1): 57–84. doi:10.1615/JWomenMinorScienEng.2020035632.

McGee, E. O., and D. B. Martin. 2011. ""You Would Not Believe What I Have to Go Through to Prove My Intellectual Value!" Stereotype Management Among Academically Successful Black Mathematics and Engineering Students." *American Educational Research Journal* 48 (6): 1347–1389. https://doi.org/10.3102/0002831211423972.

McGee, E. O., and D. O. Stovall. 2015. "Reimagining Critical Race Theory in Education: Mental Health, Healing, and the Pathway to Liberatory Praxis." *Educational Theory* 65 (5): 491–511. doi:10.1111/edth.12129.

Michelmore, K., and S. Sassler. 2016. "Explaining the Gender Wage gap in STEM: Does Field sex Composition Matter?" *RSF: The Russell Sage Foundation Journal of the Social Sciences* 2 (4): 194–215. doi:10.7758/rsf.2016.2.4.07.

Misra, J., A. Kuvaeva, K. O'meara, D. K. Culpepper, and A. Jaeger. 2021. "Gendered and Racialized Perceptions of Faculty Workloads." *Gender & Society* 35 (3): 358–394. doi:10.1177/08912432211001387.

Mora, M. T., A. R. Qubbaj, and H. Rodríguez. 2018. "Advancing Latinas and Other Women in STEM Through Dual Career Hiring." *Advancing Women In Academic STEM Fields Through Dual Career Policies and Practices*: 97–114. Information Age.

Moss-Racusin, C. A., and L. A. Rudman. 2010. "Disruptions in Women's Self-Promotion: The Backlash Avoidance Model." *Psychology of Women Quarterly* 34 (2): 186–202. doi:10.1111/j.1471-6402.2010.01561.x.

Muñoz, J. A., and I. Villanueva. 2022. "Latino STEM Scholars, Barriers, and Mental Health: A Review of the Literature." *Journal of Hispanic Higher Education* 21 (1): 3–16. doi:10.1177/1538192719892148

National Science Foundation, National Center for Science and Engineering Statistics [NSF, NCSES]. 2021. *Women, Minorities, and Persons with Disabilities in Science and Engineering*. https://ncses.nsf.gov/pubs/nsf21321/report

National Women's Law Center. 2020. *The Lifetime Wage Gap by State for Black Women*. https://nwlc.org/wp-content/uploads/2021/03/Black-Women-Overall-Lifetime-Losses-2021-v2.pdf.

Ong, M., J. M. Smith, and L. T. Ko. 2018. "Counterspaces for Women of Color in STEM Higher Education: Marginal and Central Spaces for Persistence and Success." *Journal of Research in Science Teaching* 55 (2): 206–245. doi:10.1002/tea.21417.

Padilla, A. M. 1994. "Research News and Comment: Ethnic Minority Scholars; Research, and Mentoring: Current and Future Issues." *Educational Researcher* 23 (4): 24–27. doi:10.3102/0013189X023004024.

Pew Research Center. 2018. *Women and Men in STEM Often at Odds Over Workplace Equity*. http://assets.pewresearch.org/wp-content/uploads/sites/3/2018/01/09142305/PS_2018.01.09_STEM_FINAL.pdf.

Purushothaman, D., D. M. Kolb, H. R. Bowles, and V. Purdie-Greenaway. 2022. "Negotiating as a Woman of Color." *Harvard Business Review*. https://hbr.org/2022/01/negotiating-as-a-woman-of-color.

Rideau, R. 2021. ""We're Just not Acknowledged": An Examination of the Identity Taxation of Full-Time non-Tenure-Track Women of Color Faculty Members." *Journal of Diversity in Higher Education* 14 (2): 161. doi:10.1037/dhe0000139.

Rodriguez, C. I., R. Jagsi, and C. Mangurian. 2022. "Rising to the Challenge: Strategies to Support Latinas and Other Women of Color in Science and Medicine." *Academic Medicine* 97 (3): 331–334. doi:10.1097/ACM.0000000000004558

Rosette, A. S., C. Z. Koval, A. Ma, and R. Livingston. 2016. "Race Matters for Women Leaders: Intersectional Effects on Agentic Deficiencies and Penalties." *The Leadership Quarterly* 27: 429–445. doi:10.1016/j.leaqua.2016.01.008.

Rubinstein, Y., and D. Brenner. 2014. "Pride and Prejudice: Using Ethnic-Sounding Names and Inter-Ethnic Marriages to Identify Labour Market Discrimination." *Review of Economic Studies* 81 (1): 389–425. doi:10.1093/restud/rdt031

Rudman, L. A., C. A. Moss-Racusin, J. E. Phelan, and S. Nauts. 2012. "Status Incongruity and Backlash Effects: Defending the Gender Hierarchy Motivates Prejudice Against Female Leaders." *Journal of Experimental Social Psychology* 48 (1): 165–179. doi:10.1016/j.jesp.2011.10.008.

Säve-Söderbergh, J. 2019. "Gender Gaps in Salary Negotiations: Salary Requests and Starting Salaries in the Field." *Journal of Economic Behavior & Organization* 161: 35–51. doi:10.1016/j.jebo.2019.01.019

Stromquist, N. P. 2015. "Women in Higher Education Today — Structure and Agency from a Gender Perspective." *Journal of Educational Planning and Administration* 29 (3): 287–306.

Sweeny, K., D. Melnyk, W. Miller, and J. A. Shepperd. 2010. "Information Avoidance: Who, What, When, and Why." *Review of General Psychology* 14 (4): 340–353. doi:10.1037/a0021288.

Thomas, K. M., J. Johnson-Bailey, R. E. Phelps, N. M. Tran, and L. Johnson. 2013. "Women of Color at Midcareer: Going from Pet to Threat." In *The Psychological Health of Women of Color: Intersections, Challenges, and Opportunities*, 275–286. Guilford Press.

Toosi, N. R., S. Mor, Z. Semnani-Azad, K. W. Phillips, and E. T. Amanatullah. 2019. "Who Can Lean in? The Intersecting Role of Race and Gender in Negotiations." *Psychology of Women Quarterly* 43 (1): 7–21. doi:10.1177/0361684318800492.

Toosi, N. R., Z. Semnani-Azad, W. Shen, S. Mor, and E. T. Amanatullah. 2020. "How Culture and Race Shape Gender Dynamics in Negotiation." In *Research Handbook on Gender and Negotiation*, edited by M. Olekalns, and J. A. Kennedy, 260–280. Edward Elgar Publishing. doi:10.4337/9781788976763.00024.

"Diversity is a corporate plan": racialized equity labour among university employees

Laura T. Hamilton, Kelly Nielsen and Veronica Lerma

ABSTRACT

Drawing on ninety-four interviews with university employees at two four-year publics, we identify elements of the "racialized equity labor", or efforts to challenge racial inequities in the university environment, primarily undertaken by employees of color. We argue that the amount and intensity of racialized equity labor is related to organizational logics of race, or cultural values and beliefs about race that people use to organize their activities in the university. "Diversity" logics, focusing on individual differences in experiences, values, and worldviews, are associated with identity-focused infrastructure and create greater need for racialized equity labor. In contrast, "equity" logics focus on the structural changes needed to address race as a system of oppression and are instantiated in institutionalized infrastructure that alleviates and transforms racialized equity labor. We conclude that diversity logics are profoundly limiting for addressing racial inequities in academia.

Students of color on college campuses often seek the support of non-white university employees as they navigate historically white institutional spaces (Ahmed 2012; Hirshfield and Joseph 2012; Matthew 2016; Moore 2017; Thomas and Hollenshead 2001). Employees of color are thus more likely to engage in insufficiently compensated labor in support of racially marginalized communities (Baez 2000; Gorski 2019; Wright-Mair and Ramos 2021; Zambrana 2018). This labor – what we refer to as "racialized equity labor" (or "REL") – is geared toward changing racial inequities within the university.

The REL of employees often occurs in universities that have institutionalized a visible and often benign commitment to "diversity", or the celebration of individual differences (Ahmed 2012; Berrey 2015; Byrd 2019; Thomas 2018,

2020). Diversity as a set of cultural logics shaping university approaches to race is characterized by new forms of institutional infrastructure, such as chief diversity officers and multicultural centers. As scholars have documented, diversity logics often distract from or derail efforts to address or dismantle systemic racism on campuses (Byrd 2019; Thomas 2020).

We draw on interviews with ninety-four university employees working at two campuses in the same state system to define features of racialized equity labor and document racial inequities in whom performs it. We identify the role of organizational logics of race, or cultural values and beliefs about race that people within organizations use to organize their activities, in shaping campus infrastructure and the amount and nature of employee REL. We detail the limits of diversity logics for supporting racially marginalized employees engaged in racialized equity labor.[1] Our findings expand the concept of REL to faculty and staff (see Lerma, Hamilton, and Nielsen 2020) and demonstrate how racial logics and infrastructure matter for the experiences of racially marginalized workers.

Defining racialized equity labor

Universities have historically been spaces of racial exclusion. Longstanding schools were involved in Native American genocide, grew rich from the slave economy, and were founded to serve white men only (Byrd 2017; Du Bois 1935; Wilder 2013; Wooten 2015). Today most prestigious four-year research universities in the US still enroll few numbers of historically unrepresented students. Yet, even when the student body is majority-marginalized, universities can still be white spaces. Except for Historically Black Colleges and Universities and Tribal Colleges, most Minority-Serving Institutions (MSIs) started as majority-white organizations that transitioned over time (Hamilton and Nielsen 2021). Given this legacy, staff, faculty, and administrators generally remain majority-white, and organizational practices are often modelled after predominately white institutions (Vargas and Villa-Palomino 2018; Vargas, Villa-Palomino, and Davis 2020).

The universities featured in this study are Hispanic-Serving Institutions and Asian American and Native American Pacific Islander-Serving Institutions and serve economically marginalized student populations. MSIs are primarily determined by a threshold percentage of the student body that identifies as part of a specific group.[2] They can vary in organizational "servingness" (Garcia 2019), or the degree to which the school not only enrolls the targeted population but *serves* these students, for example through the compositional diversity of faculty, staff, and administrators, engagement with marginalized communities, and the development of supportive structures. Some MSIs provide an affirming culture and infrastructure for targeted populations, while others are MSIs only in name (Vargas and Villa-Palomino 2018). Anti-

Blackness can also persist at universities not designated for Black students (Dancy, Edwards, and Davis 2018; Pirtle 2021).

On virtually all campuses, representational inequalities among employees create challenges for workers of color. Existing research is focused on racially marginalized faculty, who cope with racial microaggressions, devaluation of their research, tokenism (i.e. being asked to be a visible reminder of the presence of marginalized groups and to "speak for" a particular group), and expectations that they will contribute to the appearance of the university as a "diverse" organization in ways not expected of their white peers (Baez 2000; Matthew 2016; Moore 2017; Wright-Mair and Ramos 2021; Zambrana 2018). Many campuses also include employees whose official jobs are to make visible organizational commitment to diversity – despite university leadership's resistance to structural change (Ahmed 2012).

We offer the term "racialized equity labor" (or "REL") to describe the struggle of organizational actors, from a variety of positions, to address race-based marginalization and inequity. Previous research on REL has examined the efforts of students of color and their allies to make campus safer, more comfortable, and welcoming to racially marginalized communities (Lerma, Hamilton, and Nielsen 2020). In this article, we focus on the racialized equity labor of university employees.

We use the word "equity" rather than "equality" to signify that racially marginalized workers may need more than "equal" (or the same) supports as those who are not marginalized. Institutional whiteness – in university leadership, policies and practices modelled after historically white organizations, and the erasure of how race matters – can make universities hostile places for BIPOC (Black, Indigenous, and people of color). These individuals often experience greater harms in the university setting and shoulder a heavier burden in working to change environments (Matthew 2016; Misra et al. 2021; Moore 2017; Thomas and Hollenshead 2001). As prior scholarship documents, employees of color are more likely to engage in insufficiently compensated labor in support of racially marginalized communities (Baez 2000; Gorski 2019; Wright-Mair and Ramos 2021; Zambrana 2018).

REL is connected to other concepts. For example, Padilla's (1994) term "cultural taxation" refers to the additional service obligations of BIPOC faculty members. Hirshfield and Joseph (2012) expand this concept with "identity taxation" – acknowledging that faculty members with other historically marginalized social identities also take on extra service. Wingfield and Alston's (2013) "racial tasks" includes all forms of ideological, interactional, and physical labor that people of color perform in white spaces of employment, not just the university. Perhaps most centrally, Wingfield's (2019, 37) notion of "racial outsourcing" highlights the fact that when organizations adopt politically correct diversity rhetoric – but fail to address systematic and interactional racism – then professional workers of color may be left "to do the equity work of connecting organizations to communities of color".

Racialized equity labor is a result of racial outsourcing by universities. We define this labor as: *intentional efforts to support marginalized communities and challenge inequitable organizational structures.* REL is almost always a racial task and is often a form of identity taxation – except when performed by the racially privileged. It can be done by employees in a variety of organizational contexts. In the university, REL is shouldered not only by faculty but also by other employees. REL does not include shallow efforts to promote an organization's image as diverse or multicultural. It is often outside of employees' credentialed areas of expertise and goes above and beyond job expectations. Like racial tasks and identity taxation, REL comes at a cost to personal time, well-being, and career development – especially for racially marginalized employees.

The importance of organizational logics

Racialized organizations theory, as articulated by Ray (2019), recognizes that universities are meso-level organizational settings in which individual- and macro-level racial inequities are reproduced (or potentially challenged) through racialized practices. Racial logics are a form of organizational logics – or cultural values, beliefs, and normative expectations that people use to organize their activities. They define how universities approach race, racial difference, and racial inequities. There are at least two racial logics that organize the postsecondary sector, as summarized in Table 1.

Equity logics arose as a direct result of Civil Rights era activism and evolved in a period of high public support for postsecondary education (Hamilton and Nielsen 2021). Jayakumar and Museus (2012, 16) explain that equity logics recognize "the pervasiveness of persisting institutional racism, historic and current exclusionary institutional practices, and disparities". These logics

Table 1. Organizational logics of race.

Logics of race	Equity	Diversity
Historical roots	Civil Rights era activism	Neoliberal era
Definition	Focused on structural change needed to address race as a system of oppression	Focused on individual differences in experiences, values, and worldviews
Perspective on race	Communal and collective	Colorblind
Goal	Push back against systemic racism	Numeric inclusion
Level of focus	Structural	Individual
Associated infrastructure	Multiple, resourced, and semi-autonomous group-based centers	One-size-fits-all multicultural centers and diversity trainings and identity-based student and faculty organizations
Impact on racialized equity labor	Eases the burden of REL on employees and allows for proactive and broader efforts	Increases need for employee REL by outsourcing supports for marginalized students

highlight race as a system of oppression stretching across societal institutions and structuring organizations. On college and university campuses, they are typically institutionalized in multiple, well-resourced, group-based cultural centers grounded in marginalized communities. Equity-related infrastructure tends to be communal and collective, focused on the uplift of marginalized communities, and challenging to oppressive structures (Byrd 2019). It pushes back against systemic racism, even within the university, providing a central hub for equity work (Hamilton and Nielsen 2021).

Equity logics, and associated infrastructure, have been challenged by the diffusion of diversity logics in higher education. Thomas (2018, 141, 2020; also see Berrey 2015; Byrd 2019) argues that most universities in the US have developed a "diversity regime", or "a set of meanings and practices that institutionalizes a benign commitment to diversity". Diversity logics involve celebrating a wide range of individual differences in experiences, values, and worldviews (Ahmed 2012; Moore 2018) and are characterized by attention to numeric inclusion (Byrd 2021). A diverse learning environment may be a celebrated campus feature – if it does not upend racialized power structures (Warikoo 2016). These individual-level, colorblind logics do not recognize race as a system of oppression that structurally disadvantages/advantages some groups (Ahmed 2012).

"Diversity" was introduced in the anti-affirmative action *Regents of the University of California v. Bakke* case as the only "compelling governmental interest" for considering race in admissions (Moore 2018). The *Bakke* case was followed by state-level affirmative action bans (starting with California's Proposition 209 in 1996). The end of affirmation-action dovetailed with the withdrawal of public support for higher education, in the wake of increasing access for marginalized groups in the late 1900s and early 2000s (Loss 2012). Diversity logics are thus the dominant racial logics of what some have referred to as the "neoliberal" era of higher education. This period is defined by a belief in the need for fiscal austerity and the blocking of democratic demands on organizations (Hamilton and Nielsen 2021).

The infrastructure associated with a diversity regime is often one-size-fits-all, such as a single multicultural center, diversity training, or administrative position expected to deal with all diversity-related issues, without providing "special treatment" for any group (Hamilton and Nielsen 2021; Shotton, Yellowfish, and Cintrón 2010; Thomas 2020). Identity-based student and faculty organizations may proliferate; however, these are typically not well-resourced, similar to employee affinity groups in private companies (see Berrey 2015). Indeed, diversity logics suggest that the duty of schools is narrowly defined inclusion, not remedying inequities. Racial equity work is "outsourced" to people of color and may even be blocked by organizational leadership (Ahmed 2012; Lerma, Hamilton, and Nielsen 2020; Wingfield 2019).

Different college campuses have different constellations of racial logics, established over time and instantiated in infrastructure. In this article, we argue that campuses defined primarily by diversity logics and infrastructure produce a greater need for REL – as important student supports are outsourced to employees. In contrast, we contend that campuses that have retained equity logics and infrastructure offer an institutionalized web of supports that eases REL, such that not all employees of color must engage in this work; under these conditions, racialized equity labor can also expand beyond basic needs.

Data and methods

We draw on interviews of university employees from case studies of the University of California-Merced (UCM) and the University of California-Riverside (UCR), conducted between July 2016 and August 2017.[3] The larger project focuses on how limited economic resources shape university supports for majority racially and economically marginalized students. In 2016, over 50 per cent of the UCM student body and around 40 per cent of the UCR student body identified as Latinx. Both schools enrolled around 60 per cent Pell Grant recipients.

UCR and UCM have distinct histories. First opened in 1954 as an elite liberal arts campus, UCR transitioned to a research university starting in the 1960s. A "state-university" partnership meant greater public funding, and Civil Rights activism led to the growth of infrastructure for marginalized populations (Loss 2012). On UCR's campus continued investments in group-based centers reflect equity logics, even as diversity logics have become more present on campus. University investments continue because the centers have grown to be powerful, semi-autonomous actors on campus, in the local community, and in relationship with corporate sponsors – all of which protect them from removal. In contrast, UCM was opened in 2005, when state support for higher education had retracted and diversity was the dominant framework for understanding race. There was no existing equity infrastructure to push back against diversity logics, which defined, and were even used to justify, the limited infrastructure built at UCM.

Data collection involved interviews with employees and students, ethnographic observations, and historical work. We did not set out to study racialized equity labor, but this issue emerged almost immediately. This article centers ninety-four interviews with faculty, staff, and administrators, nearly evenly split at the two schools. Employee participants were typically selected because they had a reputation for being supportive of racially marginalized students. We sought to interview as many Black and Latinx employees as possible. Given our sample selection processes, it is likely that racialized equity labor was higher among those we interviewed than among university employees overall.

Table 2 provides the racial and gender demographics for our sample, as well as the university positions held by respondents. Although the specific racial group breakdown varies by university, 57 per cent of our total sample was BIPOC. Slightly less than half of the overall sample identified as women.

Interviews were conducted by Laura Hamilton, a cis-gender white woman, and Kelly Nielsen, a cis-gender white man. Our semi-structured interview guide included questions about the respondent's background, job duties, interactions with racially marginalized students, and race relations on campus. We did not explicitly ask about "racialized equity labor". However, we did inquire about supports that respondents (or their offices) provided for students of color. We also asked respondents how they understood the word diversity and what it meant at their university. University rules prohibited compensation of employees participating in the study.

Laura had built trust with faculty and staff over multiple years. Kelly, a newcomer to his university site, had to work at developing trust. Cultural center staff were understandably cautious of what a white man wanted from and for UCR's cultural centers. These interviews were only possible after multiple conversations and participation in university trainings. In analyzing the data, we were joined by Veronica Lerma, a cis-gender Latina scholar with expertise in this area of research.

As a group, we thought carefully about what it means for white scholars to write about race. We believe that the work of changing racist structures should not be shouldered solely by colleagues of color. At the same time, we are aware of the damage that well-intentioned white people can inflict

Table 2. Characteristics of university employee samples.

	UC-Merced ($N = 49$)	UC-Riverside ($N = 45$)
Race		
Black	9 (18%)	11 (24%)
Latinx	15 (31%)	9 (20%)
White	19 (39%)	21 (47%)
Asian or Pacific Islander	6 (12%)	4 (9%)
Gender		
Woman	21 (43%)	23 (51%)
Man	28 (57%)	22 (49%)
Position		
Administration	10 (20%)	11 (24%)
Faculty	8 (16%)	5 (11%)
Academic affairs	9 (18%)	9 (20%)
Admissions, financial aid, institutional research	5 (10%)	2 (4%)
Diversity, inclusion, equity	2 (4%)	6 (13%)
Health and well-being	3 (6%)	1 (2%)
Housing and security	4 (8%)	2 (4%)
Student affairs	8 (16%)	9 (20%)

while attempting to support communities of color. Therefore, in this article, we are careful to give voice to our respondents, whose experiences (and analyses of these experiences) are a valuable source of knowledge.

Respondents often described REL as "work", "diversity work", "effort", "building up the community", "serving", and "support". We identified ideal-type transcripts with explicit articulation of efforts to support marginalized communities and challenge inequitable university structures, as well as transcripts in which respondents indicated that they did not do REL (but others did). These transcripts helped us identify core features of employee REL and generated codes that we applied to the entire body of interviews in Dedoose (an online qualitative data software program). Later, in Excel, participants were identified by race and participation in REL. Examples were flagged and imported into Excel, revealing clear campus patterns in the nature and type of REL, consistent with our prior analyses of the racial logics and infrastructure available on each campus (see Hamilton and Nielsen 2021 for more). Finally, we coded all references to diversity and summarized each participant's understanding of diversity in Excel, with relevant quotes to support our classifications.

Results

In what follows, we first describe the nature of racialized equity labor and who participates in it. We then detail how different organizational logics of race are performed and instantiated in infrastructure on the two campuses and explain how this shaped the nature of REL for BIPOC employees. Finally, we discuss the limitations of "diversity" as a racial logic.

Racialized equity labor among university employees

"Racialized equity labor" (or "REL") describes the struggle of organizational actors to provide supports for students and employees of color and address race-based marginalization and inequities in the university. Examples of REL include working alongside student activists to demand resources from administration, organizing employee of color support groups, pushing for the translation of events into languages other than English, and working to remove curricular barriers that block BIPOC students from advancing academically.

As discussed earlier, REL is not shared equally across racial groups. This was true even in our sample, which included employees viewed as supportive of racially marginalized students. Only 6 (or 15 per cent of) white employees engaged in REL, while 38 (or 70 per cent of) BIPOC individuals did so. Women were not more likely to perform REL than men; however, we suspect that the racial equity labor performed by women involved more emotion work, consistent with prior research (Griffin and Reddick 2011; Misra et al. 2021).

Overall, REL involved *extra labor* beyond job requirements, even if the position was in diversity, equity, and inclusion (or DEI). For example, two Black employees (one in a faculty position, the other in academic affairs) were available between 5 and 7pm to offer mentorship for Black students. They would also share cell phones, provide home-cooked meals, buy interview-appropriate clothing, and offer shelter for Black students, as needed. As one of these employees described, "There was a woman who was with me today, she interviewed at the state capital .... I said, 'Let me take you shopping before you go to that interview'. She'll start in February". This kind of pragmatic support had tangible outcomes for Black students.

For many, REL was *outside of credentialed areas of work expertise*. Thus, a Latinx academic affairs employee described being "more like a social worker here on campus". A Black faculty member served as an African-Americanist in their department to ensure that Black students had access to this curriculum, even though this person would rather be their "true self ... [teaching in an entirely different area] which is my truth, that is me".[4] A Black housing and security employee was a mentor for Black men on campus. As this individual noted, "I speak to the Black young males most of the time .... I treat them like they [are] my sons".

REL was centrally about *supporting marginalized communities* – and not about promoting a personal or university image. For example, as a Latinx student affairs worker explained of REL, "This is my driving force because it represents the need for equity, not just for myself, but everyone". These individuals consulted with marginalized students and communities, rather than imposing an agenda. As an Asian faculty member explained of working with student activists, "We spent a good amount of time talking to them about their concerns and all the activisms that they had been doing .... Like how can we help support you? What can we do as faculty?" At UC-Riverside, outreach extended off campus. As a Latinx employee in DEI stated of efforts to support communities hit by deportation raids, "The community needed an ally, and they needed to feel empowered. And that's what I hope to have done".

REL also entailed *challenging problematic or inequitable structures*. Employees worked to create supports that were not institutionalized or standard practice. For instance, a white administrator known for efforts to diversify STEM argued that this labor was intended to "lay the [organizational] groundwork [for a pipeline] because I don't know if the next [person in my position] is going to find this a priority .... This is my window of opportunity to really push it and lay that groundwork". Other employees were urging administration to build staffed cultural centers to support racially marginalized students, "de-militarize" campus police, create ties to local middle and high schools with large Black and Latinx populations, build group-based living learning centers, and increase diversity in staff, faculty, and leadership positions, among other things. These individuals were the frontlines in organizational change.

Employees doing REL *expressed intentional commitments to racial equity* that could not be separated from their larger life goals and world views. As a Latinx employee working in DEI described: "Most who have worked here [in this center] have kind of made it their life". These commitments made it difficult for racially marginalized individuals to turn down seemingly endless requests from students and university leaders to provide labor toward racial equity. As an Asian faculty member explained,

> Everybody wants to diversify their committees. And so people of color get asked to serve on them. Of course they want to do that. [But] if you say yes to everything that you altruistically think that you should do with your raced body, you're going to burn out. And you're not going to get to meet the requirements of tenure ... But the hardest thing to say no to are the students.

REL frequently *comes at a cost to personal time, well-being, and career development*, as has been found in other studies of marginalized employees in academia (Hirshfield and Joseph 2012; Moore 2017; Wright-Mair and Ramos 2021; Zambrana 2018). A Black employee working in DEI described being in "constant trench warfare.... There's just a lot of different battlefronts; the mental health, the social, the microaggressions. You know it's just all of these things that are swirling around for our students.... [But] who the hell is there for me?" An Asian faculty member explained that engaging in REL "chipped away at my tenure clock and it wasn't healthy for my marriage or personal life". A Black faculty member told us about "learn[ing] the hard way that stepping in to be a resource for African American students, something I love to do and can't resist, where resources do not exist, has taken its toll on my career".

Notably, there were racial differences in the costs of REL. The labor of white employees was also time consuming and meant not pursuing other potentially promising projects. Yet, white employees were more likely to be rewarded by the university for doing REL – e.g. being tapped for high-level positions such as dean or receiving university awards for their service. White employees described facing conflict or barriers in pursuing REL but did not state that this hurt their career progression. The emotional costs were described differently by white employees, as they were not facing as many racial "battlefronts".

Our data also included individuals who reported caring about racially marginalized students but were not personally engaging in REL; they discussed campus commitments to "diversity" in vague terms. As a white student affairs employee noted,

> [Diversity is about] looking at a student's or the campus' race, ethnicity, religion, abilities; yeah, anything that makes up a person, right? And, you know, our identities, all that. I think we're very open to that and like we're very prideful [here at UC-Riverside].

Often the focus was on campus image. As this person continued, university employees were happy to "brag about [campus] diversity and what we do". Those not doing REL typically relied on others to support racially marginalized students. As another white student affairs employee indicated, "I have been very, very impressed with the ethnic program offices and their involvement with students in the ways that they outreach to students and campus in general .... I think that's really powerful".

Organizational logics and the nature of REL

Both campuses had "diversity regimes" characterized by benign commitments to individual-level differences and inclusion (Thomas 2018, 2020). This was visible in time-limited diversity trainings and multicultural infrastructure focused on celebrating all forms of difference. Diversity logics were the *dominant* framework for addressing race at Merced. However, Riverside, a much older campus, was also characterized by equity logics grounded in group-based cultural centers that emerged out of Civil Rights era activism. Different levels of organizational support for racially marginalized students shaped the extent to which BIPOC employees – especially staff – felt compelled to engage in REL, as well as the nature of that labor.

Equity logics at UCR

UCR's cultural centers ensured that "equity" logics, focused on the empowerment of groups disadvantaged by race, offered an alternative to the campus' diversity regime. As one center employee[5] described, "The work revolves around [the students'] needs and, not just theirs, but the community. Because we are part of the community. Because we are working with the community". This person noted that centers "do not operate within [the] confines ... of the student affairs model", and instead "engag[e] in the politics of our students". Their quotes highlight collective efforts oriented around group uplift, not apolitical identity-based affinities.

Equity logics on campus were thus instantiated and maintained, in large part, by the web of five distinct racial/ethnic centers: African Student Programs, Asian Pacific Student Programs, Chicano Student Programs, the Middle Eastern Student Center, and Native American Student Programs, mostly established in the 1960s–80s. Each of these centers had space in the heart of campus, paid professional staff, and a funding stream. Although separate, centers often worked together. Campus leaders were often leery of challenging cultural centers because centers supported each other and because local communities attached to the centers could be mobilized against the university. Deep historical roots on campus and in the community helped to preserve the centers, even as diversity-based initiatives developed.

Equity infrastructure allowed for the channelling of support to marginalized populations, aiding and relieving BIPOC employees on campus. UCR's cultural centers served as umbrella organizations providing race-based supports. They were, as a DEI non-center employee explained, "critical agents on campus". Centers provided cultural events, academic programming, and social functions for group-based living learning theme halls; for example, African Student Programs supported Pan-African Theme Hall and Chicano Student Programs supported Únete a Mundo. Having designated cultural centers to coordinate housing communities meant that this labor was not as heavily shouldered by racially marginalized students or employees.

Centers managed numerous student organizations; as a center employee noted, "We do a lot of student org support .... I counted it recently. We have about seventeen student orgs that we advise". Group-based graduations were also run out of centers. The year of our study, Chicano Student Programs was organizing the forty-fifth annual "Chicano/Latino graduation ceremony, Raza grad, which is the culmination of all of the achievements and all of the years [of graduating Latinx students at UCR]". Centers even organized numerous cultural, musical, social, and art-based events – such as radio stations, newspapers, BBQs, and meet ups.

At UCR, centers connected younger and older students via mentoring programmes and current students to alumni who had come through centers in years past. As a center staff member noted, "I'm programming with [the Alumni Chapter], giving our students opportunities to network and connect". Many center staff were themselves also UCR alumni and able to leverage their personal ties and knowledge. Additionally, centers were hubs for meeting students' academic needs – for example by providing letters of recommendation.

Equally as important, however, was emotional support and advice about how to navigate academia as a person of color. As a staff member explained:

> Students have to navigate dozens and dozens of microaggressions all the time, whether it's on or off campus. Coupled with the historical facts of [racially marginalized people] in education in this country, it poses a challenge on a daily basis. To help students get through those challenges ... we're here to serve in various capacities. We're not trained clinicians, but we have life skills and understanding. We're capable of letting our students know ... this is what it is [that you are dealing with], and this is how you're going to [get by] .... That's a responsibility that we have.

The emotional components of REL undertaken by university employees are often invisible and draining – but matter for students' well-being.

The robust presence of staffed, group-based centers eased the burden of REL for non-center university employees of color. While there was no variation by campus in the percentage of white employees doing REL, 58 per cent of BIPOC interviewees at UCR engaged in REL, compared to 80 per cent at UCM. In addition, REL at UCR was concentrated in particular positions. All interviewed employees in DEI engaged in REL, while no employees in admissions, financial aid, and institutional research; health and well-being; and housing and security did so. Less than half of faculty and student affairs employees, and less than a quarter of academic affairs employees, engaged in REL.

Our data suggest it was more possible to be a racially marginalized employee at UCR and *not* do REL. These employees certainly cared about racial equity and students of color but did not go above and beyond official duties. For instance, a high-ranking staff member who was "visible at this institution", was well aware of the challenges Black students faced: "There are not many of us that look like them. They can't find mentors and models, and they can't get their hair cut or done .... They can't find a church home or cultural things that are happening". However, rather than seeing it as their job to help students "plant both feet here", this employee recognized that "we have staff that helps us with that".

There were no BIPOC UCR *faculty* in our sample who stepped back from REL. The limited presence of Black, Indigenous, and Latinx individuals in tenure-track positions – especially at the highest levels – may make it harder for BIPOC faculty to benefit as much from equity infrastructure. The labor of BIPOC faculty was, however, lightened when they did not need to serve as advisors for all student of color groups on campus or plan all university events for racially marginalized communities.

For all UCR employees doing REL, equity infrastructure changed the nature of their labor: They could be more *proactive* and focus on *social issues* rather than basic supports. For instance, several staff and administrators worked with the Black Student Task Force (or BSTF) to create a town hall in which students and community members could share concerns with campus police and brainstorm strategies to prevent violence against communities of color. The event was not a result of outcry around a negative event at UCR, but rather an attempt to prevent such events from occurring. As a Latinx administrator involved explained,

> I posited to [the BSTF] that I agree, we have problems across America, we have problems here on campus. But I think it's also the case that we're better off here on campus at UCR than most, many places .... Let's do some things that others can't do.

Diversity logics at UCM

As UC-Merced was built in the twenty-first century, there was no historical legacy of equity logics or equity infrastructure. Campus leaders argued that forward-thinking universities were moving away from Civil Rights era models of infrastructure. One administrator glowingly reported that a friend recently appointed at a prestigious university decided to "eliminate the individual cultural centers and create more of a combination of a community center around culture and identity". The administrator thus also pushed for identity-based, one-size-fits-all diversity initiatives on the UC-Merced campus.

At UC-Merced, diversity logics were visible in diversity infrastructure – which, unlike at UCR, was the only infrastructure attending to race on campus. For instance, a one-time "Speed Diversity Dialogue" for first-year students focused on identifying different identities that students could have and encouraging students to develop individual "multicultural excellence". The goal was to help students to interact across difference. The training did not, however, provide targeted supports for groups grappling with racialized power structures.

UCM also provided a multicultural center, after much lobbying by students (who wanted multiple group-based cultural centers instead). All groups that sought a "safe space" would need to share the small "Intercultural Hub". The room was unstaffed, leaving students of color to manage explosive situations when white students made racialized comments in the Hub. This type of multicultural center, even if better resourced, highlights problems with diversity infrastructure. "Inclusive" spaces that do not recognize power differentials can be unsafe for marginalized communities (see Shotton, Yellowfish, and Cintrón 2010).

There was only one UCM staff member devoted to cultural programming on race: "As an office of one, I would get a phone call of 'What are you doing for Black history month? What are you doing for Native American heritage month? What are you doing for Hispanic heritage month, right?'". Because this employee was spread so thin, their efforts were mainly geared toward demonstrating inclusivity. Students would also form many identity-based student organizations and even kick-start a living learning community as noted below, but these initiatives received little university support.

A lack of equity infrastructure to help students cope with racial inequities both on and off campus meant that racialized equity labor performed at dedicated centers on UCR's campus was outsourced to employees on UCM's campus. Indeed, a greater percentage of BIPOC employees in our sample engaged in REL at UCM than at UCR. At UC-Merced, even employees in admissions, financial aid, and institutional research; health and well-being; and housing and security were doing high levels of REL. All faculty in the sample were engaged in REL, as well as a much higher percentage of student affairs and academic affairs employees than at UCR.

The lack of equity infrastructure at UCM meant that faculty and staff were primary supports for race-based student organizations. As a Black faculty member explained, "You want to do it, because it can help, but it takes energy, and it takes time. There's work that is involved, right, and I have come to learn that it'll just be pro bono (laughter)". The term pro bono was apt, as the university did not officially recognize the extensive REL faculty did to support race-based student organizations. This faculty member also played an integral role in the campus' Black graduation. Without center support, Black graduation (and the Chicanx/Latinx graduation) were a student and employee driven effort.

Absent institutionalized equity structures, individual employees became vital hubs for marginalized populations on campus. Thus, when two enterprising Black students had the idea for AFRO (Afrikan's for Recruitment and Outreach) Hall, they worked closely with two Black employees to make this happen. The amount of labor was enormous. A new Black faculty member hardly had time to unpack before students asked for help. This faculty member engaged in extensive interfacing with administration, grant writing, attending social events, and hosting office hours for AFRO students – even through family leave.

Impactful employees were known as the point-people for entire communities of color. For example, Latinx students flocked to a Latinx academic affairs employee, seeking help with everything from grades to housing and food insecurity issues. This person was also pulled into working with Black students on campus. As the employee noted: "The African American students sa[id], we want a Black [My Name]!" which resulted in the hiring of a Black employee in academic affairs – unofficially the new point-person for Black students.

Employees engaged in REL were not able to tap into a larger web of equity infrastructure to do their work. They had limits on what they could do, especially since employees had other official job obligations. Furthermore, there were concerns about what would happen when they retired or left. Because their positions were not embedded in institutionalized equity infrastructure, it was unclear that the university would replace them.

As these employees were filling unmet need, their racialized equity labor was often reactive and oriented toward basic supports. For example, an Asian and white faculty member became embroiled with administrators in pushing for the undergraduate Intercultural Hub and in arguing for protections for undocumented Latinx students. The Black faculty members mentioned above joined Black students in protesting the lack of support on campus and in writing demands for infrastructure. Rarely did employees doing REL at UCM have time and energy to think beyond what students needed from the university at that moment.

As our campus comparison illustrates, equity infrastructure – often instantiated in cultural centers, but sometimes via university-supported academic pipeline programmes, living learning centers, and summer bridge programmes – benefits more than students. This infrastructure also supports

BIPOC university employees who typically do the lion's share of REL, providing them with more bandwidth. For those doing REL, university infrastructure grounded in equity logics can also enable a proactive focus on social change.

The limits of diversity logics

A national tendency toward diversity logics celebrates a plethora of individual identities, encourages exposure to different cultural traditions (without a critical structural framework), and can lead to a single campus multicultural center (Shotton, Yellowfish, and Cintrón 2010; Thomas 2020). Our respondents on both campuses were clear that this approach is problematic: Diversity regimes do not meet the needs of racially marginalized students or employees and threaten the robustness of equity logics and group-based cultural centers.

On both campuses, employees doing REL pointed out that "diversity" is a colorblind logic. It is broad and inclusive and can decenter race and efforts to address structural racism. A Latinx student affairs employee explained,

> That's very much where the campus is: "Like, hey, we're a diverse campus. We celebrate it, we love it and I have lots of Black friends and they're gay" … But what happens when … a conversation happens in class around Black Lives Matter?

As he continued,

> Barriers lie in the illusion of colorblindness and the false reality of a diverse California. The colorblindness meaning [is], "I see people; I don't see race or ethnicity … I don't care what color your skin is". That's multiculturalism. That's not social justice …. We see the difference around us [and] it's easy to assume that … we're in a better place.

As he articulates, celebrating the inclusion of individual differences is different than, and can distract from, tackling systems of oppression, such as white supremacy.

A white faculty member working in DEI detailed the limits of diversity for increasing racially marginalized representation, particularly in states with anti-affirmative action policies:

> Faculty will try and use the language [of diversity] … to their benefit. For example, say they want to bring in a [white] person who is from Germany. They [claim this person] bring[s] diversity to the table, [noting that] they're from another country …. [But] the other side is the racial justice side where when we think about the United States and our history of colonization in Mexico, history of enslaving African Americans, genocide of Native Americans, Black opportunities for mobility, there's that side too. Because of [anti-affirmative action legislation], I can't say we want to give special attention [to underrepresented racial groups] [or that] our role as a university is to rectify these

historical inequities. Because that's not what it's about. On paper, it's about diversity, so there's that. [I am] trying to play around that line.

As this person points out, diversity becomes an inadequate tool to address racial equity, in part because it can be leveraged (both intentionally and unintentionally) in ways that work against addressing systemic racial disparities.

Those doing REL also saw diversity regimes as falling short in support for marginalized employees. An Asian faculty member described, "[The university is] using the discourse of diversity in really cynical kinds of ways .... You get all those colored bodies in and then you don't do anything for them". Similarly, an Asian academic affairs employee explained, "We want you to come so we can brown it up, so that we can say this is how diverse we are, and yet what is the action that comes along with it?". Both respondents emphasize that it is not enough to bring BIPOC bodies into universities to create numeric diversity; instead, cultural and structural change must occur so that these employees can thrive (also see Byrd 2021).

When BIPOC employees are not sufficiently supported, they may be drained by their employers, who extract far more than the services for which workers are contractually obligated. As the Asian academic affairs employee quoted above continued, diversity logics feed into this exploitation:

> I try to stay away from the word diversity because ... it's this coded word. In [some] spaces it means that we're going to have numbers and we're commodifying you. My body has been commodified for every day that I've existed, and the quantification and exotification of my body does not feel good.

For this person, "diversity [was a] corporate plan; about ... making sure that they have [a racially marginalized] presence versus this being about justice".

BIPOC faculty also discussed ways in which their racialized equity labor was commodified by the university to promote a diverse image. Even though university leaders blocked substantive change, administration was often ready to take credit for accolades that were a direct result of REL – without supporting those doing the work (also see Ahmed 2012). At UCR, respondents pointed out that the campus did not sufficiently invest in the equity infrastructure that produced such accolades.

For instance, a DEI employee at UCR argued that the cultural centers played a vital role in helping UCR to achieve public recognition: "We're the first UC to receive [the Hispanic-Serving] designation. So we have fulfilled our diversity requirements according to administration. The box is checked. We're good". This designation helps UC-Riverside to attract more Latinx students and receive targeted grant dollars. The employee indicated that, while for the administration recognition of a racially diverse student body was a sufficient end goal, further "investment [in centers] is long overdue".

Of particular frustration was university willingness to invest in emerging diversity infrastructure, rather than continuing to grow equity infrastructure. The DEI staff member quoted above continued, "In their attempt to increase programs and initiatives and create other offices, like diversity and inclusion … we have not invested in the original spaces that have cultivated this work in the first place". As racially marginalized populations have skyrocketed, group-based centers have not been cut – but they are doing more work to support more students and employees, without corresponding increases in staff, space, or funding.

What this employee describes reflects the cycle of racialized equity labor appropriation faced by students engaged in REL (Lerma, Hamilton, and Nielsen 2020). In this cycle, BIPOC identify racial equity issues in the university and work to solve them, while often encountering resistance from university leadership. However, due to external pressures such as the need to appear "diverse" or interest in receiving additional funding, university leadership may appropriate REL for university gain – but only with diluted diversity initiatives that are not equipped to support collective action and produce social justice.

As these respondents highlight, diversity logics will not lead to rich supports for racially marginalized populations. In fact, diversity infrastructure often competes with existing equity infrastructure – diluting or redirecting funding, staff, and programming away from efforts to address racial inequities.

Discussion

We described "racialized equity labor" (or REL) as intentional efforts to support marginalized communities and challenge inequitable organizational structures. Those engaged in racialized equity labor intentionally took on extra labor, beyond job requirements or areas of credentialed work expertise, and often at a cost to their time, well-being, or career development, with the goal of creating an environment supportive of people of color.

We use the concept of racialized equity labor to expand earlier work on cultural or identity taxation (see Padilla 1994; Hirshfield and Joseph 2012) beyond faculty, to look at university staff. We also highlight the possibility that white employees may join BIPOC in their efforts to create racial change in the university; indeed, this is one important way that white employees can be effective allies. BIPOC employees, however, tend to shoulder most of this work, as well as its costs.

Employees' racialized equity labor provides academic mentorship, knowledge and information, material and financial resources, emotional connection, pragmatic strategies for coping in racist organizations, and a source of affirmation for racially marginalized student populations that have historically been blocked from four-year research universities. REL is thus profound in its impact – but it is also deeply extractive. When universities rely on the REL of their employees to create safer and more welcoming campuses, they are also outsourcing central responsibilities to workers, without providing adequate compensation (also see Wingfield 2019). As many have noted, the REL of BIPOC faculty is often invisible in career reviews, or even counts against them (Matthew 2016; Moore 2017; Thomas and Hollenshead 2001; Zambrana 2018). Employees who engage in REL may also see their efforts appropriated and diluted, as diversity initiatives that maintain the status quo (Ahmed 2012).

Our analyses highlight the importance of understanding the organizational context in which REL occurs. As Ray (2019) explains, cultural understandings of race shape resource distribution and practices within organizations. Both of our campuses had developed or emerging "diversity regimes", marked by attention to multiple forms of individual difference (see Thomas 2018, 2020; also Berrey 2015; Byrd 2019). Only UC-Riverside had competing racial equity logics, grounded in longstanding cultural centers focused on collective action to challenge oppressive structures (see Jayakumar and Museus 2012).

At UCM, where diversity was the dominant logic, BIPOC employees were more likely to take on the REL necessary to address basic university supports. In contrast, at UCR, where equity logics were instantiated in infrastructure, some BIPOC employees (especially staff) could focus on doing their official jobs. Among those doing REL, equity infrastructure enabled proactive and forward-thinking efforts.

Our analyses treated the two campuses as distinct environments; however, universities are internally complex and multi-faceted. The equity logics apparent in UC-Riverside's cultural centers were not evenly spread throughout the campus; employees in some units encountered only diversity logics, and some faced explicit racism in their daily existence. In contrast, at UC-Merced, some units opposed the campus' diversity logics, instead favouring equity logics. Because parts of the university can be siloed from others, the local environments in which BIPOC labor can be greatly variable, even at the same university.

Employees performing REL emphatically emphasized the limits of diversity logics. The focus on individuals rather than groups, and on characteristics rather than structures of oppression, means that all individual differences are considered equally worthy of university attention (Ahmed 2012; Moore 2018; Thomas 2020). Diversity is easily commandeered to support groups not subject to racial discrimination and oppression. Working to create structural change within diversity regimes is thus profoundly difficult.

Our findings suggest the importance of equity-oriented infrastructure that encourages the collective empowerment of racially marginalized communities. Equity infrastructure provides vital resources to students of color *and* helps BIPOC employees who face unique challenges in the historically white spaces of research universities – spaces that remain white in their power structures and practices even as student bodies rapidly change racial composition (Vargas, Villa-Palomino, and Davis 2020). Campuses are increasingly interested in a least appearing to recruit and retain faculty and staff of color and should recognize that equity logics and infrastructure are needed to do so successfully. Change requires substantial and targeted funding for racially marginalized university communities, staff and space for equity-oriented initiatives, and acknowledgement of the ways in which universities are complicit in supporting white supremacy and settler colonialism in everyday operations.

REL should also be rewarded by universities. Many campuses implicitly rely on this labor to retain marginalized student populations at greater risk of leaving the university. As larger numbers of racially marginalized students enter four-year universities, campuses would be well-served to recognize the employee resources that exist on campus, and to provide them with incentives to continue this important labor – labor that is not equally shared by white employees. Even if university leadership is not explicitly interested in racial equity, accountability measures like recruitment of marginalized populations and student graduation rates should serve as reminders that REL is valuable.

The need for racialized equity labor is a reminder that universities are racialized organizations reflecting hierarchies that privilege white knowledge, experiences, and expectations over those of racially marginalized groups (see Ahmed 2012; Byrd 2017; Ray 2019; Smith, Tuck, and Yang 2019). University spaces often fail to reward or comfortably sustain racially marginalized students and employees, who have much to offer (Yosso 2005). Racialized equity labor will remain essential until universities fundamentally rework how they support racially marginalized populations.

Notes

1. We use the term "racially marginalized" to refer to groups who are historically excluded in the academy. The terms people of color and BIPOC are broader and encompass those who do not identify as white. Although racial groups are often associated with multiple ethnic traditions, when we refer to Black, Latinx, Asian, or white, we are referring to ascribed racial categories. We capitalize these racial categories (but not "white") to emphasize the political agency, collective identity, and solidarity of these communities in a racist society. We use Latinx when gender is unspecified, nonbinary, or to mask the gender identity of respondents to reduce identifiability.
2. For Hispanic-Serving Institutions, this threshold is 25 per cent. For Asian American and Native American Pacific Islander-Serving Institutions, this threshold is

10 per cent. Both designations also include additional eligibility requirements for economic disadvantage in the student body.
3. This study was approved by the Institutional Review Boards at UC-Merced and UC-Riverside. Participants provided informed consent.
4. We mask the gender of employees with gender-neutral pronouns to reduce identifiability.
5. In this section we do not identify the race of UCR center staff, to preserve anonymity.

Acknowledgements

We wish to thank Jovita Angel, Ashley Bennett, Maria Duenas, Darkari Finister, Rosa Hernandez, Reginald Nelson, Ana Padilla, Patrick Pascual, and Mayra Ramirez for their research support and insights. We also thank Laura Hirshfield and Tiffany Joseph for their work on this special issue.

Disclosure statement

No potential conflict of interest was reported by the author(s).

Funding

This research was supported by a William T. Grant Scholars grant awarded to Laura Hamilton and a William T. Grant Scholars Mentoring grant awarded to Veronica Lerma and Laura Hamilton. Opinions reflect those of the authors and do not necessarily reflect those of the granting agency.

References

Ahmed, Sara. 2012. *On Being Included: Racism and Diversity in Institutional Life.* Durham, NC: Duke University Press.
Baez, Benjamin. 2000. "Race-Related Service and Faculty of Color: Conceptualizing Critical Agency in Academe." *Higher Education* 39: 363–391.
Berrey, Ellen. 2015. *The Enigma of Diversity: The Language of Race and the Limits of Racial Justice.* Chicago, IL: University of Chicago Press.
Byrd, Carson. 2017. *Poison in the Ivy: Race Relations and the Reproduction of Inequality on Elite College Campuses.* New Brunswick, NJ: Rutgers University Press.
Byrd, Derria. 2019. "The Diversity Distraction: A Critical Comparative Analysis of Discourse in Higher Education Scholarship." *Review of Higher Education* 42: 135–172.
Byrd, W. Carson. 2021. *Behind the Diversity Numbers: Achieving Racial Equity on Campus.* Cambridge, MA: Harvard Education Press.
Dancy, T. Elon, Kirsten T. Edwards, and James E. Davis. 2018. "Historically White Universities and Plantation Politics: Anti-Blackness and Higher Education in the Black Lives Matter Era." *Urban Education* 53: 17–95.
Du Bois, W. E. B. 1935. "Does the Negro Need Separate Schools?" *Journal of Negro Education* 4: 328–335.
Garcia, Gina Ann. 2019. *Becoming Hispanic Serving Institutions: Opportunities for Colleges & Universities.* Baltimore, MD: Johns Hopkins University Press.

Gorski, Paul C. 2019. "Racial Battle Fatigue and Activist Burnout in Racial Justice Activists of Color at Predominately White Colleges and Universities." *Race and Education* 22: 1–20.

Griffin, Kimberly A., and Richard J. Reddick. 2011. "Surveillance and Sacrifice: Gender Differences in the Mentoring Patterns of Black Professors at Predominately White Research Universities." *American Educational Research Journal* 48: 1032–1057.

Hamilton, Laura T., and Kelly Nielsen. 2021. *Broke: The Racial Consequences of Underfunding Public Universities*. Chicago, IL: University of Chicago Press.

Hirshfield, Laura E., and Tiffany D. Joseph. 2012. "'We Need a Woman, We Need a Black Woman: Gender, Race, and Identity Taxation in the Academy." *Gender and Education* 24: 213–227.

Jayakumar, Uma M, and Samuel D. Museus. 2012. "Mapping the Intersection of Campus Cultures and Equitable Outcomes among Racially Diverse Student Populations." In *Creating Campus Cultures: Fostering Success Among Racially Diverse Student Populations*, edited by Samuel D. Museus and Uma M. Jayakumar, 1–27. New York: Routledge.

Lerma, Veronica, Laura T. Hamilton, and Kelly Nielsen. 2020. "Racialized Equity Labor, University Appropriation, and Student Resistance." *Social Problems* 67: 286–303.

Loss, Christopher P. 2012. *Between Citizens and the State: The Politics of American Higher Education in the 20th Century*. Princeton, NJ: Princeton University Press.

Matthew, Patricia A. 2016. *Written/Unwritten: Diversity and the Hidden Truths of Tenure*. Chapel Hill: University of North Carolina Press.

Misra, Joya, Alexandra Kuvaeva, Kerryann O'meara, Dawn Kiyoe Culpepper, and Audrey Jaegar. 2021. "Gendered and Racialized Perceptions of Faculty Workloads." *Gender & Society* 35: 358–394.

Moore, Mignon R. 2017. "Women of Color in the Academy: Navigating Multiple Intersections and Multiple Hierarchies." *Social Problems* 64: 200–205.

Moore, Wendy L. 2018. "Maintaining Supremacy by Blocking Affirmative Action." *Contexts* 17: 54–59.

Padilla, Amado M. 1994. "Ethnic Minority Scholars, Research, and Mentoring: Current and Future Issues." *Educational Researcher* 23: 24–27.

Pirtle, Whitney. 2021. "'I Didn't Know What Anti-blackness Was Until I Got Here': The Unmet Needs of Black Students at Hispanic-Serving Institutions." Working Paper.

Ray, Victor. 2019. "A Theory of Racialized Organizations." *American Sociological Review* 84: 26–53.

Shotton, Heather J., Star Yellowfish, and Rosa Cintrón. 2010. "Island of Sanctuary: The Role of an American Indian Culture Center." In *Culture Centers in Higher Education: Perspectives on Identity, Theory, and Practice*, edited by Lori Patton, 49–62. Sterling, VA: Stylus.

Smith, Linda Tuhiwai, Eve Tuck, and K. Wayne Yang, eds. 2019. *Indigenous and Decolonizing Studies in Education: Mapping the Long View*. New York: Routledge.

Thomas, James M. 2018. "Diversity Regimes and Racial Inequality: A Case Study of Diversity University." *Social Currents* 5: 140–156.

Thomas, James M. 2020. *Diversity Regimes: Why Talk Is Not Enough to Fix Racial Inequality at Universities*. New Brunswick, NJ: Rutgers University Press.

Thomas, Gloria D., and Carol Hollenshead. 2001. "Resisting from the Margins: The Coping Strategies of Black Women and Other Women of Color Faculty Members at a Research University." *The Journal of Negro Education* 70: 166–175.

Vargas, Nicholas, and Julio Villa-Palomino. 2018. "Racing to Serve or Race-ing for Money? Hispanic-Serving Institutions and the Colorblind Allocation of Racialized Federal Funding." *Sociology of Race and Ethnicity* 5: 401–415.

Vargas, Nicholas, Julio Villa-Palomino, and Erika Davis. 2020. "Latinx Faculty Representation and Resource Allocation at Hispanic Serving Institutions." *Race Ethnicity and Education* 23: 39–54.

Warikoo, Natasha K. 2016. *The Diversity Bargain: And Other Dilemmas of Race, Admissions, and Meritocracy at Elite Universities*. Chicago, IL: University of Chicago Press.

Wilder, Craig S. 2013. *Ebony & Ivory: Race, Slavery, and the Troubled History of America's Universities*. New York: Bloomsbury Press.

Wingfield, Adia H. 2019. *Flatlining: Race, Work, and Health Care in the New Economy*. Berkeley: University of California Press.

Wingfield, Adia H., and Renée S. Alston. 2013. "Maintaining Hierarchies in Predominately White Organizations: A Theory of Racial Tasks." *American Behavioral Scientist* 58: 274–287.

Wooten, Melissa E. 2015. *In the Face of Inequality: How Black Colleges Adapt*. Albany: State University of New York.

Wright-Mair, Raquel, and Delma Ramos. 2021. "Neutrality for Whom? Racially Minoritized Tenure-Track Faculty Navigating Resources Deficit Consciousness in the Academy." *The Journal of the Professoriate* 12: 82–115.

Yosso, Tara J. 2005. "Whose Culture Has Capital? A Critical Race Theory Discussion of Community Cultural Wealth." *Race Ethnicity and Education* 8: 69–91.

Zambrana, Ruth E. 2018. *Toxic Ivory Towers: The Consequences of Work Stress on Underrepresented Minority Faculty*. New Brunswick, NJ: Rutgers University Press.

On marginality, socialization, and lessons learned for the future of faculty diversity

Caroline S. Turner ⓘ

ABSTRACT
To improve the dialogue on the experiences of ethno-racially and gender-diverse faculty, this article draws on the author's previous research and insights from experience in academic leadership positions. Research findings and practical recommendations emphasize that marginalized faculty are talented and committed to succeed in their academic careers. However, individual efforts are not enough to counter the effects of inhospitable work environments. Organizational factors such as those within the department and the institution as a whole are crucial to support the successful development of a diverse faculty body. Higher education leadership, at local as well as national levels, must work toward the cultivation of nurturing work environments for all faculty, including those who may bring different perspectives. Individual and organizational efforts can work together to include the contributions of all faculty.

As a first-generation full professor emerita of colour[1] and as a former departmental, college and campus-wide administrator who is one year away from full retirement, I have served in various roles within several university contexts and published research spanning over four decades. These experiences have given me opportunities to gain insights into organizational structures and cultures of academia that have relevance for faculty diversity. With each rung climbed during my career and each role undertaken, I always encountered challenging transitions. Transitions are not easy, but I am now aware that transitions are far more difficult if there does not exist a space initially carved out for someone like you. At each juncture, in addition to the transition, I, as others like me, had the extra responsibility to carve out a new space and/or to fill a void because my work and I did not belong. This paper draws on insights derived from faculty of colour narratives provided by my research on faculty gender and racial/ethnic diversity and draws upon my own lived experiences to present lessons for future scholars with similar backgrounds and recommendations for those making decisions about the structures those scholars will be working within.

I am the first in my family to go to college and thus a first-generation student, faculty member and administrator. The experience of being a first continues to influence my educational path, leading me to serve for almost forty years as a professor of education at three large universities in three states (Minnesota, Arizona and California) where my work focused on the advancement of gender and ethno-racial diversity in academe. In most of my academic positions, I was the first (Latina/Filipina) woman of color to serve. In each role, my goal was to explore the experiences of students and faculty of color in order to contribute insights for increasing the representation of people of color, especially among the faculty ranks.

This paper will focus on a discussion of four overarching themes: (1) being defined out rather than defined in; (2) the importance of mentorship; (3) challenges for faculty of colour/marginalized groups in academia and (4) recommendations for improving academia.

Being defined out rather than defined in

In a previous publication, I discussed my experiences about how multiple marginality works to constrain opportunities (Turner 2002a). When I was considering graduate schools, my intersecting social identities shaped my opportunities in higher education. For example, an admissions counselor for a school of business advised that their graduate program consisted primarily of students with a profile different from mine as a woman, a minority, and a single parent with a background in the public sector. At that time, I also realized programs preferred certain social identities (i.e. male, white, experience in the private sector) that were considered to be the best possibilities for success. Others with a different profile would likely not be recruited and/or admitted. "I remember being struck by the many ways I could be defined as not fitting and, therefore, not encouraged and, more than likely, not admitted. I was so easily defined out rather than defined in" (Turner 2002a, 74). Such practices, if not contested, promote homogeneity not diversity.

How communities of color, people of lower socioeconomic background, and people who identify beyond the binary genders do not fit in the academy abound. For example, Solórzano and Yosso (2002) state that "according to cultural deficit storytelling, a successful student [faculty] of color is an assimilated student [faculty] of color ... and they identify the terms 'at-risk' and ... 'disadvantaged' ... [as part of the] cultural deficit terminology … " (31). Solórzano and Yosso (2002) also challenge the dominant narrative that educational institutions are objective, based on meritocracy, and race neutral. The assumption that institutions of higher education are neutral sites, creates a situation in which minoritized individuals must change to belong (Turner and Waterman 2019). With the current rise in hate crimes (Xu 2019), which are defined as "crimes that manifest evidence of prejudice based on race, gender or gender identity, religion, disability, sexual orientation, or ethnicity", there is heightened urgency to counter deficit narratives. During my career, I had several opportunities to interview, converse with, and read about the lives of faculty who are women and men of colour. Through the years, many continued to speak about the experience of multiple marginality and being defined out.

Research on the lived experiences of faculty of colour indicates that they feel apart from rather than a part of the workplace into which they are socialized – most feel as though they are guests in someone else's house (Turner 1994). Based on my interviews with students of color enrolled in a predominately white campus, guests were found to "have no history in the house they occupy. There are no photographs on the wall that reflect their image. Their paraphernalia, paintings, scents, and sounds do not appear in the house" (Turner 1994, 356). Guests are to maintain good behaviour and are typically not invited into all parts of the house. in someone else's house feel that they can never relax. Furthermore, guests are not part of a supportive family of origin or supportive scholarly community, whose foibles and mistakes may be used as learning experiences rather than to be judged. On the contrary, guests must follow the house rules and always be on their best behaviour. In fact, being a guest contributes to feelings of exclusion and isolation which can create a toxic environment. This lack of belonging has contributed to the early deaths and suicides of some marginalized faculty attempting to fit into a work environment not built to value them (Turner 1994; Zambrana 2018; Niemann, Gutiérrez y Muhs, and González 2020; Turner 2021a).

There are many examples of faculty and administrators of colour reflecting on this phenomenon. In Padilla and Chavez (1995), a Latina professor named Ana Martinez describes herself as a newcomer whose reality is not reflected in academe and wonders "Can I be both Latina and professor without compromise?" (74–75). In Turner (2007), university president Juliet Garcia enumerates the many ways she does not fit the profile of a campus president while "people were taking bets on how many months I would last because I was a woman, I was too young, I was too Mexicana" (10). Turner (2000), an Asian American full professor and department chair in the sciences, says "I know that their first reaction to me is that I'm an Asian American woman, not that I'm a scientist or that I'm competent" (91). This last reference to incompetence has emerged as a title of two recent volumes, *Presumed Incompetent I and Presumed Incompetent II*, which present findings of over sixty narratives, primarily by women faculty of colour (Gutiérrez y Muhs et al. 2012; Niemann, Gutiérrez y Muhs, and González 2020). Being defined out rather than defined in is an issue many marginalized faculty experience in graduate school and then as faculty. It can become foundational for the challenges they face in academia throughout their careers.

The importance of mentorship

Mentors played important roles in my career (Turner 2015a; Turner and Waterman 2019). Briefly, study findings emphasized that individual characteristics such as those related to intelligence and resilience are not enough to counter the effects of unwelcoming organizations with historical legacies of discrimination built into their policies and structures (Kanter 1977; Turner 1994; Zambrana 2018). In such environments, departmental and institutional changes that prioritize diversity are needed to promote and nurture the persistence and development of marginalized faculty (Turner 2007; Turner 2012; Turner and González 2014a; Turner 2015a). In 1989, Blackwell defined mentoring generally as a process in which a person of superior rank, achievement, and prestige counsels, instructs, and guides the intellectual development of his/her mentee(s). The mentorship relationship is built on trust and bi-directional benefits. To cultivate the next generation of diverse faculty, research underscores the importance of mentoring across race, ethnicity, and gender (Turner and González 2014) and the importance of mentoring for change. Regarding mentoring for change, Bernstein, Jacobson, and Russo (2010) state, "the goal of mentoring is not simply to teach the system, but also to change the system so that it becomes more flexible and responsive to the needs … [of] mentors and protégés" (58). Nonetheless, lacking effective mentors does not mean that faculty of colour are doomed to be unsuccessful, but they may miss out on critical career-building opportunities, connections, and resources available to those who have mentors (Patton 2009).

Like so many scholars of colour in higher education, there were few, if any, faculty who shared a similar racial/ethnic/gender/class background who were available to serve as mentors while they were students or during their years in the professoriate. In the 1960s, as a first-generation Latina/Filipina undergraduate student coming from a labourer background, I was influenced and inspired by the Farm Labor and Civil Rights Movements. At this time, I had some supportive teachers and peers on campus, but did not have mentors.

In the 1980s, as a graduate student, I was mentored by a course instructor who then became my dissertation chair. This prominent sociologist provided intellectual guidance and financial support through a research assistantship. His generosity with his time, understanding and encouragement at crucial junctures of the doctoral programme were invaluable to my completion of the dissertation as well as being selected for my first faculty position. At that time, I was also introduced to the research of faculty who, through their publications, guided my dissertation work and future research agenda. The research of Scott (1981), Kanter (1977), and Goffman (1961), led me to examine the socialization of individuals within powerful organizational and societal contexts.

As a graduate student, I also met and was mentored by a Latina who served as an Associate Dean. She helped me to overcome self-doubts during graduate school and, while warning me of potential difficulties ahead, bolstered my courage to leave California – where I was born and raised – to accept my first tenure-track faculty position. This is a very salient point as many people of colour, especially women of colour, find it hard to leave their home communities because they are a key source of financial support to their families and extended families. This situation influences where people of colour attend college and which faculty opportunities they are able to pursue. Furthermore, in my experience, due to the hierarchical nature of higher education, if people of colour take a faculty position close to home but not at a prestigious university, they primarily, regardless of their talent, are not considered for future faculty positions at colleges/universities considered above the ranking of the one in which they began their careers. Of course, there are some faculty of colour who are able to obtain a position close to home and at a prestigious university. In many of these cases, however, families make great sacrifices so that their relatives can pursue an academic career (Turner and Myers 2000; Turner 2012).

Because mentorship is so important, programmes providing opportunities for mentorship should be made available at the departmental, institutional, and national levels. Such connections within all contexts, including international professional organizations, play significant roles in the development of faculty and, ultimately, in their successful promotion and tenure (Turner, González, and Wood 2008). Campus leadership can promote a variety of mentoring programmes including online programmes, peer mentoring programmes, programmes to support women and minorities in different disciplines and fields, and programmes to support interdisciplinary academic work (Turner and González 2014; Turner 2015b). For example, in my role as interim college dean, I implemented a mentoring programme for new College of Education faculty, partly based on my research on mentoring (Turner and González 2014; Turner 2015b). One of my goals for the incoming faculty was to underscore their importance as faculty who represent the future of the college. With each new faculty member entering a different department, within a turbulent college context, I wanted to keep new faculty together for one lunch meeting a month with me to contribute to a collaborative cross-college environment and create a sense of comradery.

The new faculty drove the agenda and could inquire about further support for their projects. Other campus representatives, such as the Office of Research and the Office of Technology Support, were invited to join and present available resources. As the year drew to a close, the faculty indicated that they hoped such meetings might continue for future incoming faculty cohorts.

Challenges for faculty of colour/marginalized groups in academia

As I think about the organizational and societal processes that led me to my current role as a full professor in higher education, I marvel as to how I find myself here. How did I navigate through and around the powerful and unyielding socialization processes designed to exclude rather than include me on the journey to become a full professor? There are a multitude of studies, including my own, that focus on the various elements leading to the professoriate and beyond. Over the years, critical scholarship chronicles the experiences of faculty of colour (Chen and Hune 2011; Croom 2017; Gutiérrez y Muhs et al. 2012; Niemann, Gutiérrez y Muhs, and González 2020; Pérez 2019; Turner 2000; Turner 2002a; Turner 2015a; Turner 2019, 2020; Turner 2021a; Turner, González, and Wood 2008; Zambrana 2018). These publications demonstrate that achieving faculty diversity remains a struggle for higher education as a whole. Furthermore, in *Presumed Incompetent II: Race, Class, Power, and Resistance of Women in Academia* (2020), Niemann et al. state that despite efforts to diversify faculties, the US professoriate remains primarily white, male, heterosexual, and middle to upper class. They proceed to say that in such a context, marginalized faculty experience tokenism and devaluation of their knowledge and talents. For their race and gender, they are "tokenized" at the workplace and viewed as "strangers" and "outsiders" in their faculty and administrative positions (Hune 1998; Li and Beckett 2006; Turner 2002a). As they attempt to move up in their careers, they experience unique workplace discrimination that is classed, raced, gendered, and sexualized (Cho 1997). This also happens to marginalized faculty in international contexts (Rollock 2019; Williams et al. 2019).

Reflecting the tension between incorporation and marginalization, studies indicate that while faculty of colour may be hired in predominantly white institutions, they are provided with campus access but not access to institutional power and legitimization (Alex-Assensoh 2003; Turner 2003; Turner 2017). Furthermore, a situation described by Tracy Buenavista, a first-generation faculty member, states that, "like many minoritized people, I gained access to the academy, but was/am not able to fully participate" (Buenavista, Jain, and Ledesma in press). She describes supporting herself, family and extended family on a small salary making it challenging to attend and/or present at professional conferences. Given a lack of or limited faculty travel resources, inability to attend research-focused conferences can have negative ramifications for her promotion and tenure. In addition to hindering her career, such inequities have lifelong consequences. For example, faculty retirement is dependent on income and the ability to contribute to retirement programmes and Buenavista, Jain, and Ledesma (in press) describe some marginalized faculty's inability to do. While hiring is an important step for faculty and staff diversity, the understanding by campus leaders of such inequitable situations is imperative in order to address them, thereby promoting faculty development, retention, and institutional change.[2]

Furthermore, the 2021 tenure fight of Black journalist Nikole Hannah-Jones at the University of North Carolina-Chapel Hill (UNC-Chapel Hill) provides a contemporary example of the challenges experienced by faculty of colour attempting to advance in their careers. The John S. and James L. Knight Foundation sponsors the UNC-Chapel Hill's Knight Chair in Race and Investigative Journalism. This Knight Chair was offered to Pulitzer Prize winning journalist Nikole Hannah-Jones. However, political objections to Hannah-Jones' work, especially her Pulitzer Prize winning project that examines the legacy of slavery in America, *The 1619 Project*, prompted opposition to her tenure by members of the UNC's Board of Trustees. Acknowledging that her battle is reflective of other such battles where Black and other faculty of colour "are having their opportunities stifled", Hannah-Jones declined her hard-won tenure decision at UNC-Chapel Hill, instead opting to accept the Knight Chair appointment at Howard University. In doing so, she emphasized that despite her ability to compete and excel at the highest levels in her field within institutions "not built for you … [at some point, one has] "to decide that you are done forcing yourself in" (LDF Media 2021). Her case exemplifies the legitimacy challenges that marginalized faculty face in academia despite their many accomplishments.

Confessions of trauma in multiple pandemics

Amid the challenges of living in a pandemic and the resurgence of overtly racist discourse in the US, I want to personally thank my colleagues and the co-editors of this special issue for their patience with the writing paralysis I suffered while writing this article. I worked mostly from my small living room where I sheltered in place in the earlier stages of the COVID-19 pandemic. With little experience with online teaching, I enrolled in a summer boot camp for faculty who had to transition to online teaching for the fall semester. I was overwhelmed by at least two pandemics unleashed at this time. Each surge of COVID-19 and the pandemic of racism in this country, including the Black Lives Matter Movement and protests against anti-Asian hate created feelings of anxiety. Both pandemics revealed health inequities experienced by communities of color and the academic inequities experienced by faculty of color who felt the pandemic of racism as stressful, having an effect on their ability to be productive (Ho 2021; Melaku and Beeman 2022, this issue; Reddick 2021).

Participating in many Zoom meetings, faculty and staff of colour, including myself, talked about suffering from vicarious trauma in addition to worrying about our relatives and communities of colour. We described going about our daily tasks, pretending to be okay when we were not.

The continuing pressures and stressors described in current events and related research threatens the ability of faculty members from marginalized groups to thrive in academia. Recent attacks on teaching ethnic studies and diversity-related courses intensify an already taxing situation and accentuate feelings of being alone, overwhelmed, and depressed. In *We Can't Breathe at Work, Either: John Henryism and the Health Impact of Racism*, Reddick (2020) uses the story of John Henry, an African American folk hero who worked as a steel driver in the construction of railroad tunnels to underscore this point. John Henry raced against a machine and won but ultimately died from heart failure due to stress. Reddick describes how systemic racism permeating the workplace presents similar stressors for employees who are Black, Indigenous, or people of colour. As racism persists and change seems so far out of reach, there is a need to realize that we are not alone in our struggles. It is also vital that we reach out to one another to create supportive communities and practice self-care, including securing treatment for anxiety or depression and taking breaks from academic work as needed.

Recommendations for improving academia for marginalized groups

When studies recommend new pathways, pipelines, alternative search committee processes, and mentoring, I ask myself pathways/pipelines to what? Are new programmes meant to instil real change or to maintain the status quo? While slight changes may appear, one concrete answer appears in the consistent repetition of the relevant demographic data (Turner 2021b). Demographic data show that few scholars of colour reach graduate school, and that fewer still attain a faculty position and go on to obtain tenure and a full professorship (Myers 2016; *The Chronicle of Higher Education* 2014). For instance the National Center for Education Statistics (NCES) reported that 14 per cent of graduate students identified as Black, 10 per cent as Hispanic, 7 per cent as Asian American, 3 per cent identified with two or more races, and less than 1 per cent as Native American. NCES also reported that 6 per cent of associate professors identified as Black, 5 per cent identified as Hispanic, 12 per cent identified as Asian/Pacific Islander and less than 1 per cent identify as Native American. For full professors, percentages drop by at least 1 percentage point for each group (NCES Fast Facts 2018, 222; Turner and Waterman 2019, 138).

No matter how bleak the horizon looks, faculty of colour describe examples of safe harbours and counter spaces that serve as points from which to resist oppressive systems that work to negatively judge their work, creating self-doubt and attempting to block their progress (Turner 2002a; Turner and Myers 2000; Turner and González 2014; Niemann, Gutiérrez y Muhs, and González 2020; Hannah-Jones 2021). Such spaces provide contexts where minoritized faculty have opportunities to gather together to support and validate each other's scholarship. Within nurturing contexts, new knowledge may emerge steeped in personal, ancestral, and scholarly community experience (Turner 2000; Hannah-Jones 2021).

Bloom where you are planted: on cultivating nurturing environments and valuing self

I was encouraged from an early age to leave who I am at the doors of educational institutions because that is where my education should begin. Over years of trying to compartmentalize myself, I have learned that my power lies in bringing my whole self to whatever I do. Currently, I find myself blending the values and knowledge learned from my home community with what I have learned during my decades as a researcher in higher education. I have encountered various theories related to access and success in higher education. In contributing to these theories, I am aware of how my university learning brings me back to an understanding of the value of family and community knowledge gained in my youth. This blended knowledge helps me to think about what it means to cultivate nurturing environments in the field of farm labour and academic labour.

As a farm labourer, observing the growth of plants taught me that they must be provided with sufficient water and sunlight, fertile soil, and protection from insects and other pests that could destroy them. Lacking these, a plant may or may not survive, but it will likely not fully bloom. The environment in which you are planted matters!

Recently, I was introduced to the work of Dr Beronda Montgomery, Foundation Professor of Biochemistry & Molecular Biology at Michigan State University. Her book (2021) entitled, *Lessons from Plants*, supports the thinking I am presenting here. In her presentation, Dr Montgomery states that readers might dismiss her ideas as quaint, but they may help in reframing the issues. She states that "Plants possess numerous sensors that allow them to monitor what is going on around them and to assess the availability of resources" (139).

It may be that, in fostering diversity, working across disciplines and fields holds much hope for future progress. Continuing along this train of thought, selected elements creating an environment for a plant to bloom compared to selected elements creating an environment within which scholars of colour can bloom are presented in Table 1.

At this point in my professional journey, the importance of blending farm labor learning and academic labor learning is paramount in understanding of the creation of nurturing environments. My life as a farm laborer provided an opportunity to observe the growth of plants and the importance of providing sufficient water, sunlight, fertile soil, and protection from pests that could destroy them. Lacking these, a plant may or may not survive, but it will likely not fully bloom. The environment where one is planted matters!

However, unpredicted disasters such as storms can curtail the survival of any plant; much like how an unpredicted COVID-19 pandemic, and the #BlackLivesMatter Movement add enormous stressors that take our minds off of our scholarly endeavors to address events that remind us of the divided world in which we continue to live and work. It is important to understand the key elements needed for a plant to fully bloom and, similarly, to understand the contextual elements in which a scholar of color can bloom and reach their full potential.

Among her numerous other recognitions, in 2009, Juliet Garcia, the first Mexican American woman president of a public baccalaureate degree-granting college [University of Texas at Brownsville/Texas Southmost College (UTB/TSC)], was named by *Time Magazine* as one of America's ten best college presidents (Von Drehle 2009). President Garcia exemplifies the meaning of bloom where you are planted when she describes her campus fit: "I think there's just a good match every once in a while ... energy ... you need for a job comes from being at the right place, and doing what your soul tells you you're supposed to be doing" (Turner 2007, 29).

Table 1. Intentional cultivation of nurturing environments.

Plants bloom	Scholars of colour bloom
Sufficient water and sunlight	Sufficient encouragement, mentorship support, validation
Fertile soil	Institutional responsiveness: Intentional retention; Being Defined In
Protection from pests that hinder growth	Using and creating structural pathways for career growth and influence
	Expanding opportunities that give voice to minority faculty; creating new publication venues; need to become part of what is valued in higher education, especially during promotion and tenure discussions
Unpredicted disasters can curtail plant growth: storms, temperature fluctuations, drought	Unpredicted disasters can curtail learner growth: Hurricane Katrina, plight of the undocumented, Ferguson tragedy, a pandemic, #BlackLivesMatter social justice movement

Promoting pathways to leadership

Prior to the COVID-19 pandemic, I was asked to serve my university as Interim Dean for the College of Education, which was an unforeseen turn in my career. My Provost inquired if I would consider taking on the new assignment, as The College was undergoing a series of challenging transitions, destabilizing its function. During my tenure, to the detriment of my own health and social life, I worked 24/7 to address long-standing operational issues and to ensure a smooth transition for a permanent Dean. I would not recommend this work schedule to others. Our well-being must be prioritized (Reddick 2020).

The Provost indicated that he vetted my potential appointment with several faculty, staff, and other college administrators, including the University President. I was surprised and needed to be convinced that I was the right person for the position. After our conversation about the college needs and what I might bring to the table during a time of tumultuous change, I decided to accept. A pivotal part of my decision process to accept was my trust in and admiration for the Provost as well as the fact that my area of scholarship focused on higher education as a field of study. This experience would afford me an opportunity to view higher education leadership from the perspective of practice. When conducting research on faculty diversity, academic leadership is consistently identified as a critical element in promoting faculty diversity.

Interestingly, findings from my previous research on pathways to leadership for women of colour pointed to the use of organizational practices, such as appointment to interim positions, for their advancement. Other identified practices included the process of identifying and nominating potential faculty of colour for permanent leadership positions as well as appointing faculty of colour to head/chair influential and highly visible university-wide committees, such as a campus accreditation committee or the campus promotion and tenure committee (Turner 2007). Other scholars (Jackson and Rajai 2021) point out the need for organizations to expand the definition of leadership which, in their view, excludes women of colour. Jackson and Rajai (2021) argue that "narrow perceptions of leadership and fit … reinforce the status quo" (1). They also refer to the work of Yosso (2005), which encourages the adaptation of the community cultural wealth model to identify and invest in various forms of cultural capital women of colour may bring to leadership positions in the workplace. To cultivate the next generation of diverse faculty and academic leaders, the wide use of current organizational opportunities inherent in the structure of higher education and the creation of similar opportunities are recommended.

In addition to challenges, the interim Dean role came with many positive experiences, such as the opportunity to deliver commencement addresses to thousands of accomplished graduates and their parents – many of whom share my experience as the first in the family to attend and graduate from college. I also had the power to influence hiring and retention decisions, which I discuss in more depth later. I was also able to facilitate the endeavours of talented faculty coming from various disciplinary backgrounds. I enjoyed all of the opportunities to recognize and praise the accomplishments of students, faculty and staff. In addition, I learned a great deal about office management from the knowledgeable staff, many of whom had decades long experience serving across the university. As Dean, I was also able to recognize and support the advancement of these talented staff.

Most importantly, from a Dean's position, I obtained insights into the inner workings of the institution. Seated at a place at the table with other campus college deans, the provost, and the president, I experienced how important administrative decisions are made as university-wide goals were discussed and prioritized as part of an overall vision. In addition to an update on the status of their respective college, each Dean was also asked for their viewpoint on issues discussed. Within this context, informal gatherings and conversations with other administrators gave me another avenue in which I could learn and provide my perspective. However, in these formal and informal discussions, I was in the minority as a woman of colour.

Overall, in higher education, top academic leadership positions are typically held by White men, with women of colour as the most underrepresented group (Flynn 2021). In fact, the American Council on Education (Espinosa et al. 2019) presents data reporting that minority-group academics made up just over 10 per cent of college provosts/chief academic affairs officers with 83 per cent of college presidents across all types of postsecondary education institutions being White. Deserving a mention here, a major barrier for diversifying academic leadership is the need for the promotion of faculty of colour to the rank of full professor. Currently, full-professor status allows one to be competitive for upper-level administrative positions (i.e. department chair, dean, vice provost, provost, or chancellor) and/or to be considered for distinguished professorships (Gmelch 2013). Full professors are also eligible to participate on university-wide promotion and tenure committees. However, as noted above, recent data documents that as professorial rank increases, representation of men and women of colour decrease, making this situation especially acute at the full professor rank (National Center for Education Statistics 2018). Thus, making promotion to full professor remains an important challenge for marginalized faculty seeking to become academic administrators as well as instruments of institutional change.

The underrepresentation of marginalized groups in administration means that those voices and experiences are not often a part of deliberations when important decisions are made, strategic plans are drafted and implemented, and major institutional changes are discussed or proposed. Thus, serving in the role of Dean further highlighted the critical importance of placing those like ourselves, allies, and supporters committed to improving diversity in academic leadership roles (Turner 2002a; Turner, González, and Wood 2008).

As I write this article, I recall examples of the power academic administrators have to promote change. As an assistant professor, I had access to people of colour in academic administration so I met with them to ask for seed money for a faculty diversity project I wanted to start at the university. As a result of their enthusiastic support, I developed a national symposium focused on advancing faculty diversity in higher education (Keeping Our Faculty Symposium – http://idea.umn.edu). This gathering provides a venue for researchers and campus leaders to share their knowledge and practices as they attempt to diversify the professoriate. With sustained funding from academic affairs, the symposium was institutionalized and continues, after twenty years, to serve as a resource for those dealing with this intractable issue. Such intentional collaborative attention is important for promoting the success of faculty of colour.

Importance of campus leadership in the hiring process

In the role of interim Dean, I helped departments make the case about the necessity for new faculty and staff hires. After several years of almost no hires, significant burdens placed on the remaining faculty and staff needed to be addressed. As interim Dean, I proposed faculty and staff hires to the Provost and discussed whether requests would be honoured or not depending upon, among many other considerations, demands for faculty and staff hiring across the campus. It is a very competitive process as college deans made their case by college and, within each college, by the department. Once a myriad of paperwork was filed, faculty/staff hiring committees went about advertising a job description and deciding on a slate of finalists. Prior to the final hire, as interim Dean, I had a one-on-one appointment with each candidate. During our conversation, salary and various perks desired upon hiring were discussed. In short, once decisions are made by the department and the finalist, then they are communicated to the Provost via the Dean's office. Further discussion occurs between the Dean and Provost regarding higher salary or other requests made by the department and/or finalist in order to complete the hiring process. The Provost may also express concerns about any potential hire. With the Provost, the President makes the final decisions. Most of this discussion occurs informally, in person or by telephone. Like mentorship, research shows that strong campus leadership advocating for faculty diversity is also critical for success (Turner and Myers 2000; Turner 2002b; Turner, González, and Wood 2008; Turner 2015a). However, informal conversations and interactions among administrators around the hiring process would be a challenge to study. My understanding about the nuances of higher education institutional hiring practices increased manifold by serving in this position.

Importance of campus leadership in the retention of marginalized faculty

Interviews conducted with faculty of colour, an extensive review of the published literature on faculty diversity, and my personal experience as a faculty member document the predominant importance of campus leadership in the development and advancement of faculty of colour leading to their retention. Published literature documents a supportive administration as contributing to the creation of positive and inclusive workplace environments at all campus levels, departmental, college, and campus wide. Interviews with faculty of colour note that leadership within the academic department can set a tone of collegiality, tolerance, and acceptance of differences. The importance of financial support for their research from deans and provosts is also noted. Such support signaled to these faculty that the campus administration valued their work (Turner, González, and Wood 2008). As in the hiring process, informal conversations and interactions of faculty with administrators are described as key to the development, advancement, and retention of faculty of colour. An example from personal experience of the importance of a college dean's support is the following: during a conversation in the hallway, my dean asked me what I was working on. I described a research project for which I was in the process of seeking funding. He immediately said that his office would provide a small grant to seed the project. It was just the impetus needed to conduct the research which, in turn, was published. Campus administrators can intentionally engage marginalized faculty and identify areas where support is needed and potential resources to contribute to their development and retention.

In summary, administrators, including college presidents (Turner 2007), can create inclusive safe harbours for faculty of colour and they can fund programmes that are supportive of the hiring, development, and retention of a diverse faculty and staff. Campus leaders are also in positions from which to advocate for faculty and administrator diversity during both the hiring and promotion process. Each of us, in our own way, can use our spheres of influence to create needed change toward increasing opportunities, as well as fostering welcoming learning environments for ourselves and others. Through our experiences as academic administrators, we can open up possibilities as we push back against deficit narratives recognizing the talents and strengths communities of colour bring to academe (Yosso 2005; Turner and Waterman 2019; Jackson and Rajai 2021).

Rethinking merit for faculty advancement

Due to my long career as a faculty member in three universities, I have undergone several post-tenure reviews at the associate and full professor levels. The familiar criteria of teaching, research and service are trotted out each time, although some changes to include service in support of diversity are periodically made. For example, while applauding the increasing recognition for faculty of colour who carry the burden of diversity service, Reddick (2021) notes that "if cultural taxation exists, then so must a 'privilege payoff. If minorities carry an invisible burden, those who hold dominant identities in the academy, exempted from such diversity work, find themselves getting ahead". Continuing along the thought of burden and privilege, one of the findings emerging from *Presumed Incompetent II* (2020) is that in evaluating scholarly productivity, there is a penalty for diversity-related service, but there is no penalty for lack of diversity-related service (Niemann 2020).

While building multiple pathways for others who champion diversity in higher education is my current focus, I am prompted to ask, are there ways in which all faculty being considered for the full professor rank and/or undergoing post-tenure review can also be evaluated on how they have broadened pathways for diversity? This is especially important for full professors and others who are involved in making decisions about the promotion and tenure of marginalized faculty (Turner 2000).

Thus, I recommend that diversity-related service be more actively rewarded and included as a form of merit for demonstrating being a good department/university citizen. Reddick (2021) and Niemann (2020) delineate how faculty of colour are evaluated within an uneven playing field. In 1994, Padilla described such inequities as "cultural taxation", the unique burden placed on the few ethnic minoritized faculty on predominantly white campuses who provide diversity service. He also notes that faculty are likely not rewarded for such service and may become "overcommitted and at risk for burnout" (26). Those with influence on the promotion and tenure processes must take this research and intentionally work toward balancing the inequities revealed here. In my role as interim Dean, I took such situations into consideration as I read and advised on each promotion and tenure case submitted to the Provost's office. To begin to redress such imbalances, campus leaders must recognize and reward such service first by identifying them and then by offering support such as course releases and/or teaching assistants, providing additional research funding and/or research assistants, and addressing salary inequities as needed. In addition, diversity-related service must be prioritized in the promotion and tenure decisions for all faculty.

In other words, another way to reassess merit is to include an examination of how professors work toward broadening pathways for diversity. For example, to broaden pathways for diversity my work includes the following:

(1) Support for the development of new journals or publication venues in which the scholarship of faculty of colour can be featured. As an example, I support the development of new journals such as the *Journal of Minority Achievement, Creativity, and Leadership* published by Penn State University Press. The expansion of such venues can give voice and visibility to the research of scholars of colour (Stanley 2007; Turner, González, and Wood 2008).

(2) Promote an understanding of the additional service undertaken by faculty of colour, who while few in number, are asked to provide support for others attempting to advance, including students/faculty of colour from other departments and disciplines. For example, demographic data demonstrate how scholars of colour are especially underrepresented among the tenured and full professor ranks. These professors of colour may be asked to write more, compared to White professors who are in the majority, letters for scholars of colour coming up behind them. This includes the review of comprehensive portfolios to write letters for promotion, tenure, full professorship, named professorship, advancement to high level administrative posts, and so on.

(3) Cultivate a network of scholars of colour to support one another's scholarship and well-being. I also find it important to maintain an active communication with a large network of first-generation and minoritized scholars who are facing gender, race, and class concerns.

(4) Promote the merit of public engagement scholarship and scholar activism in academic work. For example, those faculty who write opinion pieces and blogs, such as Richard Reddick cited in this article, provide critical insights into issues of social justice and other current movements/protests/events taking place. His work, as the work of others who combine public engagement with scholarship, needs to be recognized for furnishing an important perspective for academic leaders and policymakers attempting to address such challenges (Joseph-Salisbury and Connelly 2021; Reddick 2020; Reddick 2021).

Conclusion

Becoming successful in academe, I encountered the strong socialization processes which promote advancement. In doing so, I learned not to lose sight of knowledge gained during my early life experiences. What is learned within ourselves, families, and communities is of great value and must be drawn upon as we move through academia. By doing so, we authenticate knowledge gained within our communities of origin. Knowledge gained during our early development combined with knowledge gained in school and campus settings influences our inquiries in many ways by affecting research approaches, influencing the types of questions asked, determining the kinds of issues which interest us, and guiding the ways in which we interpret our findings. Furthermore, by supporting others to see the value of their backgrounds, we can define ourselves in and create new knowledge that affirms and addresses our diverse realities and intellectual contributions.

From observing and monitoring plants that bloom, we can learn to provide what is needed for scholars of color, including marginalized faculty, to bloom. Now, it is time for all of us to take this knowledge and practice it in our everyday lives. Working together and across our differences we can intentionally create nurturing practices, policies, and programs that help all to bloom no matter where they were initially planted. Doing so, we can contribute to the development of spaces for marginalized scholars to bloom.

Notes

1. In this article, the terms "woman of color", "faculty of color", and "minority" refer to persons of African American, American Indian, Asian Pacific American, and Latina/o/x origin in the United States. I understand that "people of color" are not a monolithic group and recognize that Whites are also members of distinct racial/ethnic categories. And by using the individual racial and ethnic categories I do not intend to imply that all persons of color have a uniform experience. Rather these categories are used in order to present existing data distinguishing between these groups, identify some common themes, and making overall statements about the varying experiences of the identified groups.
2. See Hamilton, Nielsen and Lerma 2022, this issue and Ray (2019) for more on how racialized hierarchies shape organizations.

Disclosure statement

No potential conflict of interest was reported by the author(s).

ORCID

Caroline S. Turner http://orcid.org/0000-0002-4943-3873

References

Alex-Assensoh, Y. 2003. "Race in the Academy: Moving Beyond Diversity and Toward the Incorporation of Faculty of Color in Predominately White Colleges and Universities." *Journal of Black Studies* 34: 12–27. doi:10.1177/0021934703256058.

Bernstein, B. L., R. Jacobson, and N. F. Russo. 2010. "Mentoring Women in Context: Focus on Science, Technology, Engineering, and Mathematics Fields." In *The Praeger Handbook for Women Mentors: Transcending Barriers of Stereotype, Race, and Ethnicity*, edited by C. A. Rayburn, F. L. Denmark, M. E. Reuder, and A. M. Austria, 43–64. Westport: Praeger.

Blackwell, J. E. 1989. "Mentoring: An Action Strategy for Increasing Minority Faculty." *Academe* 75 (5): 8–14. doi:10.2307/40249734.

Buenavista, T. L., D. Jain, and M. C. Ledesma. in press. *First-generation Faculty of Color: Reflections on Research, Teaching, and Service*. New Brunswick, NJ: Rutgers University Press.

Chen, E. W., and S. Hune. 2011. "Asian American Pacific Islander Women from Ph. D.to Campus President: Gains and Leaks in the Pipeline." In *Women of Color in Higher Education: Changing Directions and New Perspectives*, edited by J. Gaëtane, and B. Lloyd-Jones, 163–190. Bingley, West Yorkshire, England: Emerald Group Publishing Limited.

Cho, S. K. 1997. "Converging Stereotypes in Racialized Sexual Harassment: Where the Model Minority Meets Suzie Wong." *Journal of Gender, Race & Justice* 1: 177–211.

The Chronicle of Higher Education. 2014. Almanac 2014–2015, 60, no. 45. Washington, DC: The Chronicle of Higher Education.

Croom, N. N. 2017. "Promotion Beyond Tenure: Unpacking Racism and Sexism in the Experiences of Black Womyn Professors." *The Review of Higher Education* 40 (4): 557–583. doi:10.1353/rhe.2017.0022.

Espinosa, L. L., J. M. Turk, M. Taylor, and H. M. Chessman. 2019. *Race and Ethnicity in Higher Education: A Status Report*. Washington, DC: American Council on Education.

Flynn, M. 2021. "Academic Leadership by Race: Student Diversity Grows While Leadership Remains Mostly White." https://www.investopedia.com/student-diver sity-grows-while-leadership-remains-white-5112518#minorities-are-underrepresen ted-in-full-time-faculty-positions.

Gmelch, W. H. 2013. "The Development of Campus Academic Leaders." *International Journal of Leadership and Change* 1 (1): 7.

Goffman, E. 1961. *Asylums: Essays on the Social Situation of Mental Patients and Other Inmates*. Oxford: Anchor.

Gutiérrez y Muhs, G., Y. F. Niemann, C. G. González, and A. P. Harris. (Eds.). 2012. *Presumed Incompetent: The Intersections of Race and Class for Women in Academia*. Logan: Utah State University Press.

Hamilton, L., K. Nielsen, and V. Lerma. 2022. "Diversity is a Corporate plan:" Racialized equity labor among university employees." *Ethnic and Racial Studies*. doi:10.1080/01419870.2022.2089049.

Hannah-Jones, N. July 6, 2021. *Nikole Hannah-Jones Issues Statement on Decision to Decline Tenure Offer at University of North Carolina-Chapel Hill and to Accept Knight Chair Appointment at Howard University*. NAACP Legal Defense and Educational Fund, Inc. NHJ-Statement-CBS-7.6.21-FINAL-8-am.pdf (naacpldf.org)

Ho, J. 2021. "Anti-Asian Racism, Black Lives Matter, and COVID-19." *Japan Forum* 33 (1): 148–159. doi:10.1080/09555803.2020.1821749.

Hune, S. 1998. *Asian Pacific American Women in Higher Education: Claiming Visibility and Voice*. Washington, DC: Association of American Colleges and Universities.

Jackson, M., and P. Rajai. 2021. "Does Your Definition of Leadership Exclude Women of Color?" Harvard Business Review. https://hbr.org/2021/01/does-your-definition-of-leadership-exclude-women-of-color.

Joseph-Salisbury, R., and L. Connelly. 2021. *Anti-racist Scholar-Activism*. Manchester: Manchester University Press.

Kanter, R. M. 1977. *Men and Women of the Corporation*. New York: Basic Books.

LDF Media. 2021. "Nikole Hannah-Jones issues statement on decision to decline tenure offer at University of North Carolina-Chapel Hill and to accept Knight Chair appointment at Howard University." NAACP Legal Defense and Educational Fund, Inc. NHJ-Statement-CBS-7.6.21-FINAL-8-am.pdf (naacpldf.org).

Li, G., and G. H. Beckett. 2006. *Strangers of the Academy: Asian Women Scholars in Higher Education*. Sterling: Stylus Publishing.

Melaku, T., and A. Beeman. 2022. "Black Women in White Academe: A Qualitative Analysis of Heightened Inclusion Tax." *Ethnic and Racial Studies*, forthcoming.

Montgomery, B. L. 2021. *Lessons from Plants*. Cambridge, MA: Harvard University Press.

Myers, B. 2016. "Where Are the Minority Professors?" The Chronicle of Higher Education. https://www.chronicle.com/interactives/where-are-the-minority-professors.

National Center for Education Statistics, U.S. Department of Education. 2018. "Table 315.20: Full-time Faculty in Degree-granting Postsecondary Institutions, by Race/ethnicity, Sex, and Academic Rank: Fall 2015, Fall 2016, and Fall 2017." In Digest of Education Statistics: 2018. https://nces.ed.gov/programs/digest/d18/tables/dt18_315.20.asp.

NCES Fast Facts. 2018. https://nces.ed.gov/fastfacts/.

Niemann, Y. F. 2020. "The Social Ecology of Tokenism in Higher Education Institutions." In *Presumed Incompetent II: Race, Class, Power, and Resistance of Women in Academia*, edited by Y. F. Niemann, G. Gutiérrez y Muhs, and C. G. González, 325–331. Louisville, CO: University Press of Colorado.

Niemann, Y. F., G. Gutiérrez y Muhs, and C. G. González. 2020. *Presumed Incompetent II: Race, Class, Power, and Resistance of Women in Academia*. Louisville: University Press of Colorado.

Padilla, A. M. 1994. "Ethnic Minority Scholars, Research, and Mentoring: Current and Future Issues." *Educational Researcher* 23 (4): 24–27. doi:10.3102/0013189X023004024.

Padilla, R. V., and R. C. Chavez. 1995. *The Leaning Ivory Tower: Latino Professors in American Universities*. Albany, NY: Albany State University of New York Press.

Patton, L. D. 2009. "My Sister's Keeper: A Qualitative Examination of Mentoring Experiences among African American Women in Graduate and Professional Schools." *Journal of Higher Education* 80 (5): 510–537. doi:10.1080/00221546.2009.11779030.

Pérez, P. 2019. *The Tenure-Track Process for Chicana and Latina Faculty: Experiences of Resisting and Persisting in the Academy*. New York: Taylor & Francis.

Ray, V. 2019. "A Theory of Racialized Organizations." *American Sociological Review* 84: 26–53. doi:10.1177/0003122418822335.

Reddick, R. J. 2020. "We Can't Breathe at Work, Either: John Henryism and the Health Impact of Racism." Fortune. https://fortune.com/2020/06/19/john-henryism-black-racism-workplace/.

Reddick, R. J. 2021. "Want to Combat the 'Privilege Payoff'? Here's How Inequitable Workloads Persist Across Lines of Gender and Race, but They Don't Have to." https://www.chronicle.com/article/want-to-combat-the-privilege-payoff-heres-how.

Rollock, N. 2019. "The Career Experiences and Strategies of UK Female Black Professors." https://www.ucu.org.uk/media/10075/staying-power/pdf/ucuc_rollock_february_2019.pdf.

Scott, W. R. 1981. *Organizations: Rational, Natural, and Open Systems*. Hoboken, NJ: Prentice Hall.

Solórzano, D. G., and T. J. Yosso. 2002. "Critical Race Methodology: Counter-Storytelling as an Analytical Framework for Education Research." *Qualitative Inquiry* 8 (1): 23–44. doi:10.1177/107780040200800103.

Stanley, C. A. 2007. "When Counter Narratives Meet Master Narratives in the Journal Editorial Review Process." *Educational Researcher* 36 (1): 14–24. doi:10.3102/0013189X06298008.

Turner, C. S. 1994. "A Guest in Someone Else's House: Students of Color on Campus." *The Review of Higher Education* 17 (4): 355–370. doi:10.1353/rhe.1994.0008.

Turner, C. S. 2000. "New Faces, new Knowledge." *Academe* 86 (5): 34–37. doi:10.2307/40251918.

Turner, C. S. 2002a. "Women of Color in Academe: Living with Multiple Marginality. In James Fairweather (Ed.)." *Journal of Higher Education* 73 (1): 74–93.

Turner, C. S. 2002b. *Diversifying the Faculty: A Guidebook for Search Committees.* Washington, DC: Association of American Colleges and Universities (AAC&U).

Turner, C. S. 2003. "Incorporation and Marginalization in the Academy: From Border Toward Center for Faculty of Color? In Yvette Alex-Assensoh (Ed.)." *Journal of Black Studies* 34 (1): 112–125. doi:10.1177/0021934703253689.

Turner, C. S. 2007. "Pathways to the Presidency: Biographical Sketches of Women of Color Firsts." *Harvard Educational Review* 77 (1): 1–38. doi:10.17763/haer.77.1.p831667187v7514w.

Turner, C. S. V. 2012. "Mentoring Latinas/os in Higher Education: Intentional Cultivation of Talent." In *Expanding Postsecondary Opportunity for Underrepresented Students: Theory and Practice of Academic Capital Formation, Vol. 26, Readings on Equal Education*, edited by R. Winkle Wagner, P. J. Bowman, and E. P. St. John, 89–116. New York: AMS Press, Inc.

Turner, C. S. 2015a. "Lessons from the Field: Cultivating Nurturing Environments in Higher Education." *Review of Higher Education* 38 (3): 333–358. doi:10.1353/rhe.2015.0023.

Turner, C. S. (Guest Editor). 2015b. *Mentoring as Transformative Practice: Supporting Student and Faculty Diversity, New Directions for Higher Education Journal Special Issue*. San Francisco, CA: Jossey-Bass, A Publishing Unit of John Wiley & Sons, Inc.

Turner, C. S. V. 2017. "Remaining at the Margin and in the Center." *Journal for the Study of Postsecondary and Tertiary Education* 2: 121–126. doi:10.28945/3886.

Turner, C. S. 2019. "Preface." In *The Tenure-Track Process for Chicana and Latina Faculty: Experiences of Resisting and Persisting in the Academy*, edited by P. Perez, xix–xii. New York: Taylor & Francis.

Turner, C. 2020. "I Can Only put Together Thoughts Filed Away in my Brain: Who Would pay me to do That?" *Journal of Minority Achievement, Creativity, and Leadership* 1 (1): 3–16. doi:10.5325/minoachicrealead.1.1.0003.

Turner, C. S. V. 2021a. Diverse Women as Guests in the Academic House. Book review: Presumed incompetent II: Race, class, power, and resistance of women in academia by Yolanda Flores Niemann, Gabriella Gutiérrez y Muhs, & Carmen G. González (Eds.). Academe. https://www.aaup.org/article/diverse-women-guests-academic-house#.YAn-sOhKg2w.

Turner, C. S. V. 2021b. "On Diversity, Identity and Socialization: Inequality of Educational Outcomes." *Education Policy Analysis Archives* 29 (41): 1–22. doi:10.14507/epaa.29.5329.

Turner, C. S. V., and J. C. González. (Eds.). 2014. *Modeling Mentoring Across Race/Ethnicity and Gender: Practices to Cultivate the Next Generation of Diverse Faculty.* Sterling, Va.: Stylus Publishing, LLC.

Turner, C. S., J. C. González, and J. L. Wood. 2008. "Faculty of Color in Academe: What 20 Years of Literature Tells us." *Journal of Diversity in Higher Education* 1 (3): 139–168. doi:10.1037/a0012837.

Turner, C. S., and S. L. Myers, Jr. 2000. *Faculty of Color in Academe: Bittersweet Success.* Needham Heights, MA: Allyn & Bacon.

Turner, C. S., and S. J. Waterman. 2019. "Pushing Back Against Deficit Narratives: Mentoring as Scholars of Color." *Texas Education Review* 8 (1): 138–149. doi:10.26153/tsw/7044.

Von Drehle, D. 2009. "The Ten Best College Presidents." *Time Magazine.* http://content.time.com/time/specials/packages/article/0,28804,1937938_1937934_1937914,00.html.

Williams, P., B. Sukhi, A. Jason, and L. Chantelle. 2019. "The Broken Pipeline-barriers to Black PhD Students Accessing Research Council Funding." https://leadingroutes.org/the-broken-pipeline.

Xu, Y. 2019. "Explaining the Numbers Behind the Rise in Reported Hate Crimes." Politifact. https://www.politifact.com/truth-o-meter/article/2019/apr/03/hate-crimes-are-increasingly-reported-us/.

Yosso, T. 2005. "Whose Culture has Capital? A Critical Race Theory Discussion of Community Cultural Wealth." *Race, Ethnicity and Education* 8: 69–91. doi:10.1080/1361332052000341006.

Zambrana, R. E. 2018. *Toxic Ivory Towers: The Consequences of Work Stress on Underrepresented Minority Faculty.* New Brunswick: Rutgers University Press.

Index

Page numbers in **bold** refer to tables and those in *italic* refer to figures.

Ahmed, Sara 74
Alston, Renée S. 106
American Society for Engineering Education Membership database 89
anti-Blackness 105–6
anti-black police brutality 1
anti-black systemic racism 1–2
Apodaca, E. C. 12
Arbery, Ahmaud 1
Asian American and Native American Pacific Islander-Serving Institutions 105

The *Bakke* case 108
Beeman, A. 4, 61, 70, 74–5
Berdahl, J. L. 85–6
Bernstein, B. L. 130
Black faculty, educational institutions 59–60
Black, Indigenous, and other People of Color (BIPOC) 58–9, 106, 120
Black Lives Matter Movement 1, 22, 133
Bourdieu, P. 13
Buenavista, Tracy 132

Cabrera, N. L. 12, 13
Calka, A. 84
Campbell, K. M. 61
campus leadership 131; hiring process 139–40; retention of marginalized faculty 140
Casad, B. J. 86
Center for Epidemiologic Studies Depression Scale (CES-D) 41
Chavez, R. C. 128
"Chinese flu" 2
The Chronicle of Higher Education 75
College and University Professional Association for Human Resources (CUPA-HR) 84

college-going identities 11–12
Collins, P. H. 62, 63, 73
colour/marginalized groups: retirement 133; tokenism and devaluation 132; trauma confessions, multiple pandemics 133–4
committee service 19–20
community cultural wealth model 11
contemporary population health knowledge 36
Covid-19, impact of 81
Crenshaw, K. 12, 24
critical race theory 3, 14, 37
cultural taxation 2, 3, 10, *14*, 34–5, 60, 62, 106
cultural tax credit 3, 14, *14*
culture of college framework 12, 13

diversity, equity and inclusion (DEI) 6, 9, 112, 113
diversity logics 108, 116–21
doubly disadvantaged 12

early-career faculty, mentorship of 39–40
the 2020 election 81
emotional segregation 61–2
equity and inclusion (EI) metrics 51
equity logics 108, 114–16
ethnoracial taxation 34

faculty diversity: and administrators 128; campus leadership 139–40; crimes 128; defined 127–8; mentorship 130–2; nurturing environments and self valuation 135–6, **136**; organizational structures and cultures of academia 127; pathways to leadership 137–9; rethinking merit, faculty advancement 141–2; *see also* colour/marginalized groups

Farm Labor and Civil Rights Movements 130
Floyd, George 1

Gibson, C. 23
Goffman, E. 131
grade point average (GPA) 13
Guillaume, R. O. 12

Hamilton, L. T. 4, 21, 110
Hannah-Jones, Nikole 133
Harley, D. A. 87
Harold, C. 86
Harvard Business Review 75
Haynes, M. C. 17
Heilman, M. E. 17
Henry, John 134
Hernandez, M. 85
higher education institutions: change selection processes 24–5; DEI and cultural shifts 23–4; expand access to cultural tax credits 25–6; subjectivity of students' experiences 26–7
Hirshfield, L. E. 11, 60, 70, 87–8, 91, 106
Hispanic-Serving Institutions (HSIs) 90, 105
Historically Black Colleges and Universities (HBCUs) 90

identity-focused infrastructure 4
identity taxation 2, 4, 6–7, 11, 62, 87–8
inclusion tax 4; Black women lawyers 61; defined 59; invisible labour marginalized group members 61
infrastructure addressing systemic racism 4
Inside Higher Ed 75
institutional penalty 4; defined 33; individual careers, realities on 33; see also Latino faculty
Institutional Review Board of The City University of New York (IRB) 64
intentional cultivation, nurturing environments **136**
internal events 22
international professional organizations 131
intersectionality 12, 62

Jack, A. A. 13, 20
Jackson, M. 137
Jacobson, R. 130
Jayakumar, Uma M. 107
Jones, Camara Phyllis 47
Joseph, T. D. 11, 60, 70, 87–8, 91

Kanter, R. M. 131L

Latino faculty: analytic strategy 41; depressive symptoms 41, 48; description of measures 39–40; ethnoracial taxation and discrimination 33; individuals with 32; institutional diversity efforts 35; institutional joint and leadership appointments 48; institutional socialization gaps 48; Mexican Americans and Puerto Ricans 32; non-URM Latino faculty 35–6; physical symptoms 40, 45–6, **46**; role overload scale 40; sample criteria selection 38; sample description 38–9; sociodemographic, family and employment characteristics 38; study limitations 41–2; workplace stress 48
Lerma, V. 10–12, 21
Llorens, A. 84, 85

Marks, M. 86
Martin, D. B. 91
McGee, E. O. 4, 86–8, 91
Melaku, T. M. 4, 61, 76
Mentor Facilitated Activities Scale 39
mentorship 88, 130–2
Mentorship Relationship Functions Scale 39
Min, J. A. 85–6
Minority-Serving Institutions (MSIs) 105
minority tax 61, 62
Misra, J. 87
multiple institutional taxation demands 37
Muñoz, J. A. 87
Museus, Samuel D. 107

National Center for Education Statistics (NCES) 134, 135
National Faculty Survey 39
National Women's Law Center (NWLC) 84
Native American genocide 105
Nielsen, K. 21
Niemann, Y. F. 132, 141

Office of Research and the Office of Technology Support 132

Padilla, A. M. 2, 3, 11–13, 34, 60, 70, 87, 106
Padilla, R. V. 128
parental education 41
peer advising/mentoring 20–2
people of color (PoC) 88
perceived discrimination scale 40
performative allyship 69–70
pet-to-threat syndrome 87

Physical Symptoms Index (PSI) 40
Piorkowski, G. K. 21
Pololi, L. H. 61
Presumed Incompetent II (2020) 141
privileged poor 12
Purushothaman, D. 85

racial battle fatigue (RBF) 36
racial equity work 108–9
racialized equity labor (REL) 4, 10, 11, 15–18; among university employees 111–14; defined 105–7; employees of 104–5; institutional infrastructure forms 105; organizational logics and nature 114–19; racialized organizations theory **107**, 107–9
racialized organizations theory **107**, 107–9
racial tasks 106
racial upheaval 81
Rajai, P. 137
Ray, Victor 107, 122
Reddick, R. J. 134, 141
Rideau, R. 88
Rios-Aguilar, C. 11
Rodríguez, J. E. 61
role overload scale 40, 45–6, **46**
Russo, N. F. 130

salary disparity 95–7
salary gap 84
school socioeconomic status (SES) 3
Scott, W. R. 131
socioeconomic status (SES) 9, 12
Solórzano, D. G. 127, 128
stereotype management 88–9
student labour: arbitrary intersection of identities 19; committee service 19–20; peer advising/mentoring 20–2; student organizing 22–3
student organizing 22–3

taxation: defined 34; institutional penalty, URM faculty 36; multiple experiences 35
Taylor, Breonna 1
teaching and service 88
tenure and promotion 88
theory of intersectionality 12
Thomas, James M. 108
Turner, C. S. 4, 128

underrepresented minorities (URM) 32–4, **42**, **44**
University of California-Merced (UCM) 109, 114–16
University of California-Riverside (UCR) 109, 116–19
University of North Carolina-Chapel Hill (UNC-Chapel Hill) 133
University of Texas at Brownsville/Texas Southmost College (UTB/TSC) 136

Villanueva, I. 87

white academe: Black feminist, methodological practice 62–3; Black feminist thought 63; emotional segregation 61–2; feeling unsafe/ unprotected 71–3; limitations and implications 75–6; navigating anti-racism discourse 66–9; pay the tax 60–2; performative allyship 69–70; research design 64–6
White-over-color ascendancy 37
Williams, F. 23
Wingfield, Adia H. 106
Women of Color (WoC) engineering faculty: coding architecture **91**; data analysis 90–1; data collection 89–90, **90**; faculty gender and race wage gap 83; identity taxation and stereotype management 87–9; research questions 83; risking backlash and utilizing privilege 97–8; salary disparities, higher education **92**, 92–3; salary disparity issue 95–6; salary gap 84; salary negotiations 82–6; wage disparities 93–5; women's underrepresentation, engineering **86**, 86–7, **87**; workplace development/ inclusivity 81
women's underrepresentation: percentage of all engineering faculty by race **86**; percentage of women engineering faculty by race **87**; pet-to-threat syndrome 87; STEM faculty roles 86

Yosso, T. J. 11, 127, 128, 137

Zambrana, Ruth 3–4